INDIGENIZING THE ACADEMY

CONTEMPORARY INDIGENOUS ISSUES

Series Editor
Devon Abbott Mihesuah

Edited by

DEVON ABBOTT MIHESUAH AND
ANGELA CAVENDER WILSON

Indigenizing the Academy

TRANSFORMING SCHOLARSHIP AND
EMPOWERING COMMUNITIES

University of Nebraska Press
Lincoln and London

© 2004 Devon Abbott Mihesuah and Angela Cavender Wilson
Rights to the chapters are held by individual contributors.
All rights reserved
Manufactured in the United States of America

∞

Library of Congress Cataloging-in-Publication Data
Indigenizing the academy: transforming scholarship and
empowering communities / edited by Devon Abbott Mihesuah
and Angela Cavender Wilson.
p. cm.—(Contemporary indigenous issues)
Includes bibliographical references and index.
ISBN 0-8032-3229-2 (cloth: alk. paper)—ISBN 0-8032-8292-3
(pbk.: alk. paper)
1. Indians of North America–Education (Higher) 2. Indians of
North America–Historiography. 3. Indians of North America–
Research. 4. Discrimination in higher education–United States.
5. Educational equalization–United States. 6. Indian teachers–
Employment–United States. 7. Education and society–United
States. 8. Education and state–United States. I. Mihesuah,
Devon A. (Devon Abbott). II. Wilson, Angela Cavender.
III. Series.
E97.I464 2004
378.1'982997—dc22
2003020064

To Indigenous intellectuals—past, present, and future

Contents

Preface ix
Devon Abbott Mihesuah

Introduction 1
Devon Abbott Mihesuah and Angela Cavender Wilson

1. Marginal and Submarginal 16
   Vine Deloria Jr.

2. Academic Gatekeepers 31
   Devon Abbott Mihesuah

3. Corrupt State University: The Organizational Psychology of Native Experience in Higher Education 48
   Keith James

4. Reclaiming Our Humanity: Decolonization and the Recovery of Indigenous Knowledge 69
   Angela Cavender Wilson

5. Warrior Scholarship: Seeing the University as a Ground of Contention 88
   Taiaiake Alfred

6. Seeing (and Reading) Red: Indian Outlaws in the Ivory Tower 100
   Daniel Heath Justice

7. Keeping Culture in Mind: Transforming Academic Training in Professional Psychology for Indian Country 124
   Joseph P. Gone

8. Should American Indian History Remain a Field of Study? 143
   Devon Abbott Mihesuah

9. Teaching Indigenous Cultural Resource Management 160
   Andrea A. Hunter

10. In the Trenches: A Critical Look at the Isolation of American Indian Political Practices in the Nonempirical Social Science of Political Science   174
    Joely De La Torre

11. Graduating Indigenous Students by Confronting the Academic Environment   191
    Joshua K. Mihesuah

12. So You Think You Hired an "Indian" Faculty Member? The Ethnic Fraud Paradox in Higher Education   200
    Cornel D. Pewewardy

13. Not the End of the Stories, Not the End of the Songs: Visualizing, Signifying, Counter-colonizing   218
    David Anthony Tyeeme Clark

    Appendix. Questions for Reflection   233

    Contributors   235

    Index   239

PREFACE

The reasons that spurred me to pursue a sequel to *Natives and Academics: Researching and Writing about American Indians* are simple. The book remains popular; over four thousand copies have been sold, and I continue to receive letters from faculty, staff, and nonacademics telling me they want more of the same discussions about the methods and controversies of writing about Indigenous people. And they want the truth about academia, not fence-sitting opinions intended to make everyone happy.

Natives and Academics explores methodological and theoretical questions within American Indian/Native American studies scholarship about Indian agency, author credibility, and the "New Indian History." But the book almost did not happen. I was told by numerous Native and non-Native colleagues not to pursue the idea of writing about researching Natives that takes issue with standard methodologies and interpretations of researching and writing about Natives. "You're making a very big mistake," said one. "This is a chance for everyone with a grudge to get you," said another.

My major professor at TCU, Donald Worcester, was right in saying that when you want to get ideas across, "You need to use gentle persuasion with your readers. Don't bludgeon them." I worked hard at making certain that *Natives and Academics* was as inclusive as my conscience allowed it to be, and I spent much time editing out some of the more explosive examples of poor scholarship written by non-Natives *and* Natives. Because of its political nature, the "Comment" of the special issue that later became the introduction to *Natives and Academics* is the most emotionally difficult piece I have written, and several times I considered not doing it at all. Ultimately, however, there has only been one negative public review, and it came from anthropologist Jay Miller, who wrote, "Her approach clearly has 'an ax to grind' in that the sweep and depth of the overall work is ignored in favour of highlighting a perceived flaw or insulting comment, often taken out of context." Although no one wants to come across as whining because of past wrongs, the reality of the situation is that an Indigenous scholar's academic experience—in all its facets—is not the same as that of a white man or a white woman. Yes, there are "academic grudges" that go back to graduate school, and most Indigenous scholars do encounter racism, sexism, and nonsensical commentaries about our work. Little does Miller know, however, that there were myriad examples I could have used but did not. Miller made his remarks because, clearly, he has not encountered any racism or sexism and he believes he should write about Indigenous peoples the way he wants to. The essays in *Natives and Academics* were not written because I or anyone else had grudges and wanted to get back at someone. It was written by Native intellectuals with a desire to educate people like Jay Miller.

It does not take much energy to notice that most academics side with Miller. Problematic books have appeared in the last few years. Many imperialistic non-Indigenous (and Indigenous) writers of Native history and culture choose to ignore our comments. Those scholars who told me not to pursue *Natives and Academics* are those who have become comfortable in their cushy jobs and refuse to speak out against the status quo. More than ever, I am glad I did not take their advice. Also on the positive side, Native intellectuals and our non-Native allies are speaking up, challenging methodologies used to write about Natives, in addition to the policies and behaviors of search, promotion, curriculum, and award committees -both subtle and blatant-that keep Natives subsumed.

My ideas about the reasons we should write about Natives have not changed. My overall reason for continuing with the dialogues started in *Natives and Academics* is to press home the point that as scholars we have the ability to empower Indigenous peoples. Problems among tribes continue. Poverty, anxiety, stereotyping, racism, health problems, suicides, and other issues are still the realities for many Natives. To ignore these problems while continuing to write about Natives without intending to make scholarship useful is self-serving and purposeful only to the scholar who needs a job, promotions, and book contracts. I have found out in more than one way that my stance is not a popular one, but I have not encountered any better reasons to write, teach, and research.

Every person who contributed to this work is busy and overcommitted to other projects. As a group, however, we all believed this project important enough to make time for it. This is not an "us versus them" book of diatribes. Many non-Indigenous readers know that as editor of the *American Indian Quarterly*, I have asked them to review manuscripts. They also know that I have never written or verbalized that "only Indians can write about Indians," or that "only Indian voices should be used." I have always taught and written that a balanced, inclusive methodology is ideal, that is, both Indigenous voices and archival sources are valuable when writing on any topic. Despite my very clear stance, I suppose that I will forever be labeled an "essentialist," a term misunderstood by the people who wield it for political purposes.

I asked my friend, Dakota historian Angela Cavender Wilson, to coedit this sequel mainly because I believe that her essays in *Natives and Academics* are among the most important commentaries about Indigenous studies to emerge in years. Since her essays were published, I have read new manuscripts in hopes of seeing how other authors engage her ideas, yet I have been stunned to see her work cited only a few times. And when it is, why is it usually by threatened scholars who accuse of her being "exclusive" and espousing an impossible methodology? This is a major question not answered easily, and I hope that my coeditor can help me consider the possibilities.

Angela and I find it difficult to separate our concerns about presentations of history, Indigenous voices in scholarship, and academic politics from everyday life. Our children play together and our husbands talk hunting; as we hike, cook, play with our animals, and clean dishes, we begin talking about books and movies, but our conversation inevitably comes to focus on problems in academia. This should not be surprising, since Native scholars are simultaneously concerned about job and salary, and more importantly, family, community, and tribe.

As this anthology illustrates, we are not the only ones concerned about our places in academia. If this anthology can educate or inspire scholars to focus their energies on creating a better future for Indigenous peoples, then our job is done.

Devon Abbott Mihesuah

INTRODUCTION

Devon Abbott Mihesuah and Angela Cavender Wilson

The 1996 special issue of the *American Indian Quarterly,* "Writing About (Writing About) American Indians," was the first textualized anthology by Indigenous scholars to express some of our concerns within a variety of fields in American Indian/Native American studies. That special issue came about because Devon had been aware of many of those problems for years, and after speaking with colleagues it became clear to her that she was not the only one who sought a way to address the weaknesses in methodologies used to write and teach about Indigenous histories and cultures. In addition, it was apparent that many Indigenous scholars were facing gatekeeping strategies implemented by colleagues who had no desire to make their own research and writings inclusive.

After hearing the positive responses to the special issue, we made the decision to pursue a larger volume that became *Natives and Academics: Researching and Writing About American Indians*. On the surface, the response has been positive: thousands of copies have been sold and many "thank you" letters have been received. The reality is, however, that just because someone buys and reads the book does not mean they agree with the content. Not surprisingly, the essay most quoted is the least offensive to non-Indigenous readers: Duane Champagne's "American Indian Studies is for Everyone." Conversely, least quoted are the most challenging to the status quo: Susan Miller's "Licensed Trafficking and Ethnogenetic Engineering," and Angela Cavender Wilson's two essays, "American Indian History or Non-Indian Perceptions of American Indian History?" and "Grandmother to Granddaughter: Generations of Oral History in a Dakota Family." Also pushed to the side are the essays by Devon Abbott Mihesuah, Paula Gunn Allen, and Vine Deloria Jr. that discuss the importance of linking the past to the present, using restraint when writing about religious issues, and the problems with writing about the same topics repeatedly.

Natives and Academics offered a long-needed forum for Indigenous scholars to write back to the academy, especially to our colleagues who in many ways have maintained an iron grip on the gates of power and authority. We were voicing our perceptions, our concerns, and some overdue challenges to the status quo. On reflection we have realized that many of our collegiate gatekeepers persist unfettered by such challenges; but by engaging in a more critical discourse, we found something perhaps even more valuable. We found something for ourselves. We found Indigenous scholars with similar experiences, criticisms, and agendas that allowed us to move beyond our sense of isolation and marginalization while connecting to a broader, growing, Indigenous intellectual movement. *Indigenizing the Academy* is an outgrowth of that experience, a desire to continue a public dialogue with one another and with up-and-coming scholars who will be our future allies. We believe the ideas expressed here will resonate with others with like minds and agendas, and eventually this will coalesce into a critical mass of Indigenous intellectuals and non-Indigenous allies.

This sequel is about empowering ourselves through the examination of what we can do to Indigenize the academy; to carve a space where Indigenous values and knowledge are respected; to create an environment that supports research and methodologies useful to Indigenous nation building; to support one another as institutional foundations are shaken; and to compel institutional responsiveness to Indigenous issues, concerns, and communities. As Linda Tuhiwai Smith points out, "The insulation of disciplines, the culture of the institution which supports disciplines, and the systems of management and governance all work in ways which protect the privileges already in place."[1]

Contestation over which methodologies should be used to write about Indigenous peoples remains one of the most important problems in Indigenous studies. Dissertations without Indigenous voices continue to receive approval. New PhDs who never speak to Indigenes are hired. Indigenous scholars compete with each other for fellowships, and those who win often are those with recommendation letters from non-Indigenes who do not use Indigenous perspectives in their works. Awards are seemingly presented either to non-Indigenes who write about Indigenous topics (not to those who write about their tribes), or to poets and novelists (not to Native activists or our allies who champion tribal rights). Not enough is being written about tribal needs and concerns, but an inordinate amount of attention is focused on fiction. American Indian/Native American studies programs are still based on curriculums not designed with Indigenous peoples' interests in mind. Grant and fellowship money continues to be doled out to scholars who have no intention of assisting tribes. Many Indigenous scholars are hired only because of their race and their ability to politic.

It appears that many students interested in American Indian studies are not being properly informed about research methodologies, ethics, or the needs of Indigenous peoples. For example, in an exchange during the year 2000 on the H-Amindian Web site (h-amindian@h-net.msu.edu), a message appeared calling for recommendations for books from the Native perspective around the Revolutionary period. One response was "Ruth Beebe Hill's *Hanta Yo*. Absolutely."[2] Others recommended captivity narratives, and some suggested works written exclusively by non-Natives. Indigenous scholars expressed dismay among ourselves at the answers and chalked it up to poor training.

Last year, the journal Devon edits, the *American Indian Quarterly*, sent out a query for scholars in Native studies to submit the works that have most influenced their thinking in Native studies. Of the several dozen respondents, all said that fiction writers were most important to them—rather than other Native intellectuals who focus specifically on nation building, treaty rights, or empowerment. What exactly, is the purpose of Native studies? If this particular exercise is any indication, at most schools it certainly is not to assist tribes.

At a recent American Society for Ethnohistory meeting, after a session on methodologies for researching Native females, a young woman raised her hand to express her concern that "it's about time we had some research guidelines to follow." It seems unethical that students can pass through graduate programs without knowing that institutional review boards and tribal research guidelines do exist, or that some books are simply inappropriate reading, or that Indigenous peoples do have voices and should be included in scholarship, but this lack of training is commonplace. At the same conference, after the session Devon chaired on Kennewick Man concluded, a prominent and retired non-Native historian hobbled to the front table on his cane, leaned over the table and remarked to the antirepatriation presenters about the prorepatriation sentiments of audience members James Riding In and Michael Yellow Bird: "I'm sick and tired of these Indians who think they know everything when they don't." If Natives cannot express their concerns at the very conference that is supposed to be the meshing of history and anthropological methodology (which in theory is to include Native voices), then where can they speak?

Not a lot of places, it appears. Our concerns have been voiced in *Natives and Academics*, but we have seen little evidence that our commentaries are taken seriously. We again attempted to discuss our concerns about current problems in academia in "Indigenous Scholars versus the Status Quo," which we submitted to the *Chronicle of Higher Education* in July 2002. It was immediately rejected with no explanation other than the statement that although the paper appreciated our submission, the editors would not publish it. When pressed for a more thorough reason as to why an important commentary about serious problems within academia was rejected, Jeanne Ferris, the senior editor of *The Chronicle Review*, replied that the topics of racism in the academy would not seem new to the *Chronicle* readers. Considering that these concerns in the "*Chronicle* essay" are rarely expressed by Indigenous scholars through a national, widely read forum such as *The Chronicle*, and that most of *The Chronicle*'s essays about Natives are written by non-Natives, it is astounding to read such a response. We believe this rejection is an excellent example of academic gatekeeping at a very influential level, effectively keeping a larger audience from considering our work.

We have noticed that authors and editors of recent books and anthologies not only make a concerted effort to avoid discussing the ideologies presented in *Natives and Academics*, they also purposely neglect to cite the work of prominent Indigenous scholars. There may be several reasons for these exclusions. Perhaps they do not understand tribal needs and concerns or the importance of including Indigenous voices in works about Indigenous peoples. Therefore, they have no clue as to how to engage the contributors to *Natives and Academics* and so they ignore us. Furthermore, we know from personal experience that some do understand what we are saying, but because the colonial institution does not yet require them to utilize Indigenous voices or to focus their energies on the needs of modern Indigenous peoples, they continue to churn out one-sided studies. A few of these authors have been criticized in *Natives and Academics*, and apparently out of spite they neglect to cite us where it is appropriate. This is without question purposeful behavior on the part of many scholars who are fearful of losing their control of Indigenous studies. Yet, despite what may be deemed a lack of acceptance of these Indigenous views, we must press on in our efforts.

As we reflect upon what it means to "Indigenize the academy," we are beginning from the presumption that the academy is worth Indigenizing because something productive will happen as a consequence. Perhaps as teachers we can facilitate what bell hooks refers to as "education as the practice of freedom." Perhaps we might engage in an educational dynamic with students that is liberatory, not only for the oppressed but also for the oppressors. Perhaps as scholars we can conduct research that has a beneficial impact on humanity in general, as well as on our Indigenous peoples. Perhaps the scholarship we produce might be influential not only among our ivory tower peers, but also within the dominant society. Perhaps our activism and persistence within the academy might also redefine the institution from an agent of colonialism to a center of decolonization. Cherokee scholar Daniel Heath Justice believes that Indigenizing the academy means "to make the academy both responsive and responsible to First Nations goals of self-determination and well-being." Taiaiake Alfred states that "the university is contentious ground," and that should make Native scholars seriously consider "their view on the role they are playing and on the battles they are fighting." If these visions are realized they are the consequences of a conscious desire we have as Indigenous people to transform the world around us because we are dissatisfied with the status quo, because we are tired of the tremendous injustices occurring around us, and because we are hungry for a change that will bring respect to our rights as Indigenous peoples. However, these visions also depend on our success, both individually and collectively, at establishing a continuous, visible, and active presence at academic institutions, a task that seems sufficiently achievable but proves to be much more difficult in reality.

This difficulty arises precisely because of the academy's role in the ongoing colonization of Indigenous peoples. The academy has much invested in maintaining control over who defines knowledge, who has access to knowledge, and who produces knowledge. As Indigenous intellectuals committed to our Indigenous nations, we threaten the power and authority claimed by institutions, disciplines, and peoples created, in part, from the oppression of our people. Since every academic institution sits on Indigenous land, that oppression was first corporeal; ultimately, the institutions exist because Indigenous peoples were first dispossessed. That oppression continued in a less tangible but no less destructive way with the establishment of academic disciplines that exploited Indigenous peoples as their subjects of research in ways that reinforced the superior position of EuroAmerican peoples while subjugating their subjects of study. As Linda Tuhiwai Smith argues, "In their foundations, Western disciplines are as much implicated in each other as they are in imperialism."[3] But because educational institutions are in the business of supporting the existing power structure (they are a major part of the power structure), our attempts to transform them are simply threatening. In small numbers and at the margins, our threats can be easily and effectively dismissed and silenced. Yet, in an age when perpetual white male rule (and sometimes white female rule) can become an embarrassment to a country self-righteously touting its moral superiority, diversity in the academy is also a necessity. To a certain extent, we are needed, if only for show.

It seems that the meaning of diversity is ill understood by many of our white colleagues and administrators who seem to think it is simply about skin color (or body parts in the case of gender diversity). With this in mind they believe that Indigenous individuals who have made it to their ranks and institutions now "see the light" and will think as they do, act as they do, teach as they do, and produce scholarship as they do. And because some Natives do these things, they assume all is well. While some herald the need and appreciation for diversity in color and gender, they want conformity in thought and action. They are surprised when we arrive and bring with us diversity in thought, worldview, and values and then are horrified when it affects our speech and action. When, in our consciousness of the ways colonization is perpetuated and transferred from one generation to the next, one group to the next, we attempt to interrupt that transference, we make those around us uncomfortable and angry. Clearly other scholars of color around the country are facing similar responses as they infiltrate the academy. For example, Patti Duncan is in the process of editing a volume entitled *Ingrates at the Gate: People of Color Confront Higher Education*, which addresses how these scholars attempt to preserve their integrity and their energy in the academy using multiple forms of resistance, both direct and subversive, in the face of oppression and marginalization.

All the contributors to *Indigenizing the Academy* believe, at least at present, that there is something worthwhile or salvageable within the academy, though we suspect that all of us have seriously questioned our participation on a regular basis. Some of us wonder daily if we might be more useful, more productive, and more successful if we removed ourselves from the academy and continued our research, writing, and scholarship in other arenas. Some of us feel as though we can only beat our heads against the wall so many times before the damage to our spirits outweighs whatever small gains we might be making within institutions that do not value our contributions. However, we recognize that this generation of Indigenous scholars is not the first to engage in such struggles.

In chapter 1, "Marginal and Submarginal," Standing Rock Sioux Vine Deloria Jr. traces the changes in the Native intellectual movement in the academy over the last several decades. Though a "general good feeling about Indians" has been created, Deloria laments the fact that scholars of his generation were unable to address the roots of the problem of racism in a permanent way, leaving a legacy of "regenerated racism" for contemporary scholars to face. Most important, Deloria gives a strong kick in the pants to younger Indigenous scholars whom he views as disconnected from their communities and lacking political engagement in the myriad problems facing our nations. He views political involvement as essential for Indigenous scholars, a claim echoed later in this anthology by other contributors such as Alfred, Wilson, Justice, and De La Torre. At the same time, Deloria recognizes that unlike the Indigenous scholars of the previous generation, scholars of today face "extraordinary roadblocks in their path toward academic parity," making playing the academic game a necessary component for success in tenure and promotion struggles. He advocates the formation of a new alliance of scholars to act with political force when individuals are faced with discrimination. Since Deloria began his career, many more Natives have entered the halls of academia, but unfortunately, most of the problems remain. Hence this anthology.

Chapter 2, Oklahoma Choctaw Devon Abbott Mihesuah's "Academic Gatekeeping," carries Deloria's discussion a few steps farther, laying out the realities of the workplace for scholars and students—Indigenous and not—who define themselves and their work as activist and pro-Native yet are hampered by the status quo, that is, by search committees, major professors, award committees, publishers, and other authors who fear that their control of American Indian/Native American studies is slipping. She discusses strategies used to good effect in many academic departments: artificially inflating the status of non-Indigenous and Indigenous authors who are not concerned about real issues by digging a hole under the ones who should be at the forefront of discussions about Indigenous concerns. Deloria writes that he and his colleagues did not anticipate "the reactionary posture that many scholars would take once they were forced to share the status of authority jointly with a new group of aggressive Indians." The "newer" Native intellectuals and our friends, however, have paid attention, and we know full well the strategies and ideologies of our adversaries, as well as the politics of the workplace. The irony is that no matter how alert we are, we are still blindsided by search, promotion, and tenure committees, as well as by funding agencies, book and essay reviewers, publishers, and other scholars who write about Natives—and sadly, by other Natives who have adopted the attitudes of the status quo.

Onondaga psychologist Keith James tells us more about Native scholars' marginalization in universities in chapter 3, "Social Corruption in Academe: The Organizational Psychology of Native Experience in Higher Education." While it may seem to some readers that there is much nitpicking in this volume about our workplaces, the reality is that while the university can be a fulfilling place for many—see, for example, James Axtell's *The Pleasures of Academe: A Celebration and Defense of Higher Education* (University of Nebraska Press, 1999)—it can be a place that causes extreme stress and frustration for others, especially those who are not white males (and, in most cases, white females) who support the status quo and who, like our president, George W. Bush, are staunchly set against affirmative action. While every scholar faces annoyances in the university, some face much more than others, and all of us in this anthology have tales to tell about unfair evaluations and promotion and hiring decisions. Worse, many of our stories are labeled by our privileged colleagues as "unbelievable," which results in a lack of action on the part of our administrations. While we can think of no Indigenous scholar who is actually destitute, we can say that many of us have achieved our positions and promotions only after many arduous, frustrating confrontations with those in power.

James gives suggestions for surviving nepotism, cronyism, and favoritism (those ugly, entrenched aspects of institutions), such as finding out about an institution prior to accepting a position there and building coalitions and support networks. As James reminds us, Indigenous scholars who desire to work for their tribes as well as to speak out against the status quo must expect a spectrum of challenges, so we had better be prepared. Academic struggles, he says, may also be joined by Indigenous communities that can further challenge universities to meet their own demands and expectations while improving the overall health and effectiveness of the institution.

In chapter 4, "Reclaiming Our Humanity: Decolonization and the Recovery of Indigenous Knowledge," Wahpetunwan Dakota Angela Cavender Wilson argues that decolonization is a means to "restoring health and prosperity to our people." Wilson believes that a reaffirmation of Indigenous epistemological and ontological foundations offers a form of resistance to the forces of colonialism. Like Taiaiake Alfred (who also argues for a reconsideration of traditions as a means to solve present-day problems in his *Peace, Power, Righteousness*), Wilson uses her academic training to find and organize strategies of empowerment and nation building while at the same time fighting against the entrenched standards of the academy that are usually not supportive of these endeavors (many of those who do not support these goals are Natives who have become thoroughly colonized). Like the other contributors to this volume, Wilson reaffirms our responsibility to assess what colonialism has done to Indigenous peoples. At the same time, she tells of the consequences to Native intellectual activists of speaking up and warns of potential consequences for revealing too much cultural information.

Mohawk Taiaiake Alfred carries these ideas further in chapter 5, "Warrior Scholarship: Seeing the University as a Ground of Contention." The focus of our energies, Alfred believes, should be to change our working sites of colonialism—universities—so that the institutions will incorporate tribes' values and principles into their curriculums and policies. Further, we must shake off our complacency and fight as "warrior scholars" to make certain that the academy acknowledges and acts on our concerns and shows Indigenous people respect. Before we can engage the academy in a meaningful way, however, we must first understand our identities as Indigenous peoples, which means we must be accountable to our tribal values and communities; we also must organize ourselves to fully utilize our power as Natives with specific values. Finally, we must acknowledge that change is necessary, and we must maintain our dignity during struggles for justice. This is not easy, as many of us can attest; but, because colonial policies affect not only the academy but also our communities, we don't have much choice.

Several essays focus on specific disciplines and how scholars within those disciplines can work to assist tribes. Cherokee Daniel Heath Justice discusses recommendations for finding empowerment through literary studies in chapter 6, "Seeing (and Reading) Red: Indian Outlaws in the Ivory Tower." Justice argues that as citizens of tribal nations, Indigenous literary scholars can and should find ways to empowerment through literary studies. He states that scholars and writers should ask, "Will the work we do today contribute to the health and well-being of our own Nations? If the answer is no, we're not doing our job." But as he also observes, "There are others who treat Indians—by implication or directly—as obstacles to their research about Indians." Justice recognizes that many scholars focus only on specific authors—"The Noble Nine"—and show "a good degree of laziness, discomfort, or fear regarding the exploration of other texts and traditions." This may be why we see an inordinate amount of attention placed on nonintimidating fiction writers and less attention focused on scholars who challenge traditional ways of learning.

In chapter 7, "Keeping Culture in Mind: Transforming Academic Training in Professional Psychology for Indian Country," Gros Ventres psychologist Joseph Gone discusses the dilemma faced by Native psychologists who desire to assist Indigenous peoples but who also must adhere to standards of the discipline and the academy. He argues that the discipline does not always consider that when the recipients of psychological services are culturally different, as are Indigenous peoples, the methods of treatment are also "culturally alien." He warns of the danger within the field that carries the potential for the "cultural proselytization" of Indigenous clients by "facilitating a 'conversion' to Western forms of personhood." Yet, rather than working to fundamentally challenge the discipline, Gone argues instead for the creation of a more "pragmatically beneficial professional psychology" that works within "Western rationalist and empiricist epistemologies." He does, however, envision a new conceptual and methodological training that he hopes will "facilitate and enhance cultural preservation" among Indigenous communities.

Critical problems are especially prevalent in the field of American Indian history. Repeatedly writing about the same topics, reprinting previously published essays in expensive anthologies, dwelling on historic events without considering how past events contribute to the present-day situations of modern Natives, and neglecting to cite the work of Native scholars is becoming more and more common. There also is the issue that many historians refuse to utilize oral testimonies in their data collecting and analysis. In ignoring the Native perspectives in history writing, "Indian historians" create nothing but exclusive stories of the past that are biased and incomplete. Stories of the Indigenous past are usually created by non-Natives (but also by Natives) who claim to be objective. But in ignoring Natives' perspectives of the past, they make political, subjective statements while at the same time arguing that Native writers are unacceptable because we are political and subjective. As Devon Abbott Mihesuah discusses in chapter 8, "Should American Indian History Remain a Field of Study?" these problems are symptoms of what is wrong with "Indian history," and that because few Indigenous historians write history with the goal of assisting modern Native peoples, participants in this area of study (and that includes publishers) need to reevaluate what they are writing and why.

Closely related to the study of history is anthropology, and one of the most volatile issues today continues to be the debate over repatriation of skeletal remains and sacred cultural objects that belong to tribes. Osage anthropologist Andrea A. Hunter writes in chapter 9, "Teaching Indigenous Cultural Resource Management," about how recent repatriation laws and amendments to cultural resource management laws have mandated changes in how archaeologists conduct research on private, state, and federal lands in the United States. After a decade of membership (and current experience as chair) on the Smithsonian's Native American Repatriation Review Committee (RRC), as well as participation in Native American repatriation workshops and international Indigenous cultural resource management courses, Hunter's experience shows that the time has come to establish required undergraduate and graduate anthropology courses on Indigenous perspectives in cultural resource management. Her chapter highlights the evolution of her Indigenous perspective and the programs developing at Northern Arizona University.

In chapter 10, "In the Trenches: A Critical Look at the Isolation of American Indian Political Practices in the Nonempirical Social Science of Political Science," Joely De La Torre writes that despite the intense focus on political systems, institutions, theories, and persons, the nonempirical field of political science for the most part ignores Indigenous political practices. As in many other fields of study, Indigenous writers, tribal practices, histories, and cultures are overlooked in favor of highlighting American politics and policies from the viewpoints and value systems of members of the dominant society who have little concern about Indigenous rights and empowerment. Many of those scholars who do show interest in tribal politics misunderstand cultural nuances and often lump tribes together into one group instead of considering each tribe as a distinct entity, which results in more incomplete and inaccurate scholarship. In order for Indigenous voices to be a part of the political science discourse, De La Torre, of the Pechanga Band of Luiseno Indians, recommends using three different approaches: positivist, postpositivist, and interpretive. In addition, she argues that it is up to Native intellectuals to make sure that we are not relegated to the periphery group of "minority politics" and to "define the terms of our involvement within the discipline and the direction we want to take." Ultimately she believes that the discipline is of great relevance to tribal nations of today as they grapple with issues of sovereignty and political survival, but for the field to be useful, Indigenous scholars must challenge it to include alternative Indigenous practices and knowledge. Ultimately, our goal as Native educators is to inform and inspire Native students. But how many universities have programs that focus on Native issues? Degrees and programs that feature a few courses in Native literature, history, and art is one type, but programs that deal with nation building, empowerment, and identity development are quite another. Indigenous students are very few in number, but they tend to drop out more heavily than students from other cultures.

Joshua K. Mihesuah, a Comanche and director of Northern Arizona University's Native American Student Services office, writes in chapter 11, "Graduating Indigenous Students by Transforming the Academic Environment," about the difficulties Indigenous students face in the academy. Ironically, many of those problems are similar to what Native children faced in federal boarding schools. A major reason that Natives leave school is that they do not find a course of study that meets their needs as Indigenous peoples with strong concerns about their families, communities, and tribes. The academy must recognize their requirements, adopt policies of sensitizing faculty and staff about Native students' needs, and be willing to hire Native faculty to serve as role models and to create degrees that focus on tribal issues. In so doing, students will feel empowered and will develop secure identities, two major ingredients in the mindset of successful students.

It is greatly troubling that not only do few scholars come forward and voice their opinions on issues pertaining to tribal problems, many scholars whose careers are supposed to focus on Natives appear to be in it only for the money. According to the 1998 statistics of the American Historical Association, for example, 318 members identified themselves as "American Indian or Alaskan Native."[4] Between the two of us, we can think of maybe twenty Indigenous historians, and only a few of those write useful monographs about Indigenes. Who are these other people? Why do they identify themselves as Indigenous and not contribute work useful to Indigenous peoples? One way that "Native" scholars receive attention is through what Kiowa/Comanche educator Cornell Pewewardy refers to as cultural exploitation and appropriation in chapter 12, "So You Think You Hired an 'Indian' Faculty Member?: The Ethnic Fraud Paradox in Higher Education."

Ethnic fraud is an escalating problem, and as Pewewardy quotes one concerned Native, "How are you going to decide who is Native if they aren't enrolled, but have very long, drawn out, and usually fabricated family stories? It appears that those who are not enrolled have outnumbered those who are!" And why do so many frauds find themselves employed, tenured, and even promoted to full professor, often despite the protests of Natives who know they are not members of any tribal nation? The answer is simple: universities have not enforced recognition of tribal sovereignty and tribes' rights to determine their own membership. Furthermore, if frauds have supporters in the administration, they are assured that their identity will not be challenged and they are "home free." Like other Native scholars, Pewewardy is well aware of "who is" and "who isn't," but until universities mandate requiring proof of tribal membership, frauds will continue to find jobs and security that should be held by authentic Indigenous people.

Finally, Mesquakie/Potawatomi David Anthony Tyeeme Clark sums up our concerns in chapter 13, "Not the End of the Stories, Not the End of the Songs: Visualizing, Signifying, Counter-colonizing," by stating that Indigenous scholars and our allies must recognize and overpower all forms of "anti-Indianisms." Gatekeeping, ethnic fraud, biased writings, favoritism, ignorance, racism, and exclusion are only a few anti-Indianisms we face regularly. With this volume, we draw a line in the sand. We expect our allies and opponents to consider their motivations and values, then to rationally and honestly respond with balanced narratives, lectures, and decisions.

We had great concerns about just how critical we should be in this anthology, and this was ultimately decided individually by each contributor. The authors envision themselves as political activists, and their participation in the academy is a reflection of this political agenda. Even though we were not able to include the voices of all our peers, we continue to hear from our friends about their fights over tenure and promotion, rejections from publishers, and their concerns about how some Indigenous scholars have "sold out." Quite frankly, we know how much easier it is to support and strengthen the status quo than it is to constantly dispense the energy required to fight it.

Elizabeth Cook-Lynn states that her ultimate goal for "'Native American Studies' is not interested in censorship or in delegitimizing the idea of academic freedom. It is interested only in its own search for an academic structure through which its knowledge base may become useful to its own constituencies."[5] The second part of the comment is true enough, but the first requires discussion. If those of us strongly concerned about tribal nation building, sovereignty, and empowerment do not take to task scholars who benefit from writing about Natives (but who, at the same time, could not care less about finding solutions to tribal problems), or do not challenge those who produce stereotypical, damaging works, then who will challenge them? Who will call attention to the reality that the "famous" scholars of our histories and cultures do not use Indigenous perspectives in their analyses of histories and cultures? As Vine Deloria Jr. says in his chapter, "Any challenges to anti-Indian articles must come from Indians themselves."

As Indigenous intellectuals we must ask difficult questions about our obligations and responsibilities in our struggle for freedom from oppression. Ngugi wa Thiong'o clearly articulates the choices faced by intellectual workers among the oppressed: "Intellectual workers can draw pictures of the world in harmony with the needs of the forces of human destruction; or in harmony with the forces of resistance for human survival, creativity and renewal. Intellectuals can draw pictures of the universe and its workings to instil fear, despondence, and self-doubt in the oppressed while legitimising the world of oppressor nations and classes as the norm; or they can draw pictures that instil clarity, strength, hope, to the struggles of the exploited and the oppressed to realise their visions of a new tomorrow."[6] As academics committed to our nations, we must resist institutional cooptation and continue to challenge the dominant conventions of our disciplines, and at the same time we must use whatever authority, benefits, and power that derive from our positions to further promote the causes of our peoples. Our research skills, methodological training, and access to audience and resources can become instruments of power for our nations, if we choose to wield them in that way. However, we must simultaneously work to ensure that we don't in the process become colonizing agents for colonizing institutions. This requires a reordering of the colonial power structure and an Indigenizing of the academy. In taking on this monumental task, however, we are not alone. The purpose of this book is to offer support and encouragement to those who are up for the task.

Notes

1. Linda Tuhiwai Smith, *Decolonizing Methodologies: Research and Indigenous Peoples* (New York: Zed Books, 1999), 133.

2. Beebe Hill's *Hanta Yo* is considered to be an embarrassing fake by most Indigenous peoples, making the recommendation for it particularly offensive.

3. Smith, *Decolonizing Methodologies*, 11.

4. Robert B. Townsend, "New Data Reveals a Homogenous but Changing History Profession," *Perspectives: Newsmagazine of the American Historical Association* 40, no. 1 (January 2002), 17.

5. Elizabeth Cook-Lynn, *Anti-Indianism in Modern America: A Voice from Tatekeya's Earth* (Urbana: University of Illinois Press, 2001), 180.

6. Ngugi wa Thiong'o, *Moving the Centre: The Struggle for Cultural Freedoms* (Portsmouth, NH: Heinemann, 1993), 54–55.

1. MARGINAL AND SUBMARGINAL
Vine Deloria Jr.

The first generation of Indian scholars has nearly passed from the scene now. Scott Momaday continues to teach but most of the rest are retired. They occasionally teach a visiting semester somewhere at the request of friends. No question that there were a considerable number of Indians in higher education before the 1960s. One only need remember Arthur Parker, Francis LaFleshe, John Joseph Matthews, and others to understand that there has been a tradition of Indians in scholarship ever since the early reservation days. It is doubtful, however, that any of them saw themselves as a generation dedicated to making Indians visible in significant numbers in intellectual circles. Nor did they consider that the tribal traditions they wrote and spoke about represented an alternative philosophy to Western materialism. They were dedicated to recording an accurate account of the practices of their people.

My generation was part of a movement that, facing termination and the demand for minorities to integrate into society, refused to support the further destruction of Indian communities and sought instead to offer an alternative philosophy. That feeling of the need and responsibility to ensure that Indian communities continued into the foreseeable future has now transformed itself into a general good feeling about Indians without an accompanying sense of engagement in the problems of the Indian community as a whole. We must look back at history in order to speak meaningfully about the accomplishments of the generation past. From the beginning of the literature on, about, and sometimes by Indians, we have been the subjects of white curiosity. Regardless of what the tribal leaders and elders might have wanted to say, nothing was understood as authoritative unless a non-Indian had written it. In many areas that attitude has declined, but it is by no means absent from the minds of academics and the public at large. The previous generation challenged this assumption as often and as rigorously as possible. We could offer this challenge because most of us were rooted in the Indian community in one way or another, whether it was involvement in tribal politics or working with national organizations. Unfortunately times have changed, and this important support does not hold for many of the younger generation. Many of them have been raised away from the reservation and are, sad to say, lacking any memory of reservation experience or even experience in regional and national Indian organizations and politics. The current generation of educated Indians truly needs to be called the "New Indians" because they represent the progress made in the last thirty years in bringing Indians into the mainstream of American intellectual thought.

Our goal, three decades ago, was to replace the non-Indians who performed the heavy lifting in law, medicine, social science, and education with Indians who could do the same job but with, we assumed, concerns about the future of the tribes at heart. No one figured that younger generation would make the progress they have or that they would not share the concerns we had. We have discovered that we should have tried to ensure that young Indian scholars were firmly connected to the people in the home communities. Everything developed at a breakneck speed, and before we could identify some of the problems they were already obsolete. When you consider that in 1960 there were only about 2,000 Indians in college, and in 1990 there were close to 100,000 in some form of post-high-school programs, the development of the next generation of young scholars has virtually exploded. How then do we understand the tasks of this generation of Indian scholars?

Today Indian students have a choice of many careers, and it is sometimes inconceivable how complex higher education has become with its many specialties, fields, subfields, and sub-subfields. It is no longer possible to create categories that accurately describe what Indian scholars are studying and where they will make the greatest contributions. The variety of opportunities alone makes it difficult to create a situation where the older generation can speak meaningfully to the younger people. Thus my comments may fall on deaf ears. We may have been killed by success, but if so, we must try to work our way toward a situation in which we see a modern understanding of the Indian community emerge.

Although we now have an increasing number of Indians teaching at the college level, we find extraordinary roadblocks in their path toward academic parity. While there continues to be a demand for Indian professors, opportunities continue to be restricted to entry-level positions, and within the university Indian professors are marginalized by traditional academic expectations. One obstacle that our generation did not face was gaining a solid foothold in academia. It was relatively simple to move into the college and university scene thirty years ago because most of us already had already acquired formidable reputations from activist work. We were identified as movers and shakers before we even approached the university scene. Under pressure from outside forces and the tenor of the time, colleges sought not simply Indian scholars but visible Indian scholars, people the Indian community and the news media would recognize. That kind of leverage does not exist today for most Indian scholars wishing to make a career in higher education. Quite honestly we were not recruited as scholars but as high-profile Indians. We had already challenged authority outside academia and therefore had no difficulty raising issues inside the ivy-covered walls, too.

It was, to be sure, a pleasant and satisfying time. I once made Margaret Mead back away from referring to the Indians she interviewed as informants. She claimed instead that she had always believed the Indians she had interviewed were colleagues and not tattletales. This change of heart was, of course, a barefaced lie designed to change the image of the noisy intruding scholar to that of benign friendship and collaboration. We did not call Margaret to account publicly but were satisfied that she had given up the argument so easily. We hoped that the rest of the anthropologists would follow her lead and see themselves differently, perhaps even treat Indians as colleagues. With these kinds of changes the content of Indian studies moved swiftly toward a more realistic posture. Standard archaeology and anthropology classics that had been offered as "Indian" courses were dropped, and courses dealing with federal Indian policy and contemporary affairs took their place.

This change was swift but it also raised a backlash that we did not anticipate, a change that has not been beneficial to this generation of Indian scholars. Many non-Indian scholars resented the elevation of contemporary concerns to academic status. They were content to perpetuate the old stereotypes of Indians that they had learned in graduate school decades before. Academia has often been a hotbed of racism because scholars are taught to pretend that they can observe phenomena objectively. In fact they observe data through culturally prescribed categories that restrict the possible answers and understandings to a predetermined few selections. With Western thought primarily a binary, yes/no method of determining truth, so much data is excluded, and so limited are the possible answers that Western knowledge might be regarded as a mere classification system devoid of valid conclusions.

Race has been the primary criteria in gathering and determining data about Indians. Debates over whether Indians fit into one of Aristotle's minor categories of subhuman ensued shortly after discovery of the New World and was not really settled until cultural evolution placed us at the bottom of the scales and described us as comparable to Europeans but with a Stone Age understanding of the world. We were able to remain in the human category because we were subjects of scholarly inquiry and represented man's climb toward a mechanized culture. This belief continues to be held by many people in the universities today.

We realized that we were offering a direct challenge to the entire framework of social science. We were attacking the status of academics who believed they were the ultimate source of authority on Indians. We did not anticipate the reactionary posture that many scholars would take once they were forced to share the status of authority jointly with a new group of aggressive Indians. It should have been noted by these scholars that the old framework for understanding human societies was breaking down and cultural diversity was being recognized. The problem was that each scholar held tenaciously to the little bit of doctrine he or she had mastered and had no idea that change in one area would have a ripple effect and require changes all along the line. Indians would no longer sit by and hear derogatory descriptions of their culture and religion.

One need only read Stephen Jay Gould's *The Mismeasure of Man* to understand the degree to which racism was embedded in science and what a task it was to raise these issues. Gould outlines the history of the study of human skulls and demonstrates that where data was not deliberately faked to conform to preexisting doctrines, scholars showed obvious bias and were oblivious to their own racist assumptions. The idea that measuring the shape of the human skull could determine intellectual and cultural potential and accomplishments and even identify race was absurd from the beginning. Yet for the better part of a century scholars devoutly believed this nonsense. I mention this theory because when the Kennewick remains were found, James Chatters immediately argued that because the skull was relatively narrow, it had to be Caucasian. This belief continues to thrive today in the minds of many scientists. The scholars who filed suit to get possession of the Kennewick remains must surely have endorsed this view. These scholars, several informally described as members of the so-called Clovis Police, threw doctrine to the wind in an effort to take the skeleton away from the tribes of the Pacific Northwest even though that belief in skull shape had been discredited half a century before. With few exceptions the vast majority of scholars said and did nothing to correct the record. Thus whatever change we were able to create, we certainly didn't go to the roots of the problem in any permanent manner.

Unfortunately, part of the legacy we might have left for another generation of Indian scholars is regenerated racism. One need only glance at the intellectual landscape in higher education to understand how deep are the effects of race. In the advanced degree programs in every college and university there is an engrained belief that Indians are not only inferior but also that they know virtually nothing about their communities. It is a cherished and unexamined doctrine in many advanced degree programs that a non-Indian student can spend a few weeks in the summer living at the margins of an Indian community and, because of his or her training and the innate ability of whites to be objective, accurately understand what Indians are doing and why they are doing it. One need only look at the record of the Newberry Library Indian program to see how pervasive this attitude is. Some time back when they offered major fellowships to do graduate work, the ratio of awards to whites as opposed to Indians was an embarrassing forty to two at one count. Indians were confined to summer workshops and received virtually no year-round awards for research leading toward publication. During the program, a large number of non-Indians received sufficient financial support to enable them to write books that launched them into the university system on a very high level.

The timing of Paul Martin's ridiculous idea that Indians with an insatiable blood lust came marching across the Bering Strait into North America and completely exterminated thirty-nine species of large animals may be no coincidence. His book *Pleistocene Extinctions* was published in 1967, just as Indians were becoming visible as a distinctive group in the eyes of the public. The absurdity of such a theory should be manifest to anyone who has spent any time hunting wild animals. It is simply not possible for a limited number of hunters to eliminate animals completely from a vast landscape, since the animals' response to hunting is to avoid the area where the hunters are. Each fall multitudes of modern hunters with the latest weapons invade forests and take a considerable amount of game. Yet the supply of deer remains reasonably stable and even increases in some locations. How then could a handful of ancient hunters threaten great numbers of large animals using the most primitive of weapons?

Very few of the megafauna supposedly killed by these proto-Indians were edible, and many species that perished around 12,000 B.C. were predators, competitors of humans, not prey for the hunters. Most animals as a rule do not stand around waiting to be killed, although killing buffalo by hunting them downwind did often have this result—but high-powered rifles from a distance killed these buffalo. The ancient hunters were not equipped with powerful rifles but at best had to drive animals off cliffs. What is so totally disconcerting is that so many scholars promptly and enthusiastically adopted Martin's scenario so that it became a standard explanation of the loss of large animals in textbooks and in lectures, without a shred of evidence to support it.

We did not anticipate that these absurd anti-Indian theories would soon be offered without the slightest hesitation and apparently with the full support of the academic community. By the time we realized that academics were determined to besmirch Indians through any means the reaction was well underway. The idea of complaining of anti-Indian scholarship was not understood by many Indians, and so response was piecemeal if it existed at all. The revolt against sharing authority with Indians crystallized in James Clifton's *The Invented Indian*, in which a number of disgruntled third-rate scholars wrote essays disproving popular myths about Indians. Whites on the frontier or later academics, as a display of their enlightenment and knowledge of Indians, created these myths. Some Indians, in an effort to please inquiring whites, adopted these fictions. Essays in *The Invented Indian* said as much, but the authors of the pieces blamed Indians for perpetuating the myths. A submarginal theme in some of the essays was the complaint that the authors as scholars knew more about tribes than did the contemporary Indians who were members of the tribes. Some scholars complained that the Indians got preference in hiring when it came to the new social programs of the 1960s and 1970s, when the jobs should have gone to scholars who had "studied" them.

Once the academic community accepted this anti-Indian attitude without a strong response from Indians, the floodgates were opened for almost any ridiculous idea. Thus Indians have been accused of being the primary actors in killing off the buffalo. All available historical data shows that white hunters, taking only the hides for the European leather market, virtually exterminated the animals in a three-year period. The most absurd accusation was made by Elliot West, who argued that the Cheyennes occasionally wintered in the Big Timbers, a twelve-mile stretch of cottonwoods in the Arkansas River. In doing so they deprived the buffalo of grass and cottonwood bark during the wintertime, thereby lowering the reproductive rate of the animals. West offered no evidence whatsoever. Currently there is a popular notion that the buffalo were safe only in areas where there was incessant warfare between tribes, the belief being that Indians were so busy killing each other they didn't have time to kill animals.

Little emphasis is given to the fact that several tribes in fact herded the buffalo within their own territories, and there were few herds outside their areas that they hunted. Several commentators reported Kiowa and Comanche efforts to protect the buffalo herds within their reservations led to Indian herding practices and the so-called Buffalo War of the 1870s. As to warfare, horse-stealing expeditions of a few people from each tribe can hardly be called a war and more resembled the mountain feuds of the Appalachians.

With the rising concern for the environment the Indian was pictured as one of the few peoples who acted properly toward nature. Iron Eyes Cody's ad of the weeping Indian looking at trash along the highway became a symbol of ecological concern. This image suggested an ecological perspective far superior to the acts of the frontier pioneers, but it also hinted that perhaps contemporary Indians still had some knowledge of how to live on lands without destroying them. The younger generation of Indian scholars must deal with this situation. How did Indians treat their lands? People are today undecided whether the practice of some tribes in firing forests and grasslands was a wise or frequent Indian activity. Burning grass would certainly cause better growth during the next year but it would also eliminate feed for the animals in the winter. The actual historical evidence indicates that many fires were started by careless whites that let campfires get away from them. The historical record, whether good or bad, is hardly sufficient to make the accusatory calls against Indians that we have seen in recent years.

The epitome of anti-Indian propaganda is represented by *The Ecological Indian* by Shepherd Krech, which is very popular among academics although it demonstrates an almost deliberate avoidance of relevant scholarship. Krech accuses Indians of many venial sins at the beginning of his chapters, reviews his evidence, which is scanty if it qualifies as evidence at all, and generally concludes that Indians could not have had any impact on the environment. A certain tone carries throughout the book in which Indian behavior is viewed through dark glasses and malevolent motives are subscribed to the Indians in contrast to the assumed purity of white environmentalists who sit in judgment over them. Prominent scholars endorsed the book even though it was filled with factual errors and illogical reasoning, and book reviewers chortled that Indians were no better environmentalists than the polluting industries of today. The watchword was the belief that every group of people has totally destroyed its lands and there is no reliable model for environmental ethics.

Krech often bases his accusations on anecdotal evidence of three hundred years ago and suggests that Indians have not improved since that time. Based on studies of the white farmers in the Salt River valley, Krech hypothesizes that Indian farmers engaged in the same commercial monoculture agriculture as did the whites of the 1890s and thereby made their lands sterile because of leaching salts in the water. He also suggests that Indians stripped bare the lands around some of the ancient ruins in the Four Corners, reducing the lands from a fertile forest to create deserts, when the lands have plainly been desert lands for countless millennia.

There is an almost automatic acceptance of anti-Indian themes in academia. White scholars will not, as a rule, defend Indians against the attacks of their colleagues because it is assumed that Indians are unworthy of defense. So any challenges to anti-Indian articles must come from Indians themselves. Not only are there attacks overturning familiar stereotypes, but many attacks are aimed to destroy or undermine whatever positive images Indians may have been able to generate in the last thirty years. So the Indian as a positive person becomes reduced to a submarginal existence in many people's consciousness. He becomes a creature without common sense or concern for the environment. Indeed, he becomes a creature devoid of moral and ethical behavior. We are encouraged to believe that Indians acted thoughtlessly and in a deliberately negative way whenever the opportunity presented itself. A prominent historian who was promulgating one of these ideas told me that she was only trying to level the playing field by pointing out that Indians were people with frailties. If that is the contemporary game, then frailties should be examined. The discussion, however, should be confined to topics for which there is ample evidence to carry the argument.

The academic image of Indians carries forward to the general public view of Indians. A good deal of the literature on Indians is generated by freelance writers and Indian buffs. Indians are regarded as secretive, mysterious people who possess some kind of knowledge not available to ordinary people. To validate this belief the writer must generate some status as an authority on Indians that is not available to him in an academic setting. The most common avenue for achieving this status is the "best friend" syndrome. Thus, a white writer comes to Pine Ridge, Taos, Hopi, or Nez Perce and becomes acquainted with a few people in the community. He or she attaches themselves to an elder or a group of people and pries out of them the information they want to believe. We next meet the writer during a publicity tour when the story of his or her reception by the Indians is revealed. As it turns out the elder or the traditional group has been preserving stories of immense importance that they have refused to share with their relatives or the local community. Upon seeing the writer coming down the road, however, they have eagerly embraced him or her and quickly revealed information of immense secrecy, sacredness, and sanity.

This format must have begun with John Neihardt's visit to Black Elk at Manderson, South Dakota, because prior to that book there were numerous Indians publishing books, recounting their lives, and talking about tribal customs and culture. Neihardt, as you will recall, claimed to have been perceived by Black Elk as having such a high moral and ethical profile that he was to be given information that not even the people of Pine Ridge could share. At least that's how Neihardt described it. But there was no reciprocity. Neihardt kept the money, Black Elk continued to be poor. The book, as we all know, has received immense support from its readers. It has survived efforts to debunk it and even sporadic efforts by Roman Catholic priests and scholars who try to argue that the best thoughts of Black Elk were the result of the teachings of the priests.

After Neihardt's achievement at becoming Black Elk's best friend the pattern was set for authenticating the non-Indian writer, and people uncritically believed that casual white visitors, if they were morally sound, would be showered with tribal secrets if they visited a reservation. They not only become the authority on a tribe or ceremony but their status is elevated above that of tribal members because of their innate moral superiority. Look at a partial list of "best friends": Stan Steiner, Peter Matthiesson, Frank Waters, Richard Erdoes, Thomas Mails, and so on. The list of morally correct writers who have fatefully become confidants of wise old Indians, have been forced to write books lest secrets be lost, and have become famous for their knowledge of Indians may be endless.

It is good to have friends with whom traditional people can share secrets. However, this claim of intellectual discipleship and inheritance eventually enables these writers to become authorities within academia because, if nothing else, they are at least decent writers who speak in a relatively comprehensible style without the academic jargon that negates most of the studies done on Indians. Here is a problem with authority that is most difficult to resolve. These writers have succeeded in sharing our authority as Indian scholars through their best-friend relationship and in the process have elevated themselves above Indian scholars. The simple reasoning is that Indian scholars as a rule do not often claim to have this ecclesiastical blessing but are rather oriented toward getting the approval of their white academic colleagues. Indians are at best a marginal group within American society, but we are submarginal in terms of academia and the reading public. This condition must be confronted and resolved.

Within the academic community, as we all know, are networks of people who attended graduate school together and are tightly bound together in a mutual support system that virtually eliminates a fair playing field. They constitute a feudalistic society in which there is competition only between competing networks of scholars. A scholar's academic pedigree begins with his supervising professor and continues with his peer group during his or her graduate years. In my contacts with scholars over the past three decades I have been struck by the casual way non-Indian scholars validate each other. Usually the major accomplishments of new scholars have been simply that they studied with a well-known scholar of the previous generation. No analysis is offered whether the person was a good student, whether he or she has produced anything significant in the years since, or whether the professor bent all the rules to get the student a degree—and that happens more often than we would like to believe. Employment at the professorate level is more often a reward for personal loyalty than an acknowledgement of the competency of the former student. I know of several professors who, while they had the necessary credentials with prominent professors of the past generation, had to have their classes listed as required because they could not teach a lick.

When the idea of affirmative action came along it did not sit well with most academics because it suggested that the academy was obligated to look, if but for a brief spell, at the credentials and accomplishments of minority scholars who had faithfully followed the prescribed path to academic employment and had met the requirements of the discipline. No established scholar was willing to look at the actual employment practices of departments, and so it was easy to continue to hire one's friends by simply announcing that the minority candidate did not meet the qualifications. For this reason universities have been forced to hire young Indian scholars as "targets of opportunity" or affirmative action candidates, implying that the minority scholar could not possibly qualify for employment otherwise. The younger generation of Indian scholars should perceive this status most critically because their academic careers depend on transforming an affirmative action hire into a positive, contributing member of otherwise staid and conservative departments.

Most Indian scholars of this generation have not had the benefit of these informal academic networks. Even if they have studied under a prominent white professor, little is done to keep them connected to the scholar and his progeny. Meeting objectively stated academic goals, then, does not really qualify Indians for positions in the university. We are now seeing Indian scholars failing to gain tenure and promotion because they have no connection to influential white scholars who can be mustered to plead their case. Since it will be difficult to make this connection in the future, Indian scholars must spend considerably more time planning their academic futures, developing allies within academic circles, and cultivating contacts outside the institutional setting in which they find themselves. They cannot, as many have done, try to walk the path of the previous generation of Indian scholars because that path no longer exists.

What then is the task of the current generation of Indian scholars? Minimally there must be new alliances, perhaps even mutual assistance pacts, made between scholars that can eventually be extended outward to embrace an increasing number of people. The same principle that tribes have followed must be adopted by this generation of scholars— an attack on one is an attack on all. This attitude sounds difficult and unfair and not within the scope of professional academic practice—but it is not. Imagine what would happen if an Ivy League or Jewish scholar were criticized unfairly and denied tenure. Those communities would immediately come into the issue and without hesitation support their colleague. Their response would be clothed in the proper academic language, but it would be strong, quick, and effective, and definitely political.

There is quite a bit of nonsense regarding the idea of community in academia today. I understand that some Indian professors, freshly endowed with Ivy League degrees, have rejected any discussion of the idea of community on the basis that such an entity no longer exists—if it ever did. Apart from parades designed to increase tourism, white American communities do have a hard time surviving in the larger society. Rural areas, whether white, brown, black, red, or yellow still have this strong sense of being a unique people, but even they are being undermined by the electronic universe of instant communication and Wal-Mart stores that destroy small businesses for hundreds of square miles. In the urban areas there are increased efforts to develop and sustain a sense of the neighborhood, but urban neighborhoods, which were traditionally based on ethnic and language similarities, hardly exist at all unless they are composed of racial minorities.

That there is a national Indian community should be evident in the powwows, basketball tournaments, and so forth that take place every year. Indeed, expenditures for some powwows could easily resolve some poverty problems if spent for that purpose. We invest heavily in social interaction and entertainment. Much of what passes for Indian political rhetoric originates at the grassroots level and works its way up to the national organizations. We already have some organizations of Indian scholars, but they are in the formative stage. They do not, as a rule, exert any influence on behalf of programs or individual scholars who are being removed by budget cuts and reorganizations at the university level.

Some members of this generation of scholars have told me that they find "politics" distasteful and will not engage in it. Yet the world is political and everything in it is political. How many of the decisions affecting younger scholars are based on merit? It is ludicrous to refuse to engage in politics at whatever level one finds oneself because that guarantees that you will unquestionably be a willing victim and the gracious gesture of playing "fair" will rebound against you. I know of no scholar, Indian or non-Indian, who does not have some contacts at the higher levels of university administration, within the professional journals, or at competing universities that were cultivated in part as a means of protecting themselves. So it becomes a measure of whether you can play the academic game with a minimum amount of political activity, not whether you can avoid politics altogether. You may never be disturbed during your academic career, but to rely on that probability when the specter of unrelenting racism is always going to affect your fortunes is foolhardy.

One absolute requirement in protecting minority scholars would be to make clear to scholars and administrators alike the radical difference between the demands placed on minorities and the demands on the white-majority scholar. The white professor arrives at his office. He or she may get a few phone calls from students or other professors, may call colleagues on committees or journals, may complain about no parking places, or may just fritter away the time before or after class. The minority professor, on the other hand, generally finds a mass of telephone calls from people who want to know the Indian word for "encouragement," who want a bibliography or books on Indian art, who ask where they can get Indian music, or who simply want to tell the professor of the nice Indians they met on their summer vacations. There will be several calls from Indians seeking assistance in some personal problem, who want the professor to find scholarships for their children, who are distant relatives come to say hello, or who are stranded in town and need gas money to get home.

The Indian professor will always be on a variety of committees so the university can claim that Indians were consulted and represented in whatever harebrained scheme the administrators have conceived. Since the Indian professors will be junior they will probably have to serve on departmental committees, and if there is a protest about anything affecting Indians and the university they will be expected to support the university without question. The Indian professor's day will be disrupted countless times as he or she will be regarded as an authority on anything remotely dealing with Indians. And university fundraisers will pester the Indian scholar whenever there is a chance for the university to get grants. They will expect scholars to enthusiastically endorse proposals even though they know that the majority of people who will be hired will be non-Indians.

The white scholar often lists as his or her community service and outreach some activity that requires only a willing presence, and department or university activities are given great credence since everyone knows that the category is false and designed to soften the image of the academic as totally irrelevant to society. Indian and other minority scholars, however, have community service as an almost overwhelming burden. They must continually prove to Indians and to university personnel that they are an active part of the local community. In spite of this vast difference in the allocation of time and energy, Indian scholars will be judged by wholly inappropriate criteria. They will be required to publish in prestigious journals even though those journals are closed to anyone outside the journal "in" group. Their writings will be judged on the basis of whether they are making a contribution to the latest theoretical fad in the discipline.

The older generation of scholars had some authority and avoided some of these pitfalls because we were willing to engage the practical problems of the ordinary people of our generation. Many of the problems of today are found inside academia. A whole new task awaits this generation of Indians. Today with the multitude of anti-Indian publications inside academia it would behoove younger scholars to raise a strong Indian voice against some of the nonsense as a first step in protecting themselves. It takes very little effort to refute poor scholars like Krech or Clifton; and to the degree that Indian scholars are willing to enter the lists and speak back, the majority of scholars in a discipline will offer support and also speak out. The practice at the university level, however, is to remain silent on issues until a clear trend is spotted so that the scholar can always be in the majority. When I criticized anthropologists in *Custer Died for Your Sins*, there was an outcry of unfairness by scholars, Indian and non-Indian. The Indians were the most vocal, and they accused me of trying to destroy the good relationships they had with white scholars. They were content to be good house pets in anthropology, but the sentiment at the grassroots level, where I had heard numerous complaints from elders who were tired of being studied, made many "anthros" admit that I had hit a nerve in both Indian and academic communities. It was delightful to see anthros confiding to me in deepest secrecy that they were really ethnohistorians, not anthropologists, and had always wanted to tell the people in the discipline the same thing—but never did.

Leadership today is governed by public opinion. Politicians do not move on any issue unless pollsters have assured them it is safe to have an opinion. Then they move half-heartedly behind an issue and offer a compromise that doesn't work and only slightly offends people. It is good to see so many young Indians appearing in the colleges and universities but it is very discouraging to see so few leaders. Why aren't we seeing Indian scholars engaged in serious debate about some of the anti-Indian articles and books being published? Why are there no responses to some of the nonsense that the anti-Indian scholars are offering? How many young scholars are known to reservation people so that instead of hiring non-Indians to do their historical research they can hire an Indian scholar? What are the goals, if any, of this coming generation? What would they like to see at the end of their careers?

It is not difficult to become engaged in the problems of our time.

The national Indian newspapers are filled with articles on projects and programs of the respective tribes. Can no one become interested in the progress of tribes raising buffalo and step forward and counteract the frequent articles accusing Indians of destroying the buffalo? What about the continuing struggle over the use and access to sacred lands? The Mormons are able to purchase a tract of historically important land now sacred to their church. We see no Indian scholars stepping forward to offer a proposal to return some sacred lands to tribes as part of a general settlement. What about the problems of repatriation and the uncovering of human remains in various parts of the country? Sports mascots? The world we live in is full of choice opportunities for the young scholar to make his or her mark. It sometimes seems as if the next generation of scholars is waiting for people to define everything before they can move forward.

Budget cuts today threaten programs straight across the board at the university level. Programs that have no community or national outreach or reputation will quickly be regarded as superfluous. Already at many universities Indian studies is being merged into ethnic programs that are token efforts to maintain a shred of visibility and a hint of racial parity lest the university be criticized for failing to serve minorities. Unless the Indian presence in higher education becomes productive in publications and community service, we can look to the dissipation of the movement to gain status for Indians in the academic world. Our scholars must step forward and occupy a prominent place in the national Indian community. By doing so they will ensure that they have viability and a place in American intellectual life.

2. ACADEMIC GATEKEEPERS
Devon Abbott Mihesuah

The colonization of Native America[1] has been documented extensively, and we like to think that most scholars are aware that the experience has been—and still is—crushing and brutal for many Indigenes.[2] Many scholars continue to document atrocities of the past, and a growing number discuss problems in the present. Despite all this writing, however, many professors, administrators, publishing houses, authors, and committees comprised of scholars are still contributing to the oppression of Natives.

They argue otherwise, but by purposely ignoring Indigenous voices, publishing repetitive monographs that offer little to tribes, hiring unqualified faculty, graduating unprepared students, and devaluing Indigenous programs and concerns on campus, many scholars and universities are still supporting, promoting, and acting upon many of the same colonial ideologies.

In 1940, Walter Benjamin (a German-Jewish writer) wrote about the opportunistic nature of rulers who inherit power: "All rulers are the heirs of those who conquered before them. Whoever has emerged victorious participates to this day in the triumphal procession in which the present rulers step over those who are lying prostrate. According to traditional practice, the spoils are carried along in the procession."[3]

The sentries guarding the gates of academia double as standard-bearers of the status quo and are in essence the "rulers" Benjamin discusses. They take advantage of the oppression of Indigenous peoples, and from their positions of power they decide who is amiable enough to be hired, neutral enough in their writings to be published, and Euroamerican enough in their outlooks to earn awards or qualify for grants and fellowships. In other words, in order to be acceptable to gatekeepers, Indigenous scholars and their work must be nonthreatening to those in power positions.

Every scholar, regardless of race, culture, or gender, is aware of academic gatekeeping because they have either run into blockades or they are gatekeepers themselves. Indigenous scholars are by no means the only ones victimized by gatekeeping: gays, females, and African, Asian, and Mexican Americans (and their supporters) are all well aware of who runs their universities and who maintains the status quo.[4] This piece addresses gatekeeping created specifically to monitor, dispel, and discourage Indigenous scholars and our allies.

I begin with the search committees who hire the professors who teach, write, sit on promotion and tenure committees, review manuscripts submitted for publication, and are elected to their professional organizations' conference committees; the discussion then moves to the publishing houses and writers of books used in classrooms. In practice, all of these positions meld into the others, ensuring successful gatekeeping in every aspect of Indigenous studies. An understanding of the subtleties of gatekeepers' strategies to protect the status quo is also crucial for every student, professor, and administrator who is either involved in Indigenous studies or who has Indigenous faculty or students in their departments.

Before proceeding, it is important to state that the relationships between Indigenous and non-Indigenous scholars (and indeed, among Indigenous scholars) are complex and not all the same. There are many friendships between Indigenous and non-Indigenous scholars, including respect and genuine concern on personal levels. The problems referred to here revolve around two major situations.

First is the behavior of many scholars who resent having to work with Native scholars who often have empirical knowledge that the gatekeepers will never acquire, and who also insist that Native studies exist for the betterment of tribes' situations. Gatekeepers rarely confront us to our faces; rather, they act out their frustrations behind the scenes through annual merit evaluations, promotion and tenure decisions, search and curriculum committees, and countless other academy portals through which they strike, do their damage, and plot the next attack.

The second are the gatekeeping strategies that keep Indigenous voices subsumed so that the gatekeepers' opinions representing the status quo emerge at the forefront of discussions about how Indigenous histories and cultures should be written and for what purpose. Examples of their behavior include neglecting to invite appropriate Native scholars to participate in anthology projects, refusing to cite our works where they should be mentioned, not asking us to speak at conference sessions and lecture series—in addition to making the inevitable defensive comments upon reading this essay that this is gatekeeping on my part designed to bar all non-Native people from writing about "Indian topics" and that I am setting up imaginary straw men to make my points.

Much is at stake for both sides of the controversy. Gatekeepers are concerned about their jobs, promotion, profit, and power. Most scholars are concerned about those things, but the major difference between the camps is that Native and non-Native scholars fighting the status quo are concerned about the welfare of tribes, empowerment for Indigenous peoples, inclusive stories of the past and present, and overturning the colonial structure, including the gatekeepers. Indigenes who do not strive for those goals only help to reinforce the power structure that subsumes all Natives,[5] and so do those "friendly" colleagues who stand by and watch gatekeeping occur.

Search committees on the lookout for candidates in an American Indian/Native studies position are usually given mandates by the deans of their colleges and their office of affirmative action to advertise in numerous publications most likely read by Indigenous scholars, to invite applications from specific individuals, and to keep all deliberations confidential. (The strategy of protecting the internal candidate who will win the position no matter who else applies is not addressed further here.) An obvious strategy in the game of gatekeeping is to hire a non-Indigenous person to teach courses under the umbrella of American Indian/Native American studies despite the existence of qualified Indigenous scholars in the pool. Very often, if the Indigenous candidate is viewed as a threat to the committee and department in question (that is, he or she is more published, is an advocate of utilizing Indigenous voices in their work, and promotes studies that benefit tribes), the search is cancelled, subversive measures are taken to discredit the candidate, or the qualifications of the other candidates are artificially inflated.

Sometimes the committee wants to avoid a strong Indigenous voice among the candidates and will not advertise widely enough in order to avoid obtaining a qualified pool. If they must advertise according to their affirmative action office's standards, the committee alters their game plan and will not notify the campus that the search is underway and announces the status of the search after the final candidates are chosen. This strategy ensures that few people know who was in the original pool and allows the gatekeeping search committee and department supporting it to hire a person to maintain the status quo. The goal is attained of keeping power and authority out of the hands of threatening scholars who are the most qualified.

At most universities it is not legal to state that the job is only for an Indigenous person; nevertheless, committees often know they are destined to hire only a Native, regardless of the qualifications of the rest of the pool. Admittedly, this is often a positive gatekeeping strategy for Natives. Sometimes administrators purposely move a Native candidate from the bottom of a list to the top and insist that person be hired. In some instances, this is a good thing because the Native candidate should have been at the top of this list in the first place. But in other situations, it can be a disastrous move if the person is not qualified.[6]

Similarly, sometimes universities hire candidates who say they are Native, but are not tribally enrolled (even though they may say they are; few universities require proof of tribal membership), or are enrolled with no cultural connections to their tribe, or are poorly qualified Indigenous people who are easily manipulated. These scholars will in turn sit on future search committees, and because they are an "authoritative voice" in the department about Native issues, they have a major influence in hiring candidates who are nonthreatening to them, and hence nonthreatening to the department.

This situation is common and the rationale frightening: by hiring a second-rate Indigenous person or a Native scholar with no concerns or knowledge about decolonization, the committee has satisfied the affirmative action office, the naïve supporters of Indian studies, local tribes, and the administration. More important, the "hire the mediocre scholar" strategy takes the power out of the hands of Indigenous and non-Indigenous scholars who preferred a candidate who challenges the status quo and who is not intimidated by those in power (quite often representatives of the power structure are on the search committee).[7] The symbiotic relationship works for many on campus because the Indigenous scholar plays on the white guilt of his or her colleagues to achieve promotion and tenure while the white professors know that they cannot be faulted for not supporting minorities, and they know they can keep the Indigenous scholar in an ineffective tactical position.

Professor gatekeepers then take their place in the classrooms, where they choose the books students read, compose lectures students hear, and determine who has the "right stuff" to graduate with terminal degrees. The number of complaints I have heard from students about some professors (and some are supposedly Natives) who teach topics dealing with Indigenous studies is staggering, and they can be grouped into categories that often overlap: ignorance, arrogance, racism, and jealousy.

Under the heading of ignorance are those professors who know little about Indigenous histories and cultures, yet nevertheless charge ahead and teach about savage wagon burners and innocent settlers who die at the hands of savages, and who assign books like Ian Frazier's *On the Rez*, Ruth Beebe Hill's *Hanta Yo*, and the complete works of Frederick Jackson Turner, and are completely unaware of the concepts of decolonization or Nation building. Some who are "pro-Indian" are known to "smoke" (using sage or cedar, or both) their classrooms prior to the start of each semester and to require that students attend at least one sweat lodge "ceremony." Ignorant professors are usually non-Natives, although it is ironic how often Native students tell me that the Indigenous professor who was hired as a mandate from the university is also clueless about tribal issues.

Ignorant professors also include many of those who may be well-published in the realm of AIS. They have won fellowships, grants, and scholarly awards, and they are known as "experts on Indians." They cannot define, much less discuss, concepts such as empowerment or sovereignty. They are idolized only by other ignorant people, but the latter are often in power positions.

Arrogant professors do not allow students to ask any questions except to clarify a point, and they will award inquisitive students with lesser grades. Arrogant professors not only dismiss Natives students' complaints, they also refuse to seek advice from activist, knowledgeable Native scholars, preferring to credit nonthreatening Indigenous professors who tell them what they want to hear. Arrogant professors will not attend diversity or sensitivity seminars and workshops, and if they must, they will argue with the moderators about the atrocities of "political correctness."

Also in this category are professors who are well aware of the concerns Native scholars have over their propensity to ignore Native voices yet require their graduate students to write according to the status quo (that is, to ignore Native versions of the past and present and not to focus on tribal concerns), and they tend to dwell excessively on Euroamerican theory and will not approve students' theses and dissertations unless they adhere to those standards. These professors are particularly difficult to combat because of the established power base that has been created from their politicking abilities and published works about Native peoples that make money for publishing houses.

There is also the über-arrogant professor who believes that tribes are too stupid to remember their histories (despite having extensive oral traditions) and who asserts that he or she is the chosen one who can single-handedly document the information for the mentally challenged Indigenes. This list includes the anthropologist James Clifton, whose publications suggest that few, if any, Indians remain today, and even if there are, they are too close to the topic to accurately write about themselves, and the German-American professor Ekkehart Malotki, who continues to write about sensitive and sacred aspects of Hopi religion and culture despite Hopis' objections to his work and being declared persona non grata on the reservation.[8]

Racist professors' gatekeeping strategy is best described by Brazilian educator and thinker Paulo Freire: "Projecting an absolute ignorance onto others, a characteristic of the ideology of oppression, negates education and knowledge as processes of inquiry. The teacher presents himself to his students as their necessary opposite; by considering their ignorance absolute, he justifies his own existence."[9]

Indigenous students have complained to me that professors say a variety of prejudicial statements to them, but because the students usually do not assert themselves and complain, the professor continues his or her behavior. One professor I know is notorious for telling his students that "Navajos had no civilization until whites brought it to them," while another tells his class that "students may write a term paper on any topic, but Indian students cannot write about Indian topics." This type of professor insists that the students keep quiet in class, not ask questions, and regurgitate facts and figures on exams without thinking about what the answers really mean. They consciously attempt to control the students' beliefs and behaviors, for, as Freire observes, "the more the oppressed can be led to adapt to the situation, the more easily they can be dominated."[10] In other words, accepting the versions of histories created by non-Natives keeps Indigenous students passive and under control.

Other professors are not racist, arrogant, or especially ignorant. But they are jealous, which may be the worst kind of gatekeeper, and they are well known across all spectrums of academia. Jealous gatekeepers are determined to keep power out of the hands of scholars of all races and cultures, especially those who are highly published, awarded, and secure in their stature outside the university. These gatekeepers do much harm because their behavior is calculated and purposeful; they routinely rumor-monger and lie about their object of jealousy. This type of behavior devastates Native programs and Native professors' careers, especially when it comes from an Indigenous professor who is insecure and suffering from intense internalized oppression. Looking for relief from their psychological distress, the best targets for troubled Indigenous scholars are other Indigenous scholars whom they see as fairer game than the "superior" whites. Their own gatekeeping strategy is simple but unrelenting: they question other Indigenous scholars' identities. Often they claim that only rez Indians or those who have worked for a tribe "really know" about important issues, and they volunteer for every committee they can. The latter ploy puts them in decision-making positions such as on search, award, internal university grant fellowship, and lecture series committees. This strategy turns the focus away from scholarship and actual knowledge and toward their real talents: the ability to politic and function as inadvertent roles as pawns for gatekeepers.

Professors also compose curriculum committees, entities that decide whether a proposed course meets their standards, regardless of the committee members' knowledge of the subject matter. Some years ago, we had one university curriculum committee member object to proposed courses on Indian history because, she rationalized, if a nutrition course can include discussion about all the food groups, then a history course surely can include lectures on all ethnicities. When it comes to courses on Indigenous histories and cultures, department curriculum committees and chairs often do not question the syllabi content, nor do they ask if the instructor is qualified to teach the course. This is why we often see stereotypes, incorrect information, inadequate reading lists, and inappropriate instructors in classrooms. Ironically, however, another college curriculum committee made an unprecedented demand before they would approve a course I taught on Native women: obtain approval letters from four different departments, a requirement that up until that time no other professor had to meet.

Representatives from all these categories serve on award, fellowship, and conference committees. Because of their lack of sensitivity and knowledge about tribal issues and methodologies about writing about Indians, and the reality that racism still affects Indigenous people, many of these committees proceed to give awards to authors who maintain the status quo they seek to protect and defend. Hence, we see award-winning books that include no Indigenous perspectives or contributions toward decolonization; they come to conclusions that please gatekeepers, and often the authors are friends with members of the awards committee. It is also curious that the few awards given to Native writers are almost always presented to fiction writers. Is this because voters know nothing about the importance of nonfiction work? Or is it because fiction writers—some with hazy tribal connections—truly contribute more to decolonization with their imaginary scenarios (although to be fair, some "fiction" is based on reality) than do scholars who devote their lives and careers to Nation building? Most likely, many fiction writers are apolitical and do not threaten readers; therefore, "lit-critters" can make careers studying Natives without lifting a finger to help solve tribal problems.

Fellowship-granting agencies in the humanities also tend to ignore Indigenous candidates in favor of white scholars who write about Indigenous peoples. In their view, white scholars are oh so noble to devote their scholarly lives to writing about poor Indigenous peoples. Ironically, judging by the numbers of Native people who have been turned down by the same foundations, Indigenous scholars, especially activists, apparently are not perceived as doing anything important.[11] It is also becoming clear that if fellowship committees are faced with a choice of deciding among a pool of Indigenous candidates they will select those candidates with letters of recommendation from white professors who maintain the status quo (and who have won awards bestowed by some of the aforementioned book awards and fellowship committees). Occasionally we see a deserving Indigenous scholar receive an award from a "nonminority" agency, but they are rarities and are usually in the field of literature.

Promotion, tenure, and merit committees are composed of gatekeepers armed with extraordinary powers over the careers and lives of candidates who often are more qualified than the people judging them. Horror stories could fill volumes about unfair tenure decisions and merit evaluations decided by a subjective group of jealous, racist, and misogynist peers. In the department where I worked for ten years it was not uncommon for allies to conspire for weeks over the voting of committee members to ensure that the status quo remained intact. I know from personal experience that committee members pass judgment on course material they know nothing about, books they have not read, and ideologies they have never heard of before. Colleagues at other institutions tell me that committees comment on things like "collegiality," a category Indigenous scholars often do not fare well in for the simple fact that they have been ostracized to various degrees since beginning their jobs. Ironically, whenever a university balks at giving an Indigenous scholar tenure, the rest of us know about it and make the decision not to apply to that university, thus denying the school a few qualified candidates for future position openings.

When we enter the world of publishing, including the way authors write and how reviewers of submitted manuscripts control who gets published, the issues become more disturbing because of the apparent freewheeling authority some writers have over their topics.

Few writers who submit manuscripts and essays to publishing houses and journals receive reader commentaries that recommend publication without any changes. Much of the time the comments are made in good spirit, that is, the reader wants to help the writer create the best manuscript possible. And as I like to tell writers who submit essays to the *American Indian Quarterly*, you want criticism before, not after, publication. As an editor who sends out numerous essays to even more reviewers each year, however, and as a fairly prolific writer myself, I can speak to the reality that many reviews are not done in good spirit. Some negative reviews are written to keep the status quo alive, and some are obviously written in retaliation for perceived past wrongs perpetrated by the writer against the reviewer, such as writing a bad book review, or as I found out, not accepting a lunch invitation and rejecting essays for *American Indian Quarterly*. As an editor, it is my responsibility to sort out retaliatory comments. As a writer, it is my job to try to educate my publishers as to the politics behind nonsensical comments.

An obvious and common way to retaliate publicly is to vent in published journal book reviews. Another form of gatekeeping (that can also be called "territoriality") in the review process is to discredit any submission that threatens the reviewer, that is, a submission that is on the same topic the reviewer focuses on. The reviewer then lists criticisms—rational or not—then checks the "not recommended" box. The editor of the press immediately notes that there is a problem with the submission regardless of the motives and qualifications of the reviewer, or even if there are other positive reviews; often the editor is ignorant about the topic. According to rules of the university press game, the editor often must then find another reviewer or tell the writer he or she must revise according to the negative review, then resubmit and the process begins once more. The result is a delayed review process, frustration for the writer, and satisfaction for the vindictive reviewer.

Authors are effective gatekeepers of the status quo. They make conscious decisions about source material, contributors to their anthologies, and theories they incorporate. A prominent example of author and publisher gatekeeping is Nancy Shoemaker and her books published by Routledge and Blackwell. One of her latest efforts, *Clearing a Path*, is a particularly condescending anthology that purposely ignores prominent Indigenous writers and their ideas. Quickly noticeable is that she mentions *Natives and Academics*, as well as Fixico's *Rethinking American Indian History*, in her introduction, but dismisses both in one sentence (Phil Deloria and Neal Salisbury do the same thing in their *A Companion to American Indian History*, only they refer to *Natives and Academics* as a "noteworthy" book, along with a variety of books that do not address the crucial issues *Natives and Academics* does).

In Shoemaker's *Clearing a Path*, the only Indigenous theorists mentioned outside of Craig Howe's chapter (and a handful scattered in the endnotes with no discussion about them in the text) are non-Natives. The same can be said about *A Companion to American Indian History*. Here we see a gatekeeping strategy at work: mention Indigenous scholars in the introduction, and that way you might not offend them and at the same time appear to be "cutting edge."[12] And hopefully, that named person won't present the book with negative reviews. A related gatekeeping tactic in which Shoemaker excels is to throw in statements here and there about the importance of including Indigenous voices, yet she only includes two.[13] In *Clearing a Path*, Craig Howe's interesting piece is one thing, but the essay by Choctaw Leanne Howe is quite another. Howe begins her essay with a mystical vignette about a flock of red-tailed hawks landing in her grandmother's back yard, evidently believing that an essay about Natives is not valid without throwing in a few stereotypes.[14] But because Howe is an Indigenous writer with talent for authoring fiction, Shoemaker probably feels her anthology is legitimized, much like James Clifton used Penny Jessel, the Shawnee woman who claims that an eagle landed on her shoulder prior to positively reviewing his *The Invented Indian*.

While utilizing non-Indigenous ideologies is not problematic in itself, it does become an issue when they are used exclusively and Indigenous voices are not included. It is obvious gatekeeping when the author purposefully ignores them. Shoemaker has repeated opportunities to discuss previously mentioned concepts and topics in all her essays. So do her authors. In the *A Companion* piece, "American Indian Education: by Indians versus for Indians," the author snubs notable works on education. The essay "The Sacred Black Hills" in Shoemaker's *American Indians* again brings to mind essays in *The Invented Indian* in which the contributors do their best to disprove tribal beliefs and stories. The author does not bother to discuss the sacredness of the Black Hills with Lakotas, the very people who could best inform her. The *Companion*'s "Primary Sources: Indian Goods and the History of American Colonialism and the Nineteenth Century Reservation" neglects to mention Indigenous authors and prefers to use biased nineteenth-century sources, apparently not grasping the reality that writers she cites merely repeat what historians before them have written.[15] Only a modicum of Native scholars appear in *A Companion's* "Wanted: More Histories of Indian Identity," a piece that excludes works by Indigenous writers who have written extensively on the topic. Unfortunately, the list of incomplete essays goes on, in addition to chapters that have little bearing on modern tribal life.

For examples of how the disjointed anthology *American Indians* fails readers, consider these questions: how can Nanih Wayah be discussed without including its importance to modern Choctaws? Why discuss gender issues without addressing how patriarchal thought continues to undermine tribal attempts at egalitarianism? Why talk about the benefits of European culture without acknowledging the devastation from the dependence on it? Why include statistics on the Cherokees without analysis or Cherokee perspectives of their complex past and present? How can one accept phrases like "survival, resistance and accommodation" or "we made it our own" in regards to boarding schools without also acknowledging the reality that internalized colonialism, insecurity, and acceptance of the status quo are also glaring results of the experience? Why was the essay on Alcatraz selected without also including Troy Johnson's knowledgeable discussions about the politics of AIM, the aftermath of Wounded Knee, and how modern Indigenous peoples define activism? For some reason, Phil Deloria praises this anthology as "extraordinary" and the "best in contemporary scholarship," an assessment which is just as disconcerting as the book.

With the exception of Craig Howe's essay (which ironically is the only commentary that matches the title of the book), and the pieces by the dependable Julie Cruikshank and James Brooks that belong in a more reputable anthology, *Clearing a Path* does not clear a path. The problem surfaces on page vii in the introduction, where Shoemaker makes the dubious claim that "few historians ever mention the word 'theory,'" despite the reality that "theories" are precisely what Indigenous scholars are concerned about, although not in the same way as Shoemaker. She claims about *Clearing a Path* that "this book will serve as a *starting point* for further discussion of what role theories should have in studies of the past" (emphasis mine). On the contrary, Shoemaker incessantly kicks around the same archaic ideas while simultaneously failing to give credit to Indigenous scholars who have previously articulated "her" new ones.

What is the use of studying history and culture if you cannot assist those alive today? Anthologies dealing with Indigenous histories, cultures, and writing methodologies cannot be considered complete without discussion of methodologies and Indigenous perspectives—not just one or two token voices within a quagmire of the same old history topics, but a chorus of input that completes the stories. To see even more how repetition abounds and which strong voices are missing, compare authors, essays, and topics in the above books to numerous other anthologies about Native history, culture, and methodologies of study, such as Sterling Evans's *American Indians in American History, 1870–2001* (Westport: Praeger, 2002).[16] Indigenous scholars want more-inclusive versions of the past and present and are disturbed about the overuse of historical and anthropological theories, such as those presented with great flourish in *Clearing a Path*.

Another noticeable trait about recent anthologies is how the same authors are quoted repeatedly, without consideration of criticisms of those works. The Shoemaker and Deloria anthologies consistently highlight Richard White's *The Middle Ground: Indians, Empires, and Republics in the Great Lakes Region, 1650–1815* (New York: Cambridge, 1991) without considering Susan Miller's important critique of White's book.[17] Patricia Galloway's *Choctaw Genesis* (Nebraska, 1995) is also cited repeatedly, despite the reality that she includes no source material from Choctaws.[18] With the exception of Taiaiake Gerald Alfred's essay on sovereignty, and to a lesser extent, Sidney L. Harring's piece on Indian law, neither the Routledge anthologies, the Blackwell readers, nor dozens of other recently published books address the crucial issues that Indigenous peoples are concerned about: decolonization, Nation building, and how the past impacts the present. Despite their posturing otherwise, these books are simply the same tedious, "comfy history"[19] that clogs library shelves.

It appears that many authors hope that by not mentioning our ideas readers will instead turn to them as the authoritative voices in Indigenous studies. Some of them have created a small dynasty of redundant anthologies that are evidently popular among the uninformed masses. Until academic journals start sending these books out to brave readers who will give thorough, intelligent critiques, publishers will be encouraged to publish the same material over and over.

Another major problem with publishing gatekeeping involves the review of published books. Peter McCormick, the book review editor of the *American Indian Quarterly*, has noticed that AIQ has not received any of the aforementioned books for review. Nor have we received much of anything in 2001–2 since Peter has been editor, but I have noticed that at least since I began editing the journal in 1998, AIQ has received mainly noncontroversial manuscripts that we have dubbed "Little Golden Guides." The majority of books we receive are not sent out for review because they offer no new ideas and no suggestions about decolonization or empowerment. Why do publishers send only select books? Why do they not send us books even after we make personal calls to their publicity department and ask for specific titles? Every author information form I have filled out contains a section on where my books should be sent for review. Unless the publicity people at over a dozen presses I can name are cleverer than we think, authors are purposely keeping certain journals off their lists because they know they will receive critical reviews of their controversial books.

On the other hand, as some of these anthologies illustrate, publishers don't necessarily care what critics think. Rejected manuscripts, if shopped around long enough, will find a publisher, and even if the press's publicity person receives negative responses to her invitations to blurb a book, there is always someone willing to give positive statements for the back cover.[20] Some manuscripts do not even go through a peer-review process. One does not have to include Indigenous voices in their work to be published, nor does one have to cite the work of Indigenous intellectuals. And, as Blackwell and Routledge show us, many publishers know nothing about writing about Natives and are only concerned about making money. As Blackwell has illustrated, many books are not published with Native people in mind; among all the readers of Indigenous histories, Indigenous people (and tribal colleges) are least likely to afford their outrageous prices. This is quite different from anthropologist Luke E. Lassiter's decision to donate all royalties from his *The Power of Kiowa Song* (University of Arizona Press, 1998) to the Kiowa Education Fund.

Tearing down the barriers erected by gatekeepers will be difficult, if not impossible, in many cases. Scholars who challenge these gatekeeping strategies, especially those with few or no allies, will be subject to retaliatory action because often they are the only ones who will speak up. Even though many of us serve as "window dressing" (that is, universities want us, but not our opinions), that does not mean that we and our allies will stop trying to do what is right.

Notes

1. That is, the loss of land and populations; erosion of lifeways; intrusion of religions and patriarchal thought that have destroyed traditional gender roles, disrupted tribal value systems, and caused rifts between tribal members; introduction of material items and policies from the Old World that resulted in dependency and unprecedented intertribal warfare; Indigenous women suffering abuse and sexual violence at the hands of Euroamericans and later from Indigenous men who suffer from the insecurity and displacement brought about by colonialism; and creation of stereotypes and false images of Natives, in addition to poverty, racism, cultural confusion, and psychological problems. All the effects of colonialism were and still are used to the colonizers' benefit.

2. I now use the terms "Indigenous," "Indigene" and "Native." "Native American" refers to anyone born in the United States. In Texas, Oklahoma and Arizona, at least, I see bumper stickers that read "Native," usually referring to a white person born in that state; but Native "Indians" also sport that same sticker in protest. "American Indian" is a thoroughly American term that does not recognize the first peoples of the continent. I like "Indigenous" because it is a clear stance as to the traditional beliefs of most tribes: their stories tell them that they were created here, not that they were created elsewhere and then migrated to the New World.

3. Walter Benjamin, cited in David Getches, Charles F. Wilkinson, and Robert Williams Jr., *Federal Indian Law: Cases and Materials*, 3d ed. (St. Paul MN: West, 1993), 44–45.

4. For discussions about African Americans in academia, see Joy James and Ruth Farmer, eds., *Spirit, Space and Survival: African American Women in (White) Academe* (New York: Routledge, 1993). For a revealing commentary on how gatekeeping works in social work specifically (but actually applies to all fields), see Robert A. Wertkin and Linda Cherrey Reeser, "Uncollegial Relationships Among Social Work Educators," *Journal of Teaching in Social Work* 11, no. 1/2 (1995), 101–17.

5. For example, a tribally enrolled acquaintance told me "I have never faced difficulty in the academy" and "I do not approve of this anthology." Of course, this person has repeatedly demonstrated an alliance with the status quo by expressing a resent-

ment of Native activists and discussions of decolonization, in addition to wholeheartedly supporting the self-identification of fraudulent Native colleagues (and not tribes' rights to determine who their members are), and by protesting potential activist guest speakers and courses focusing on recovering Indigenous knowledge.

6. I have served on numerous search committees in which we have been told that the finalists can be from any racial group or geographical area, but the final choice must be Native. On occasion, we have been told that the person must be Native and from a specific geographical area. This has caused much frustration because according to the rules of the game, sometimes we have only one (often unacceptable) choice.

7. For a powerful narrative of how these traits, in addition to territoriality, come together to form a stunning display of paranoia and racism, see Haunani-Kay Trask, *From a Native Daughter: Colonialism and Sovereignty in Hawai'i* (Honolulu: University of Hawai'i Press, 1999), 151–68.

8. Recently, Malotki proposed to give a talk on "Hopi cannibalism" and was censured by NAU's president, causing an outcry among faculty and students that his "academic freedom" had been violated. See "NAU Censors Prof's Title of Hopi Lecture," and "NAU Censors Professor," NAU *Lumberjack*, Feb. 21–27, 2001, 1, 2; "Professor's Actions Undermine Freedom," (the president's response), *Lumberjack*, Feb 28–March 13, 2001; "Letters: Professor's Reputation Speaks for Itself," *Lumberjack*, March 14–20, 2001, 9.

On the Salt Trail incident see: "Hopis Want to Block Historian's Book," *The Arizona Republic*, Aug. 19, 1990, D8; "Hopis Against Book's Printing," *Arizona Daily Sun* (Flagstaff), Sept. 16, 1990, 1, 4; "Dispute Between Scholar, Tribe Leaders Over Book on Hopi Ritual Raises Concerns about Censorship of Studies of American Indians," *Chronicle of Higher Education*, Oct. 17, 1990, A6, 8, 9. See also D. Mihesuah, "Suggested Guidelines for Researchers who Study American Indians," *American Indian Culture and Research Journal* 17, no. 3 (1993): 131–39.

9. Paulo Freire, *Pedagogy of the Oppressed* (New York: The Continuum International, 1970; reprints 1993 and 2000), 72.

10. Freire, *Pedagogy of the Oppressed*, 74.

11. Thanks to Angela Cavender Wilson for this observation.

12. I have found myself the object of thanks in several works of the past few years, despite the fact that my work was not discussed in the manuscripts, nor was I consulted about the books' contents. Another example of "introduction padding" is Morris Foster's *Being Comanche: A Social History of an American Community* (Tucson: University of Arizona Press, 1991). Until I spoke with my husband's family as to just how much time Foster spent with them, I had been under the impression (from Foster himself) that the book was in large part based on Comanche voices. Foster does utilize some Comanche sources, but he also slyly thanks some of my husband's family in the introduction, thus racking up a large list of apparent Indigenous informants. One puzzled cousin stated just last year that he still does not know why Foster thanked him.

13. For examples: in regards to American history beginning in 1607 she writes in *American Indians* (Malden MA: Blackwell, 2000), "By implication, Indians have no history outside of a European presence" (p. 3); in *Clearing a Path* (New York: Routledge, 2002), she says, "The individuals who come to mind as the world's most significant theorists are almost all European (Marx, Freud) and usually French (Foucault, Derrida, Lacan, Bourdieu). Even those theorists (Said, Fanon, Spivak, Bhabha) writing from the perspective of the colonized, or postcolonized, seem foreign and distant from North American Indian studies" (p. x), yet she allows the essay authors to mainly discuss these theorists.

14. Howe claims on page 30 that red-tails can grow up to ten pounds, when in reality large ones reach only two and one-half pounds. In regards to red-tails landing in flocks in someone's yard, Northern Arizona University wildlife biologist Paul Beier is not aware that these birds of prey ever rest and roost in proximity to each other. Of course, because the scenario Howe describes is not normal, the passage is appealing to many readers who fully expect Indians to be mysteriously capable of attracting birds of prey into their yards.

15. Other authors who write about Comanches and cite each other, use the same references, and do not incorporate Indian voices are: Gerald Betty, *Comanche Society: Before the Reservation* (College Station TX: A&M Press, 2002); Dee Brown and Martin F. Schmitt, *Fighting Indians of the West* (New York: Ballantine, 1978); T. R. Fehrenbach, *Comanches: The Destruction of a People* (New York: Knopf, 1974); William T. Hagan, *United States–Comanche Relation: The Reservation Years* (New Haven: Yale University Press, 1976); Charles L. Kenner, *A History of New Mexican-Plains Indian Relations* (Norman: University of Oklahoma Press, 1969); Ernest Wallace and E. Adamson Hoebel, *The Comanches: Lords of the South Plains* (Norman: University of Oklahoma Press, 1952); Thomas A. Kavenaugh, *Comanche Political History: An Ethnohistorical Perspective, 1706–1875* (Lincoln: University of Nebraska Press, 1996); Colonel W. S. Nye, *Carbine and Lance: The Story of Old Fort Sill* (Norman: University of Oklahoma Press, 1937); Dan L. Thrapp, *Encyclopedia of Frontier Biography*, vol. 2 (Glendale CA: Arthur H. Clark, 1988).

16. Evans's book is curious in that he published essays without authors' permissions (although getting permission only from the original publisher who owns the copyright is adequate, asking permission from the authors should be common courtesy). Also included are published conference speeches, one of which I know was submitted to the *American Indian Quarterly* and was quickly rejected. The editor at Praeger also has removed all endnotes that help further explain the text and did not bother to ask "contributors" what their current positions are.

17. Susan A. Miller, "Licensed Trafficking and Ethnogenetic Engineering," in D. Mihesuah, ed., *Natives and Academics: Researching and Writing about American Indians* (Lincoln: University of Nebraska Press, 1998), 100–110.

18. Galloway's award from the American Society for Ethnohistory, in addition to the James Mooney Award and McLemore Prize, also brings into question exactly what

is ethnohistory? If one can thank Choctaws in the introduction, yet not use their voices in the work, does this count as being inclusive?

19. "Comfy history" is also known as "flag-waving history," or history according to those in power. Comfy history makes one feel good because it is thoroughly controlled by the ones who write it and it helps them to maintain their privilege and power.

20. I was invited by Routledge to donate a back-cover statement to *Clearing a Path*, but declined. A year later, the finished product appeared with positive blurbs on the back cover.

3. CORRUPT STATE UNIVERSITY

The Organizational Psychology of Native Experience in Higher Education

Keith James

A particular university department with one Native faculty member had a faculty position to fill. A search committee was duly formed, applications solicited, and a short list of candidates selected for interview. After the last of the interviews had been conducted, a meeting was called to discuss perceptions of the candidates and decide whether to seek administration approval to make an offer to any of them. The chair of the search committee began the meeting by announcing that he had talked to all of the department faculty members in their offices or in the halls and all had agreed to make an offer to a certain candidate. Neither the search committee chair nor any of the committee members had, however, discussed the candidates prior to the "decision" meeting with the one Native member of the faculty. The Native faculty member pointed this out. The search committee chair acknowledged having missed the Native faculty member in advance of the meeting, but argued that this violation of procedures did not matter because, since everyone else was in agreement, the decision would have ended up being the same in any case. The chair further argued that getting fast approval to make an offer ahead of potential competing universities needed to be the most important consideration, and he forwarded the name of the applicant who had been selected in advance of the decision meeting to the university administration.

Events like that just described do not seem to be aberrations, according to discussions I have had over many years with Native faculty and staff at a number of mainstream higher education institutions. While the specific details may differ, Natives in academe often seem to find themselves excluded from access to important information, excluded from important decisions, and excluded from important resources. There is a logical argument to be made for discussing options and analyzing facts outside of the temporal and structural constraints of formal meetings.

When some groups or individuals who supposedly have a right to participate are systematically excluded, however, informal decisions pervert the official organizational system. When lines of inclusion and exclusion are based on social group membership, friendship, or conjoint cover-ups of unethical or unfair practices, the result is a corrupt, discriminatory system.

What causes such a system to develop and what sustains it? Why, moreover, are the goals and needs of Native students and Native communities often given little attention by colleges and universities? How should Native people, individually and collectively, deal with corrupt academic systems? In this chapter, I attempt to answer those questions by turning theories and research on the dynamics of social identities and institutional systems reflexively onto academe and the experiences of Native individuals and Native communities with it. I also offer some suggestions for how Native students, staff, and faculty can overcome social and institutional barriers to success in academe, as well as suggestions for how Native communities might get colleges and universities to better serve their needs.

Cultural, Genetic, Identity, and Psychosocial Causes

The image of an institution of higher education that many of us have internalized includes ideals of dominance of reason, meritocracy, free exchange of ideas, and humanistic support for the downtrodden. In higher education, as in organizations of other types, however, emotion, informal identity, and culture- and social-group-based norms frequently trump formal institutional ideals, goals, and policies. While colleges and universities have the stated missions of education, research, and service to the community, the reality is that they often put much more effort into rule making, paper shuffling, internal politics and game playing, resource grabbing and hoarding, rewarding of friends, and empty gestures than into any activities directly related to their mission.

Procedures for decision making and resource allocation may be devised and written, committees and task forces created, forms documenting the process completed and filed, but the real decisions are very often made behind the scenes thorough informal discussions and vote buying and trading. Professing one set of policies and procedures while actually operating under another is the essence of corruption. In fact, the tendency of groups whose members share a common identity to share information and decisions among themselves and withhold it from outsiders is a major corrupting force of bureaucratic systems. These "hall-talk" decisions (which can happen in places other than hallways) are, in fact, a favorite tactic of the powers that be in corrupt institutions.

Norms, Values, Identities, and the Implicit Academic System

Academic faculties and staffs bring to higher education implicit cultural and class values, norms, social identities, and social statuses. The structures and procedures of higher education flow from, build on, and reinforce the values, norms, identities and status systems of the mainstream majority. Identity, norms, and status converge to produce profound effects on individual thinking and behavior, as well as on group dynamics. Individuals and groups often fail to consciously recognize those effects, however, because these forces operate at unconscious and emotional levels. Values, norms, identity, and status largely operate nonverbally, in the mental background. They are, in short, informal systems.

Both Native and non-Native individuals often fail to recognize the disjunction of the formal and informal academic systems. Differences in implicit norms and identities from non-Native colleagues in higher education may make the informal system of academe difficult for Natives to deal with. The result is that Native individuals frequently find themselves in the "out" group in the dynamics of departments and academic institutions, as well as at the bottom of the academic-status hierarchy.

The Genetic Bases of Academic Identities

"With the weight of available information and evidence, it is difficult to deny the flagrantly apparent fact—from Auschwitz to (communist totalitarianism), and from Vietnam to racism—that our intelligence is the victim of a persistent, hereditary, genetic flaw in our brain, of which our intelligence itself is unaware at the very moment it carries out the orders it receives from that original defect."— Romain Gary, *Chien blanc. White Dog*

Everything about humans and everything humans do has a genetic basis and an environmental basis and is an outgrowth of the interplay of genes and environment. One's sense of who one is and with whom one shares elements of identity each have a genetic (inherited) basis. The whole functioning of the (relatively normal) human brain may, in fact, be designed to allow for and capitalize on the dialectic[1] between genetic and environmental inputs. Groups of humans who share a common genetic heritage also share, to some extent, values, behavior patterns, identity, and biochemistry, and those things differ to some extent across groups with different genetic heritages. An ability to unconsciously recognize apparent genetic similarity seems to occur among humans. Research with both animals and humans also indicates that individuals seen as relatives are substantially more likely to be on the receiving end of positive behaviors, and those seen as unrelated substantially more likely to be on the receiving end of negative behaviors.[2]

Cultural and Value Bases of Hostile Academic Climates

"How sad you can be, Truth, and how stupid you often are, (Science)."—Romain Gary, *Chien blanc. White Dog*

Values seem to provide an organizational framework on which all aspects of perception (self-perceptions included), cognition, belief, motivation, and complex behavior are built. Native cultures and individuals are varied and show a range of values and behavioral norms; mainstream, Canadian, or U.S.-born whites may have less cultural variability, but they also have some. There seem, nonetheless, to be some broad general differences in values between Native and non-Native people that contribute to Native difficulties in academia.

Value similarities and differences are fundamental to our understanding of who we are, who we are not, where we fit in social systems (with all of the preceding constituting our sense of identity), and how the world operates.[3] Together with racial differences, they provide the fundamental basis for the difficulties that Native people experience with academic institutions: Those institutions are controlled and populated largely by people who differ from Natives genetically, in values, and in the sense of identity that both of the latter underlie. This predisposes members of the majority and the institutions that they control to a fundamental lack of sympathy, support, or understanding of Native individuals or communities.

Perhaps most important, however, genetic and value-based identity influences who will receive *positive* treatment in the form of encouragement, nonverbal and verbal support, information, and resource and opportunity access. Those who are perceived as similar are more likely to be liked, helped, treated fairly, and to be supported with social and material resources.[4] Individuals who do not fit the surface image of professional or unit subcultures can be seen as threatening all of the functions they serve for the members. Such a threat promotes stereotyping of both in-group members (including self) and out-groups. Perceived differences are exacerbated and negative feelings about and behaviors toward out-groups become likely.[5]

The tendency to favor groups to whom one is linked racially and by a strong common in-group identity is favoritism. When favoritism is made systematic by a cluster of people, it morphs into cronyism, that is, a group of people working together to develop and maintain a corrupt informal system that benefits them by circumventing or supplanting formal rules and procedures. Some of the factors that encourage identity-based favoritism to be systematized in higher education are detailed in later sections of this chapter.

The most extreme version of cronyism is nepotism, and it seems all too common in academe. For example, I had the misfortune early in my career to be part of a program that also had a married couple. That couple formed an unshakable voting block in the program and attempted to control all of the faculty and students even in matters such as course content that are supposedly governed by the principle of academic freedom. Their behavior was perceived to be abusive and threatening to those they perceived to be of lower status. For example, the husband at one point told a graduate student they did not like that he was too stupid for graduate school and should not be in the program. This occurred in a public setting in front of several other students. The wife of that couple put up a picture of a pizza with a swastika on it to represent an Italian American faculty member with whom she had been arguing.

I opposed their behavior and they attacked me, and the department and university leadership sometimes passively and sometimes actively backed them. Academic administrators do not like people who complain, do not like to have to take a stand, and cronyism leads them to rally around those who are most similar to them regardless of the nature of a dispute. In this case, the administrators involved in the story were also, themselves, engaged in questionable mixings of family interests and job responsibilities. The department head was about to marry a woman who had been a graduate student in one of his classes. The university president had gotten his wife hired in a university job where she promptly deleted an important database for which there was no complete backup. That incident was covered up.

So nepotism and its weaker cousins, cronyism and favoritism, are important sources of corruption of the academic ideal of equability of procedures and treatment. Because they operate largely at the emotional and unconscious levels of much of identity, however, those in their sway often fail to recognize their influence or that it has corrupted the principles they profess to believe. Thus, many people in academics would argue that it is the part of modern society that is most welcoming to Native people. A line of study of what is called "Aversive" or "Modern Racism,"[6] however, sheds light on the accuracy of any protestations that discrimination rarely occurs in academia. That research indicates that many people who consider themselves to be tolerant of group differences and who would be horrified to have to acknowledge racist behavior will still engage in discriminatory behavior and prejudicial thinking when circumstances allow them to justify those actions as unrelated to group membership.

The Values of Science and the Values of Academic Institutions

There are also specific values of non-Native North America that help produce Native difficulties in higher education organizations. The mainstream science ethos is derived from cultural tendencies within mainstream Canadian and U.S. society. Those background cultural tendencies also directly affect how higher education structures and systems are designed and how they operate over time. For instance, relatively strong valuation of social group memberships (i.e., collectivism) and relatively strong valuation of independence and individuality (i.e., individualism) seem to be two fundamental approaches to life that help to define cultures and individuals. Native cultures have generally been characterized as relatively collectivistic[7], and non-Native North American ones as relatively individualistic.[8]

While, however, the ideal of mainstream U.S. individualism that is presented is one of self-sufficiency and independence of thought, all too often in recent decades, mainstream individualism has been more self-serving and hedonistic than independent. Much of the behavior of academic administrators and faculty is driven by desires for personal comfort, power, and money along with conformity to group norms that are perceived as likely to produce those outcomes. Corporate scandals at companies such as Enron and Xerox illustrate how hedonism and conformity can promote greed and abuse of employee and public trust among organizational leadership. University leaderships and power elites are not immune to these effects. Universities and science are actually rife with conformity pressures and normative patterns of thinking and behaving. In fact, Miner[9] found that university faculty members were, contrary to stereotypes of critical and independent thinking among academics, as inclined toward conformity as business professionals or students.

The ideals of science also dominate academic institutions even in most nonscience departments because science departments have historically had the political clout to control university policies and resource systems.[10] The consensus seems to be that scientists are oriented toward mastery of nature; priority to the technically sweet; progress (a better future); independence; and personal prestige and achievement. Science and science education are also inclined toward reductionism and specialization such that issues and problems are addressed in isolation from each other.[11] Interestingly, the real cutting edge of science does recognize integration and complexity as critical.[12] This has not yet, however, affected how most of the mainstream of science nor has it affected how science education is organized at colleges and universities.[13]

Reductionism and specialization have some worth. For instance, when knowledge, skills, and techniques are rapidly shifting (as they are in most scientific and technical disciplines), great pressure for functional specialization occurs because it greatly assists training and continued mastery. While there are clear benefits of some specialization, however, excessive functional specialization has also been shown to reduce creativity and the coordination of the multiple types of knowledge and skills that are necessary to address complex issues and goals.[14]

One of my Native student advisees used to constantly rant against the linearity and reductionism of academia. Those emphases simply did not fit with her tendency to see "not things, but the connections among things."[15] To my mind, however, she overreacted to the extent that she wanted to avoid all reduction and all linearity, even when it would be helpful to developing and presenting her work so that others could understand what she was saying. As I have argued elsewhere, it is not that linearity and reductionism are evil a priori, it is just that they tend to be overly valued by mainstream science and mainstream academics such that complexity and integration are often ignored or greeted with hostility even when circumstances really demand them.[16] Problems result because analyses and judgments tend to have very narrow foci regardless of the breadth of the issue(s) at hand; and those, such as many Native people, whose values tend more toward integration and synthesis, tend to be driven away from scientific and technical fields and higher education in general.

Another implicit value in science and engineering is what has been called the technological fix mentality. A significant part of mainstream North American society sees technology as capable of solving almost any problem, and technical virtuosity is often admired in and of itself. These values are so strong among many scientists and engineers that problems are often immediately defined in technological terms, and technical solutions are sought regardless of the true nature of the issue. In recent research, I have found that Native students and adults with strong Native identities are less likely to accept the technological fix mentality.[17] Thus, the technological fix value of science and higher education can help create negative climates for Native people.

A more general problem with mainstream science is hubris and frequent assertion of objectivity and orientation toward "the greatest good for the greatest number." The problems that scientists and engineers address, far from being the universal want of some amorphous general society, more typically reflect the issues that particular groups possessed of significant economic and political power desire to have addressed. Not surprisingly, the benefits of addressing those problems typically go more to those powerful groups, and the costs typically fall more on less-powerful social groups, such as Native communities. Scientists and engineers, far from being objective in this process, are generally part of the very elites that benefit.

Bureaucratic Culture in Higher Education

Bureaucracy is characterized by an effort to cluster organizational functions and activities into logically related groups of tasks that are then assigned to partitioned organizational units. Each unit is (ideally) composed of experts on the set of functions and tasks the unit has been assigned, and it is supposed to use a systematic set of formal rules and procedures to guide execution of unit activities and achievement of unit goals. Units are then clustered into bigger organizational subsections, and a hierarchy of professional managers supervises their operation. Deriving from the same Western orientation toward specialization and compartmentalization that informs the sciences, the bureaucratic form of organization gained impetus from nineteenth- and twentieth-century efforts in Western cultures to apply scientific ideals and strategies to the design and management of human institutions. Formal bureaucracy is one, probably *the* most widespread, of a group of systems for "scientific management" of organizations. Informal bureaucratic approaches were, however, around long before formal science or scientific management.

Obviously, to the extent that bureaucratic values are elaborations on Western and scientific ones, they also contribute to identity and climate problems for Native people in higher education.

The bureaucratic model of organizations was adopted to try to eliminate favoritism in organizational hiring, resource allocation, decision making, and dealing with outside entities. It was intended to professionalize workforces rather than having positions filled by spoils system rewarding of family members, friends, and political supporters. It was also intended to promote consistency and efficiency of operations by systematizing procedures and making them transparent by documenting and distributing them. As is often the case with human systems, however, the designs that look good in the abstract are frequently perverted in actual operation, and such is the case with the bureaucracy of a corrupt university. Bureaucracy and entrenched cultures, entrenched systems, and entrenched turfs often actually result in the exact opposite of what they are supposed to achieve. At the extreme, they essentially yield academic cults.

Professional Cultures, Bureaucratic Compartmentalization, and the Formation of Academic Cults

Departments, programs, and other functional academic groups can develop cultlike qualities. Cults are characterized by strong efforts to bind members' time and effort within the program and isolate them from outsiders; an authoritarian yet familial pattern of social organization; unique rituals and symbols; an orthodoxy of opinions that have polarized toward extremity to which members are pressured to conform and that mark them as distinct from non-members; and a sense of superiority and the right to flaunt rules in service of the goals and values of the group.

The development of academic cults is made more likely because members of bureaucratic systems are frequently screened for, and in large part hired on the basis of, acquiescence to and comfort with, hierarchy, dominance, and rote rules. An inclination toward bureaucracy seems to naturally occur among a sizable segment of the human race. Those with extreme bureaucratic orientations have what is known as authoritarian personalities.[18] In corrupt academic institutions, self-selection and external selection processes in favor of authoritarian personalities tend to extend to faculty as well as administrators. Thus, hierarchic control is made easier and dissention less likely. This facilitates the spread of corruption, once introduced, throughout the institutional system.

Specialized units within bureaucracies are also often linked to procedural mechanisms and requirements and allocation of resources (e.g., physical space and faculty teaching time) and rewards. Identifications with groups serve psychological and emotional needs, but they also provide opportunities for gaining accesses to physical and social resources. Identification is likely to occur, therefore, with the level (i.e., subgroup versus full group) of social organization and type of social group best able to meet whichever of these needs is most salient for an individual. Proximity is a major marker of group boundaries and in-group status. Thus, individuals are likely to begin to strongly view themselves at least partially in terms of unit identities because these are what are associated with interpretable differences in activities and outcomes. Focus on the overall organizational mission is, therefore, often lost, and unit goals and tasks and maintaining unit power come to be seen as *the* mission. Individuals with a strong Native identity are less likely to accede to the unit identity focus, and this adds another reason that they are unlikely to fit in well with corrupted bureaucratic systems.

The damaging potential effects of bureaucratic compartmentalization were illustrated when it was publicly revealed that the FBI, the CIA, defense intelligence, and the State Department had not effectively shared information or coordinated action regarding possible terrorism prior to the September 11, 2001, attacks because of turf fights and historic antipathies. Bureaucratic compartmentalization can also hinder effective academic functioning. For example, a particular Native faculty member had a course, the enrollment limit on which was raised from one semester to the next from 80 students to 120 students without any prior input from or notification to her. In addition, only 70 textbooks were ordered for the two sections of this class even though total potential enrollment was 240. Changes in course limits were neither routinely reported to nor considered by the bookstore in deciding the number of copies of any particular book to order. The result was that many students in the class had no textbooks for several weeks, the faculty member had an unanticipated increase in workload (more students), and the whole course suffered. When the faculty member got low student evaluations, however, the department blamed her, not itself or the university bureaucracy.

Another negative result of bureaucratic compartmentalization is that problems such as Native student dropout or Native community outreach tend to be ignored by most segments of academia if there are specialized offices assigned to address those things. Thus, Native (American Indian, or First Nations) student service or cooperative extension offices often become the symbolic salve that allows the rest of the institution to escape responsibility for Native issues.

Rigid Rules and Mission Corruption

Bureaucratic culture, structure, and systems promote rigid and hyper-cautious thinking and behavior that often bear no relation to real (and complex) organizational missions. Rules also tend to multiply and interact to the point of promoting paralysis. An example occurred when I once, using grant funds, brought a Native Canadian graduate student to my campus to make a presentation. The Internal Revenue Service (IRS) had recently sent a form letter to all organizations in the United States that stated that foreign nationals who were being paid for consulting work must have either a U.S. Social Security number or a taxpayer I.D. number. Organizations were then to use that number to report the payment to the IRS. Foreign consultants were often paying no taxes on U.S.-derived income. As was the university bureaucracy's inclination, however, the narrow IRS policy was interpreted in the broadest and most rigid way possible.

My Native Canadian student speaker drove to my university. Since he drove, though, I had to reimburse him for gas and lodging expenses for the trip. This gave the university accounting bureaucrats an opportunity to (mis)apply the new IRS policy. They decided that travel reimbursement constituted "payment" and that a student from outside the United States being brought to campus to speak at an academic conference was a "consultant." They refused, therefore, to issue travel reimbursement unless the student provided a U.S. Social Security number or taxpayer I.D. number. He had neither and would have had to put substantial time and energy into filling out and filing paperwork to obtain either. I tried to reason with the university bureaucrats. I tried contacting the IRS directly asking for a clarifying ruling, and got the same results as from the university bureaucracy: none. It took invocation of the Jay Treaty, intervention by a member of the U.S. House of Representatives, and a threat to take the story to the media to get a letter (unsigned: "maintain deniability" is a prime unwritten rule of bureaucracy) from the IRS indicating that it was all right for the university to reimburse the student.

Power Corrupts

The example just given shows how bureaucracy, when combined with control of resources, tends to make some feel entitled to dictate to those they are officially supposed to be serving. When power and status hierarchies are added to bureaucratic control systems, arrogance and abusive behavior by those with power are often the result. Power and status differentials are associated with multiple forms of institutionalized social discrimination and other types of organizational corruption.[19] For instance, one new Native PhD found that a member of her doctoral committee (not even the committee chair) who controlled hiring for a postdoctoral position she wanted had, without consulting her, submitted her dissertation for publication with himself as first author. Another Native student who worked for a megalomaniac medical school faculty member was denied access to what was supposed to be his dissertation data because the student refused to give free time to a particular project the faculty member wanted to carry out. Aside from the direct effects they create, such abuses of power often trigger strong feelings of stress in the targets, which can disrupt their performance and lead them to withdraw from the setting. Those indirect effects often seem, in fact, to be what the power abusers intend to achieve.

The extreme of corruption by power and status in academic institutions comes with faculty-student sexual affairs. For instance, one of my friends who is on the faculty of another university told me about a group of male faculty who, when he began his academic career in the late 1980s, had an ongoing competition to see who could seduce the greatest number of female students. Similarly, one of my former graduate advisees, a Native woman, told me that at her undergraduate institution there was even a special term (i.e., a piece of identity-reinforcing jargon) used among male faculty members to describe the behavior of seducing vulnerable female students: "grazing." Her understanding was that minority female students in general, and Native females in particular, were favored targets of the "grazers." Social and legal pressures have led many faculty members who once would have pursued such activities relatively openly to be more discreet. The issue has not gone away, however, and formal university policies in this regard and others are often not enforced in practice. It is part of the cronyism and corruption that sometimes lie behind the façade of openness and objectivity that institutions of higher education present to the public.

An additional twist to the hall-talk hiring story I told at the beginning of this chapter illustrates this. An incoming department chair (i.e., already selected by the administration in a hall-talk decision that subverted of the "official" chair selection process but not yet officially in office) backed up the search committee chair and his faculty cronies in subverting the formal decision process. The incoming department chair had, however, himself been reported to the administration a short time before for engaging in sex in his university office after being seen by someone who happened to walk past the open office window. The woman he was trysting with met him while volunteering on research being conducted by a female faculty member in order to gain experience to support an application to the department's graduate program. So, she was the nearest thing possible to being a graduate student. There were apparently discreet informal inquires made about the complaint, but no formal investigation was conducted. Other members of the faculty covered up for him, and he, in turn, supported them in their corruption of the official process for selecting new faculty. In drawing conclusions from this, I find myself repeating myself even if in slightly different words: sleazy individuals incline toward cronyism, cronyism corrupts institutional systems, and corrupt systems support cronyism and sleazy individual behavior.[20]

Lack of Adequate Administrative Power Can Also Corrupt

Often lacking power to make changes or influence outcomes within the official procedures and policies, supervisors and administrators can easily be tempted to exert influence through under-the-table means, trading of favors, coercion, and bribery. One near-fatal example occurred when a group of Native higher education staff members who also formed the core of a nonprofit community group were asked to put on a dinner of traditional foods for a national meeting of Native academics. They contacted the powers that were to try to arrange details and were run over various hurdles and made to jump through numerous hoops. An insurmountable barrier finally arose when the university's environmental protection officer (EPO) told them that they would have to document the handling of every item of food along every step of the way, from its production to their bringing it to the campus to get approval, even though they held a government permit for preparing and selling food. They could not meet that impossible burden of documentation, so they moved the dinner to an off-campus location, where it went off without problems. The EPO revealed his true motivation when he said, hearing that the dinner would be held off-campus instead of on, that he had to "protect the special status of the student union" (as the primary food supplier on campus). The vice-president who controlled the student union was both crony and ultimate supervisor of the EPO.

The near-tragedy that underscored the hypocrisy of the scuttling of the dinner came about two weeks later when heavy rains led to flooding the lowest two floors of that same student union. Several workers just managed to escape the building after nearly being swept away. Another building flooded in the same incident was the library, where about 50 percent of the holdings had been moved to the basement only a few weeks before to facilitate renovation of the upper floors. Among the books and other materials lost in the library flood were maps that showed that both the student union and the library stood in a floodplain. Similar floods had occurred over the same area in the 1920s and 1950s. One would have thought that someone (i.e., the EPO) whose job was supposedly to protect the safety of the campus would have been aware of the flood hazard and focused on addressing it rather than hindering nonprofit events in order to curry favor with his crony who controlled the food empire on campus. The flood was, though, spun to the public as an act of God, a one-hundred-year flood that could not have been anticipated. In corrupt colleges and university the buck often stops . . . nowhere.

Aside from favoritism, bribery, and coercion, another strategy that academic administrators use to help enhance their power is divide-and-conquer tactics to keep people who are being treated badly from banding together, as well as to give them a target for anger other than the administration. The compartmentalization of bureaucracy and some of the values of mainstream society and mainstream science make this easy to do in academia. However, I have seen and heard of it being frequently employed relative to Native employees or students. I have heard, over the years, stories of Native infighting at a number of institutions that gave the administration an excuse for not addressing Native concerns. Administrators sometimes intentionally stir up hostility between factions of their institution's Native members as a way of controlling—or an excuse for ignoring—all of them.

Corrupt or Merely Flawed?
Though I have used the phrase "corrupt" in describing a number of examples of problems in academia, are academic institutions really ever corrupt in the sense of morally degenerate or depraved and evil, or are they simply imperfect and subject to faults like all humans and all human creations? I would argue that some of the examples I have given, such as "grazing" by male faculty who attempt to prey on young women away from their families for the first time, are, in and of themselves,

enough to convict an institution of corruption. If those behaviors persist and the institution's leadership fails to act, the entire institution is liable to experience spreading corruption. In many other cases, however, my examples were intended to illustrate *corrupting influences* that move an institution closer toward becoming fully corrupt but that are not enough, singly, to signal the depravity of the entire institution. Higher educational organizations range along a continuum of having varying degrees of corrupting influences. None, I would argue, however, are completely free of them relative to how they deal with Native students, Native employees, and Native communities. As I have also argued earlier in this chapter, corrupting influences often tend to occur together because each of them helps support the development of others.

What Native Individuals Can Do
An initial consideration for any Native person contemplating affiliating with an academic organization has to be to try to get as clear a picture as possible of the nature of that organization. How corrupt is it? Does it provide a good climate for Native students and employees? Has it reached out to Native communities and worked with them on their goals, or has it either ignored them or exploited them for its own ends? Rather than relying solely or largely on the faculty or staff members of the department, talk to people in other departments, to students, the janitors, and anyone else who might offer a different perspective. Seek out records that cast light on internal functions and external relations. Search the local newspaper archives for stories about the institution. You may find several about discrimination lawsuits or several about projects with Native communities. Go to the school's library and ask what documents on the institution they have. Is there, for instance, information about the ethnic and gender composition of the entire institution and of particular units within it? Often at state institutions, at least, the titles and salaries of all employees will be on record at the library or perhaps on-line. Are there discrepancies between the salaries of Native and non-Native employees? What about student graduation rates and average years to graduation?

Native individuals must also *be realistic about their perceptions of academia*. Promoting such realism has been a main focus of this chapter because, as I said early on, the very real problems of academia are exacerbated in their effects by the fact that people (Native and otherwise) and communities (especially Native ones) often have an idealized view of what academic institutions stand for and how they function.

If you entered or are contemplating entering academia because you think you can accomplish important things for Native individuals, families, and communities, be prepared for a difficult challenge. You will need to work around and through the politics, inertia, narrow values, discrimination, cronyism, and corruption of higher educational institutions to achieve your goals. Steel yourself for difficulties and work out strategies and tactics that will allow you to survive and succeed. Build coalitions and support networks. Never join an academic institution unless you can see potential allies within it. Try not to let political games disrupt your performance or your focus on your goals. In a corrupt institution, never trust a promise from an academic administrator unless you have witnesses or have it in writing—and be skeptical even then. To paraphrase Mark Twain, the hierarchy of human deception is lies, damn lies, and every word an academic administrator utters.

The reality is that most Native people are no strangers to nepotistic, cronyistic, externally manipulated, disingenuous, corrupt systems. These are endemic among tribal governments, in tribal communities, and among federal programs targeted to Native people. Native students, faculty, and staff should, therefore, be well prepared to deal with the same systemic characteristics in higher education. That they often are not is partly because they do not expect those characteristics and so generally do not focus on diagnosing and managing them until a major problem occurs, and partly because they are away from family and friends and the familiar context that helps them deal with those systemic characteristics in their communities. It is also the case, though, that people in academe often have higher levels of skill and knowledge that allow them to put corrupt practices in effect in a more subtle and sublime fashion.

What Should Native Communities Do?

Native individuals sometimes chafe under the burden of having to educate academic colleagues and administrators about the cultural, historic, and community realities of Native people. We may have to do it, though, and we might want to work out ways of attempting to do it systematically. For example, wider understanding of the implications of cultural values such as consensus-seeking and humility for native leadership styles and self-evaluations might be effective in assisting Indian success in mainstream organizations. Native communities also need to, individually and collectively, demand that higher education assist them with their goals and needs, especially in state schools and especially in land-grant institutions. Community service is supposed to be part of the mission of and rationale for both of the latter. They often focus community service on the largest or most politically powerful communities and often think of Native communities only when the academic institution can gain funds from them. Native communities need to define what they want and need and systematically communicate it to higher education institutions, their governing boards, and the media. Instances of exploitation or high Native student dropout rates or other damaging actions by colleges and universities should be taken to the board of directors or trustees, to the press, and to the public, and should be consistently pursued over time.

Perhaps Native community collectives or Native nonprofits could begin to issue regular ratings of institutions of higher education on the quality of their service to Native students and communities and on their hiring and advancement of Native faculty and staff. Related ratings of television networks seem to be working to some extent in getting more minority characters into programs, getting more minority writers, technicians, and managers hired, and promoting development of more minority-focused programs.

Certainly Native communities should put their resources behind pushing higher educational institutions to serve their needs. For instance, to receive tribal student scholarships, research and grant collaboration, and media endorsement, higher education institutions should be required to document success at educating Native students and serving Native communities. To receive resources from tribes, they should have to have good records of retaining and graduating students; hiring and retaining Native faculty and staff; working collaboratively and effectively with communities on applied projects; and supporting ethical and participative approaches to research involving Native issues, people, and Native intellectual property. Mainstream institutions should also be systematically encouraged and coerced to work collaboratively with tribal colleges on educational, research, and applied projects. Tribal colleges are closer to communities but generally lack the resources and the expertise to do many of the things that they want or need to do for Native students and Native communities. Mainstream institutions need to support them more.

What Systemic Reforms in Higher Education Should Native and Non-Native People Support?

Based on examination of a number of different cultures, Wallace[21] identified five basic strategies for handling differences among groups in goals, values, norms, identification, and beliefs. Wallace's first type of strategy is what he calls the zero principle. This states that groups can attempt to deal with diversity by reducing it, with reduction being more effective the closer it gets to yielding zero diversity. Clearly this would run counter to my entire focus on how to turn higher education toward better service of Native people. Academic systems often, though, implicitly or explicitly try to zero out difference. That tendency needs to be recognized and opposed. While it is impossible and harmful to try to totally eliminate all difference, it is certainly important to avoid instituting differences where they need not exist. Use of unified, open structures and procedures along with minimizing power hierarchies would not only keep new differences from being created, it would keep unavoidable differences in things like area of focus from being exaggerated in apparent importance by a system and structure that makes them more salient and more closely linked to outcomes than are shared goals.

The second approach Wallace identifies as ad hoc (i.e., casual; unstructured) communications to cement relations. Although this type of communication cannot, by definition, be mandated or systematized, it can be facilitated or inhibited by organizational and professional cultures, structures, and procedures. Certain individual and group actions can also promote it. For instance, Native community leaders and parents of Native students could simply show up in the offices of department heads, faculty, and administrators rather than being seen only at prearranged formal meetings primarily with members of the central administration. Similarly, institutions could arrange to send representatives to talk, with no structured agenda, with tribal government leadership or grassroots community members. Wallace's third approach is inclusion. Lack of inclusion in decision making, goal setting, power structures, norms, and values is one of the major problems for Native people relative to mainstream higher education. Effective academic leadership is needed in framing new visions of education and science, couching them in terms that make them inspiring, keeping them salient, and reforming institutional structure and systems to support real and comprehensive Native inclusion.

Wallace's fourth type, what he calls end-linkage, is closely related to inclusion, vision, and mission. End-linkage involves creating formal connections among the activities, goals, ideas, and identities of the groups within a group. Within academic institutions, this would involve things such as rewarding cross-department faculty and staff collaboration in teaching, research, outreach, and professional development. One possibility that I proposed once at my university without success was to allow, encourage, or require two or more students to do theses or dissertations or other degree requirements collaboratively across degree programs. This would obviously directly encourage communication and integration among students with different foci, but the students would also, of course, drag their advisors and departmental staffs and administrations along, so that there would also be a broader institutional impact. Strategies might also be attempted to promote end-linkage in academia and between academia and communities. One obvious idea would be to broaden the representation of the oversight boards for colleges and universities, and therefore, the goals they focus on.

The last of Wallace's unifying strategies he calls the administrative approach. In this, some individual or set of individuals is given the role of facilitating and coordinating intergroup relations. Universities and professions could designate individuals or committees to plan and coordinate interarea ferment and synthesis. We lack enough individuals focused on weaving together different strands of content by engaging in synthesizing research and theorizing. We have been like Einstein's hypothetical individuals throwing bricks into heaps in hopes that they will spontaneously form houses. Few of us get training on synthesizing among areas; it should be provided to students, faculty, staff, and administrators. Research results indicate that effective boundary spanners promote creative and noncreative organizational performance and facilitate communication of important information among members.[22] To move higher education organizations and fields toward valuing and emphasizing boundary-spanning activity also requires vision or mission articulation and exhortation, along with application of supportive structural and systemic levers. For instance, allocating some control over important resources (decision-making power, information, materials, and money) to boundary spanners can facilitate their acceptance by others and their influence over them. Accreditation of higher education institutions could be partly based on inclusion of theory, research, or practice integration efforts throughout an institution; this might be an effective step to take to promote end-linkage. Native faculty and Native professional organizations (e.g., the American Indian Science and Engineering Society; the Society of Indian Psychologists) might consider forming their own accreditation boards that would develop and apply standards for certifying inclusion of Native perspectives (including cross-area synthesis), existence of Native supportive climates and systems, and attention to Native community goals and needs.

Conclusions

Academia is a combination of an economic enterprise and a calling. It also mixes many goals, missions, professions, and types of people. What we study and teach should inform how we who live in academia operate. If it does not, then, like an "integrity" expert I once encountered who was willing to lie and cheat for personal gain, we will ultimately be failures regardless of how much fame or wealth we gain. On the other hand, if we can turn our theories and knowledge reflexively on ourselves and deepen them and improve the health and effectiveness of our institutions by doing so, we can be more confident that they will be of genuine value elsewhere. This chapter is one small effort toward achieving those ends.

Notes

1. V. Turner, "Brain, Body and Culture," in *Brain, Culture and Human Spirit: Essays from an Emergent Evolutionary Perspective*, ed. J. B. Ashbrook (Lanham MD: University Press of America, 1993), 77–108.

2. J. P. Rushton, "Genetic Similarity, Human Altruism, and Group Se lection," *Behavioral and Brain Sciences* 12 (1989): 503–59.

3. H. Tajfel and J. C. Turner, "An Integrative Theory of Intergroup Conflict," in *The Social Psychology of Intergroup Relations*, ed. W. G. Austin and S. Worchel (Monterey CA: Brooks/Cole, 1979), 33–47.

4. Tajfel and Turner, "An Integrative Theory." See also K. James, "The Social Context of Organizational Justice: Cultural, Intergroup and Structural Effects on Justice Behaviors and Perceptions," in *Justice in the Workplace: Approaching Fairness in Human Resource Management*, ed. R. Cropanzano (Hillsdale NJ: Erlbaum, 1993), 21–50.

5. J. Greenberg, T. Pyszcynski, and S. Solomon, "The Causes and Consequences of Need for Self-esteem: A Terror Management Theory," in *Public Self and Private Self*, ed. R. F. Baumeister (New York: Springer-Verlag, 1986), 189–212; see also James, "Social Context of Organizational Justice."

6. S. L. Gaertner and J. F. Dovidio, "The Aversive Form of Racism," in *Prejudice, Discrimination, and Racism*, ed. J. F. Dovidio and S. L. Gaertner (Orlando FL: Academic Press, 1986), 61–89.

7. See, e.g., E. Badwound and W. G. Tierney, "Leadership and American Indian Values: The Tribal College Dilemma," *Journal of American Indian Education* 28 (1988): 9–15; and K. James, "Fires Need Fuel: Merging Science Education with American

Indian Community Needs," in *Science and Native American Communities*, ed. K. James (Lincoln: University of Nebraska Press, 2001).

8. G. Hofstede, "Culture and Organizations," *International Studies of Management and Organizations* 10 (1981): 15–41.

9. J. B. Miner, "Conformity among University Professors and Business Executives," *Administrative Science Quarterly* 7 (1962): 96–109.

10. A. Pacey, *The Culture of Technology* (Cambridge MA: M.I.T. Press, 1983).

11. Pacey, *Culture of Technology*.

12. See, e.g., N. Goldenfeld and L. P. Kadanoff, "Simple Lessons from Complexity," *Science* 284 (1999): 87–89; S. Wolfram, *A New Kind of Science* (Champaign IL: Wolfram, 2002).

13. Wolfram, *New Kind of Science*.

14. See, e.g., M. J. Dollinger, "Environmental Boundary Spanning and Information Processing Effects on Organizational Performance," *Academy of Management Journal* 27 (1984): 351–68; see also James, "Social Context of Organizational Justice."

15. H. Carruth, *The Selected Poetry of Hayden Carruth* (New York: Macmillan, 1985).

16. K. James and J. Eisenberg, "Personal Identity and Group Identity Influences on Algorithmic and Original Task Performance," *Creativity Research Journal* (in press).

17. See, e.g., K. James, "Identity, Values, and American Indian Beliefs about Science and Technology: A First Wave of Data," *American Indian Culture and Research Journal* (in press).

18. T. W. Adorno, E. Frenkel-Brunswik, D. J. Levinson, and R. N. Sanford, *The Authoritarian Personality* (New York: Harpers, 1950).

19. See, e.g., K. James, "Indian Identity, Indian Values, and Science," in *Research on American Indian Education*, ed. D. Chavers (Albuquerque: Catching the Dream Foundation, 2001), 121–140; F. Pratto, J. H. Liu, S. Levin, J. Sidanius, M. Shih, H. Bachrach, and P. Hegarty, "Social Dominance Orientation and the Legitimization of Inequality across Cultures," *Journal of Cross-Cultural Psychology* 31 (2000): 369–409.

20. G. Burrell, "Eco and the Bunnymen," in *Postmodernism and Organizations*, ed. J. Hassard and M. Parker (Thousand Oaks CA: Sage, 1993), 71–82; W. H. Hegarty and H. P. Sims, "Organizational Philosophy, Policies, and Objectives Related to Unethical Decision Behavior: A Laboratory Experiment," *Journal of Applied Psychology* 64 (1979): 331–38; M. Anderson, *Impostors in the Temple: A Blueprint for Improving Higher Education in America* (Palo Alto CA: Hoover Institution Press, 1996).

21. A. F. C. Wallace, *Culture and Personality*, 2nd ed. (New York: Random House, 1971).

22. Dollinger, "Environmental Boundary Spanning."

4. RECLAIMING OUR HUMANITY

Decolonization and the Recovery of Indigenous Knowledge

Angela Cavender Wilson

As Indigenous[1] scholars long exposed to intellectual imperialism, we often search for rational justifications to defend our cherished worldviews against attack by those who consistently wish to denigrate them. In the academy, this is a common occurrence. We realize that it is not just our individual academic freedom or right to an opinion that is at stake. We know that in our home communities our people are continuing to die at exceptionally early ages and that our lands and rights as Indigenous peoples are under constant threat. Our empirical and scholarly understandings substantiate the connection between the reality of our circumstances today and the five hundred years of terrorism and injustice we have faced as a consequence of European and American colonialism. In entering the academy most of us hope that our skills and research will contribute to bettering circumstances for Indigenous people. A growing number of us believe that as Aboriginal intellectuals we can best be of service to our nations by recovering the traditions that have been assaulted to near-extinction. For us, our traditions provide a potential basis for restoring health and dignity to our future generations.

In recent years I have been enormously influenced by the writings of Frantz Fanon and Paulo Freire. Fanon's argument regarding the necessity of decolonization and the overturning of the colonial structure in realizing freedom from oppression resonates strongly with me as a member of an Indigenous nation. In addition, Freire's commitment to the notion of praxis (reflection and action upon the world in order to transform it)[2] in his liberatory pedagogy also carries a vibrancy applicable to the struggles we face. After all, for what had I been continually seeking an education if not to transform the world around me and create a place where justice for Indigenous people is more than an illusion? Their teachings have given me a language to articulate my own struggle and what I perceive as the struggle of First Nations people to fight against our ongoing colonization. Unlike many of the previous theorists I had been exposed to in academia, their writings refreshingly offer hope for real-world change.

However, despite the tremendous importance of these great teachings for revolutionizing society, as Indigenous people our strategies for decolonization and empowerment are in some ways necessarily markedly different. For example, Freire's renowned and extraordinarily successful literacy program was predicated on the anthropological distinction between nature and culture in which culture is a characteristic specific to human beings and created by them. In thoroughly discussing this assumption with nonliterate people he hoped they would come to the understanding that many of the conditions of their lives are man-made and therefore capable of change.[3] For Indigenous people, while we certainly recognize characteristics of something called "culture" (the production and exchange of shared meanings including such things as language, ceremonial life, food, values, kinship structure, etc.) that might make adaptations through time, most of us have been taught that our core traditions were given directly to us from a divine source. Furthermore, we do not deny consciousness or "culture" to the other spiritual beings that inhabit this universe with us. Our attempt to elicit among our people a recognition of our power as individuals and as a collective group to transform our world, then, must emanate from a different assumption, and one which also considers respect for our nonhuman relatives. A return to the roots of our traditions will help define a new liberatory framework for the future.

Similarly, though Fanon argued that the Third World should not "be content to define itself in the terms and values which have preceded it,"[4] his hope for the future of Algerians in their postcolonial world depended on the abandonment of the folk beliefs of the past.[5] In this instance Fanon had assumed the colonizer's dismissal and hatred for Native traditions, a view that fundamentally clashes with our Indigenous decolonization strategies. At the same time, his own fierce struggle against colonialism compelled him to argue that "the underdeveloped countries ought to do their utmost to find their own particular values and methods and a style which shall be peculiar to them."[6] Indeed, as Indigenous people we must embrace the traditions of our past and advocate a return to those ways, beliefs, and values (many of which our oppressors have long disparaged) that formed the basis of our once strong and healthy nations.

Decolonization becomes central to unraveling the long history of colonization and returning well-being to our people. As Cree scholar Winona Wheeler explains, decolonization offers a strategy for empowerment: "A large part of decolonization entails developing a critical consciousness about the cause(s) of our oppression, the distortion of history, our own collaboration, and the degrees to which we have internalized colonialist ideas and practices. Decolonization requires auto-criticism, self-reflection, and a rejection of victimage. Decolonization is about empowerment—a belief that situations can be transformed, a belief and trust in our own peoples' values and abilities, and a willingness to make change. It is about transforming negative reactionary energy into the more positive rebuilding energy needed in our communities."[7] Decolonization in its farthest extension moves us beyond mere survival and becomes a means of restoring health and prosperity to our people by returning to traditions and ways of life that have been systematically suppressed.

The strategies we develop as Indigenous people of North America toward decolonization and empowerment must be distinct to us and developed from the guiding principles that allowed us to live a sustainable existence for thousands of years. When considering the plethora of social problems plaguing Indigenous communities today (including poverty, chemical dependency, depression, suicide, family violence, and disease), it is profoundly clear that these are the devastating consequences of conquest and colonization. For Indigenous nations, these problems were largely absent prior to European and American invasion and destruction of everything of value to us.[8] A reaffirmation of Indigenous epistemological and ontological foundations, then, in contemporary times offers a central form of resistance to the colonial forces that have consistently and methodically denigrated and silenced them.

For example, Kanien'kehaka scholar Taiaiake Alfred in his courageous work *Peace, Power, Righteousness* has called for a return to traditional forms of Indigenous governance as an alternative to the now-advocated European conception of "sovereignty" and as a necessity of long-term survival. He stands as an excellent example of an Indigenous scholar utilizing academic training to address the concrete needs of our communities. In addition, Alfred articulates the need for an Indigenous intelligentsia rooted in tradition and states that, "As intellectuals we have a responsibility to generate and sustain a social and political discourse that is respectful of the wisdom embedded within our traditions; we must find answers from within those traditions, and present them in ways that preserve the integrity of our languages and communicative styles. Most importantly, as writers and thinkers, we should be answerable to our nations and communities."[9] Clearly, as Native academics with intellectual strength we would be wise to heed this call and work toward the recovery of Indigenous traditions as part of our scholarly agenda and commitment to our tribal communities.

As Alfred has begun on the topic of Indigenous governance, so too must many aspects of Indigenous knowledge be studied, articulated, preserved, and adapted for effectiveness in the modern world. The recovery of traditional knowledge is deeply intertwined with the process of decolonization because for many of us it is only through a consciously critical assessment of how the historical process of colonization has systematically devalued our Indigenous ways that we can begin to reverse the damage wrought from those assaults. The revaluing of our ways through alternative knowledges becomes a consciously political act in which we actively resist the forces of colonialism while at the same time building Native nationalism. Native Hawaiian Haunani-Kay Trask explains that, "Indeed cultural hegemony is the cutting edge of the imperial enterprise, which explains why cultural nationalism becomes such a crucial Native strategy in the battle for decolonization."[10]

Some of the greatest resistors to the recovery of Indigenous knowledge are our own Native people who have internalized the racism and now uncritically accept ideologies of the dominant culture. As I worked to develop a Dakota language program within my home community, it became apparent that the boarding school experience coupled with Euro-American society's purposeful and complete denigration of our language had successfully destroyed the belief among many of my own people regarding the importance of our language. When the program crashed and burned after two years of success (including a Dakota language immersion preschool program where the children were beginning to express their thoughts in complete Dakota sentences after six months), I realized an important lesson. Because of the extent to which colonization had taken root, any efforts to restore our traditional ways would have to be matched with a strong community decolonization agenda. While developing a critical consciousness aimed at understanding precisely how colonialism has affected our health and mindset, and thus how we might meaningfully challenge that oppression, we can begin to reaffirm the richness and wisdom inherent in our traditional ways. Through a consciously critical adaptation, these ways can then provide the foundation to carry our people through the twenty-first century and beyond. Because these are ways that have been systematically suppressed, our alternative ways of seeing, being, thinking, and acting are necessarily political and a challenge to the dominant society. Sustained resistance to the status quo requires such energy that fostering a crucial mass of support for decolonization efforts in a community is necessary for long-term success at recovering Indigenous lifeways.

As Native academics, we are in the position to use our academic research and writing skills (as well as the available academic resources) to assist in the recovery of Indigenous knowledge. However, this presents its own particular challenge, as the academy has not historically valued or respected our knowledge. Often, the university has accepted only what it can appropriate for colonial purposes (the field of anthropology alone, notorious for their Indigenous data collecting, offers endless examples of this) and dismissed any knowledge that challenges the status quo and Western ways of knowing. As Indigenous scholars we simply cannot reject that which is unacceptable to the academy (because we value all Indigenous knowledge), so our task is to challenge the academy as an agent of colonialism and carve a place for our own traditions as legitimate subjects of scholarly study, but on our own terms. This means defying the disciplinary boundaries that dissect and categorize our traditions, as these boundaries simply do not exist in Indigenous ways in which the physical, spiritual, emotional, and intellectual are inseparable. We can specialize and narrow our efforts of concentration, but none of us may lose sight of the holistic traditions from which we have come. So while scholars like Alfred and De La Torre specialize in Indigenous governance, I focus on oral tradition and language, and others are concerned with additional areas of Indigenous knowledge, I think we would all agree that our work is part of a larger movement toward the recovery of the Indigenous ways that have provided sustenance and nurturing to our ancestors for thousands of years.

Engaging in an activity within the academy such as the recovery of Indigenous knowledge also presumes that to some extent Indigenous knowledge can be effectively transferable to an institution. This is a great presumption, and certainly we as Indigenous scholars would agree that there is much tribal knowledge that is inappropriate for the microscope, manuscript, or classroom. For example, Native human remains, grave goods, and other sacred objects are inappropriate for scholarly study. Many of us also believe that anything else dealing with the sacred, such as ceremonial life, should not be shared with those outside our communities or studied. As more militant activists, some of us might also suggest that particular decolonization strategies should not be revealed in scholarship. Therefore, each of us must distinguish what kind of knowledge can be respectfully researched, documented, and analyzed in the academy while aiding the long-term goals of our communities. This is an issue that simply cannot be defined by non-Native people.

Recovery of Indigenous knowledge is survivalist in nature, not only because of its potential to restore health and dignity to our people, but also because of how it will assist us in advancing our political aims against our oppressors. It originates among Indigenous people and openly endorses an Indigenous agenda. This flagrant dedication to Indigenous goals is openly political because it defies those who have been defining our existence for us and who have attempted to make us believe we are incapable of self-determination. This means that our first obligation as Native scholars engaged in this kind of work is not to the academy, but to our nations. This is similar to the kind of obligation Dakota scholar Elizabeth Cook-Lynn has faithfully argued is necessary for any scholars engaged in Native American studies: "Our responsibility is to the tribal nations that have survived terrible wars, that have signed solemn treaties with our enemies, that possess vast resources, the rivers people live by, the lands where our relatives are buried. This legacy is our constituency."[11]

Belief in the relevance of traditional knowledge in the twenty-first century is predicated on the notion that no matter how ancient our traditional knowledge may be, it offers a potential basis for rebuilding our Indigenous communities. While generalizations are sometimes difficult across tribal boundaries, some commonalities remain. For example, Indigenous people seem to share a belief that our way of life, land, ceremonies, and language are of divine origin. That is, a divine force placed each Indigenous nation, or guided us, to a specific place that would be our own, and provided us with a set of original directions about how we were to live. This is at odds with anthropological explanations of how our "cultures" have been constructed, and in response to such an explanation some anthropologists would likely condescendingly argue that this is simply how we "believe" our cultures have come to be. But as Indigenous people we "know" differently, we know these things are not imagined but are a reflection of our reality. I have heard some of my elders express the idea that it is precisely because we have been forced to stray so far from our original divine directions that we are experiencing so many difficulties in the modern world.

If these ways of life were given to all of us, those of us advocating their return are making a declaration about their relevance for contemporary Indigenous people. In this way our stance is not so different from the one taken by those involved in the early era of the National Indian Youth Council (NIYC). As Osage scholar Robert Warrior cites: "They sought a nationalism that would draw its strength from the cultural, political, and religious traditions that the U.S. government had tried to stamp out, a nationalism that would at the same time adapt itself to the contemporary situation."[12] While none of us seem prepared to reject everything from the modern world and return entirely to old ways even if this were a possibility, it is only reasonable to critically assess the outside colonial influences that have so miserably failed to improve our lives and have instead subjugated us to such despairing levels.

While Warrior links our contemporary struggle for sovereignty with a way of life that "is not a matter of defining a political ideology or having a detached discussion about the unifying structures and essences of American Indian traditions,"[13] I would argue the opposite. Our struggle for self-determination is precisely about examining (in a very attached way) the unifying structures and essences of American Indian traditions. We do need to sort out that which has been imposed on us, consciously and critically assess whether it supports or harms Indigenous value systems and worldviews, and make appropriate changes. While our traditional forms of knowledge may not have begun in a modern, hi-tech, capitalist society, existent in that traditional essence is a world in which our communities thrived and in which our people were healthy in mind, body, and spirit. We must look at the truths within our forms of knowledge and bring them forward to the modern world while simultaneously working to transform the modern world to create a society more in tune with our traditional values. As Vine Deloria Jr. and Alfred have elsewhere argued, our Indigenous societies have much to offer the rest of the world.

Commitment to Indigenous knowledge recovery also presumes that there is more to Indigenous survival than physical survival through a high enough blood-quantum and that this survival is linked with traditional forms of knowledge. It is an acknowledgment that other factors are intrinsic to the forging of an Indigenous identity that cannot be measured by blood level but are no less important; thus language and worldview, oral tradition, ceremonial life, values, and relationship with the land and other beings are all important in shaping Indigenous consciousnesses and ways of being.

Those who might be biologically Native but who are thinking and acting as colonized peoples assimilated into the dominant society may not become white, but what do they become? This question is answered by Indigenous scholars in differing ways. Alfred, for example, relates that, "Our bodies may live without our languages, lands, or freedom, but they will be hollow shells."[14] Similarly, Anishinaabe language activist Anton Treuer has stated that losing the Ojibwe language is tantamount to losing identity; without it they would become just descendants of the Ojibwe people.[15] At a conference in 2001, Vine Deloria Jr. used the phrase "genetic Indians" to apply to those who might be biologically Native, but who were thinking and acting like white people.[16] Those of us who realize the importance of a strong connection to our Indigenous communities in shaping our way of being would argue that this traditional knowledge is central to counteracting colonialism and the genetic Indian. Certainly without developing ourselves in this area, self-determination will be impossible and our nations will crumble. There is no way to build Native nationalism without the basis of that which makes us distinct peoples.[17]

This is not to suggest that there is no hope for the colonized genetic Indian. On the contrary, this is an area where our actions can work to bring others into the fold. Sahnish/Hidatsa scholar Michael Yellow Bird suggests a proactive alternative for Indigenous people who want to abandon colonialist practices for determining membership requirements and replace them with more consciously traditional standards of tribal membership. As an antidote to colonialism he recommends that tribal membership requirements shift from blood quantum to tribally developed concepts of citizenship.[18] An attempt to determine membership beyond standard blood quantum requirements would challenge Indigenous nations to identify distinctive core cultural traits that could be transmitted, fostered, measured, and used as a means to build Native nationalism and solidarity. As a protective measure in the contemporary world, Indigenous people must also maintain some requirement of blood quantum or lineal descendancy, otherwise exploitative New-Age groups or other opportunists could seek Indigenous nation status on the grounds that they had become culturally Indigenous (or "Indian at heart" as Pewewardy discusses in his essay on ethnic fraud). Membership determination has been a key component in the exercising of Indigenous self-determination, but as Indigenous nations engage in the process of decolonization, it is likely that tribes will begin to move beyond a racial determination as their sole criteria.[19] As Indigenous scholars it is legitimate for us to raise the question among our own people: how is it that our spiritual ancestors will recognize us and claim us? The recovery of Indigenous knowledge will help us to answer that question and work toward building future generations whose essence will be recognizable to the elders who came before us.

Though intellectuals such as Deloria have been arguing for decades the importance of traditional knowledge, and this has been a tenet of American Indian studies programs, this notion has been seemingly difficult for Indigenous scholars to promote in the academy. Previous generations of scholars were so few in number, many of them were pressured to adhere to their disciplinary strictures regarding appropriate topics and methods of research. Since the recovery of other forms of knowledge requires abandoning or challenging existing academic norms, many Indigenous scholars have chosen to protect their institutional status rather than risk being denied tenure and promotion because their research and publication was not "scholarly enough." Fortunately, there seems to be a growing number of us who are less concerned about our status in the white world and more concerned with helping our respective nations with long-term survival, and who also realize the value of our traditional ways of knowing. In addition, white individuals in some parts of the academy are acknowledging that there is much to be gained in exposure to and understanding of this traditional knowledge.[20] As we make inroads to the academy in this direction, we must also be aware that the old guard will be on the attack.

While many of us organize our research agendas based on directives from our communities, the academy often resists responsiveness to those directives. The following story is offered as an example. In March 1995, I was invited to participate in a conference at Western Michigan University on "Methodologies in American Indian History." It was a daunting experience: I was still a graduate student at the time, not even A.B.D., and I was presenting alongside Theda Purdue, James Axtell, and Richard White, scholars who had been adjudged the "New Indian historians" (a distinction intended to identify the newness of their approach to the writing of our history rather than an Indigenous identity). While all of them had the prestige of winning prizes, fellowships, and awards to complement the numerous books they tucked under their belts, I had only two short essays published in *American Indian Quarterly*. This was not entirely unimpressive at this early stage in my academic career, but in comparison with the other senior scholars, my publishing record was lean indeed. Still, I was appreciative that Don Fixico had asked me to present on the topic of methodologies in American Indian oral history, even if I would be offering the lone Indigenous perspective.

I knew my paper would be controversial as I was advocating such earth-shattering ideas as the importance of including Indigenous voices in the writing of history, the need for historians to get out and talk to Indigenous peoples to hear those voices, and the obligation historians have to learn Indigenous languages. Perhaps most challenging was my suggestion that because Indigenous people have other means of validating our historical record, historians should not subject our oral traditions to the same historical verification process as they would documentary evidence from their own written tradition. I expected that differences of opinion would arise at the conference stemming especially from this particular challenge to one of the cherished cardinal tenets of historical research and writing.

However, my presentation went smoothly, without any serious confrontations or disputes, and I thought the most difficult part of the conference was over. The next morning, however, it was Richard White's turn to present and it was clear to me that he was intent on defending those cherished tenets. Though historians across the country were touting his work as new, it was for the most part a reification of the same historical canon. In the discussion session, I followed up on his statements about the need to verify all evidence before it can be included in a historical text, astounded that he might dismiss the millions of Indigenous oral historical accounts because they might not be verifiable using standard historical methods. When I questioned him on this he was quite prepared and proceeded with a lengthy denunciation of what he termed "privileged information," that is, information that one person might have from any given source that cannot be validated. He stated unequivocally that such information had no place in historical writing. As someone who had already worked extensively with the oral tradition and knew firsthand how important our stories were but also that they stood little chance of being verified by some piece of paper somewhere, I was furious. After the session I retreated to the restroom and while crying I contemplated my withdrawal from the Ph.D. program in history. It wasn't just that I'd had a fierce exchange with a senior scholar in my field, it was that I had heard essentially that the only work I really cared about would have no place in history from *the* leading scholar in the field at the time.[21]

This was my first public entanglement with a prominent scholar in my field, but it would not be the last. Fortunately, I recovered from that experience and realized that more than ever it would be important for me to stay in the field of history to attempt to break down the barriers that have allowed historians to dismiss our languages, our voices, and our stories in order to perpetuate their colonialist versions of history that facilitate the continuing subjugation of our people.[22] This experience clarified for me the particular challenges that occur when attempting to reconcile Dakota knowledge and worldview contained in our oral tradition with the world of written history dominated by our colonizers. Ultimately I have realized that on the most basic level this was about seeking justice by challenging their power to define our humanity; or as my grandfather, Eli Taylor, stated about wanting his stories published, "I want them to know we are human." As humans, we have the right to argue that our ways of knowing are equal to any on earth and we have a right to challenge colonial claims to superiority.

Since then I have had ample time to reflect on my anger toward the vast majority of white historians who engage in research and writing about our past. Many have assisted in our colonization and the perpetuation of our oppression in myriad ways, including celebrating the myth of Manifest Destiny, making light of the genocide and terrorism experienced by our people, and holding firm to a progressive notion of history that forever locks our people's past and our "primitive" existence into a hierarchy where we occupy the bottom. More recently, many historians are guilty of focusing solely on the resiliency of Indigenous people while refusing to offer an honest and critical indictment of state and federal governments, leaders, and all the citizens of America who have been complicit in our bodily extermination, cultural eradication, and assaults on our lands and resources. Most historians have been accomplices in a great conspiracy to ensure Indigenous subordination.[23]

Aside from these already mammoth issues, historians are most offensive when they refuse to acknowledge our peoples' ways of knowing and being as legitimate and as worthy of academic attention as their own. In so doing, many scholars continue to dehumanize us by imposing a near-neanderthal mentality on our people. Not only is this racist and insulting, histories stemming from this dangerous misconception of Indigenous peoples have very real consequences for living First Nations people. For example, the tribal administrator on my home reservation estimated in 2002 that our young people had an eighty percent dropout rate in the public school in the town bordering our reservation. While a racist school curriculum is by no means the only factor affecting this outrageous statistic, it is certainly an important one.[24] The painful denial of self necessary for many to be successful in white academic institutions has been referred to by some scholars as "forced racial suicide," indicating the extent of violence to the identity of children.[25] In the area of history, then, it is essential for Indigenous scholars to put forth stories from our oral traditions that will undoubtedly challenge the myths of America and provide alternative perspectives largely unavailable in written documents. However, the advancing of paradigmatic shifts is not achieved without conservative backlash. As Smith quoted from Gayatri Spivak, "I would say that if one begins to take a whack at shaking the structure up, one sees how much more consolidated the opposition is."[26] This became apparent in the field of history with the formulation of a new organization, The Historical Society (THS). Upset by the relativistic doctrines of postmodernism, as well as the attack on the notion of objective history, this group was founded in 1999 as a means of restoring traditional ideals of historical scholarship (based, of course, on *documentary* evidence and *their* ideals).

Attacks come from more liberal-thinking scholars as well. Disappointingly, Phil Deloria argued in a recent historiographical essay that it is untenable for Native people "to write history through a strictly native lens."[27] While it is often useful for us to examine both Indigenous and white records of history, Deloria's assertion suggests that Indigenous oral traditions are not viable on their own. This is absurd considering that the majority of our history has little or nothing to do with white people and that our traditions thrived for thousands of years without white documents to validate them. In making such an argument Deloria is doing the work of our colonizers and delegitimizing the traditions from which we come. It is because of examples such as this that it is essential for Indigenous scholars and our non-Indigenous allies to identify and locate one another so that we can stand in support of one another.

One aspect of Indigenous knowledge recovery integral to Indigenous survival is the resuscitation of our languages. Federal government and church boarding schools in the United States and Canada are the primary perpetrators of the violent and unforgivable assaults upon this foundation of our cultures. As a result, Arapaho scholar and language activist

Stephen Greymorning has stated that "If we are not able to effectively pass our languages on to our youth, within the next 15 years we could witness the loss of as much as 85% of the Indian languages that are still presently spoken."[28] This bleak prognosis of language loss matters tremendously because the language is the key to worldview and values, much of which simply cannot be translated into English. Not only is our ceremonial life for most of us reliant upon our Native languages, so to do our languages reveal conceptions of all aspects of social and political life. Our stores of linguistic knowledge also teem with valuable information regarding the natural world in which our nations have lived for millennium. Our people had names for and a relationship with all the flora and fauna around us. It is these facts that make the loss so devastating. The generations of our elders who were punished for speaking our languages either had the ability to speak literally beaten out of them, or if they were fortunate enough to retain their language after years of abuse, they often chose not to teach it as a first language to their own children. Darrell Kipp, cofounder of the Piegan Institute of the Blackfeet Nation in Browning, Montana, reminded a group of language activists that while it is a hurtful reality that recent generations were not gifted with Native languages, ultimately, parents made that decision out of love. This was a way to protect their own children from the hurt and humiliation they were forced to endure as children.[29] This is one of the most painful consequences of colonization.

The damage done even among those who retained their languages after boarding school or even day school experiences has yet to be accurately assessed and quantified. The problem is that when young people cease to speak a language, the language ceases to change and adapt, and the language of imperialism closes in. Rather than making sense of the changing world through the lens of the Indigenous language, the world begins to be viewed through the dominant imperial language, and everything that implies. Fighting for language survival and recovery becomes a political challenge to the colonizing forces that worked so methodically and extensively to eradicate our cultural identity in this way. It makes sense that language revitalization has played a prominent role in the Indigenous cultural revolutions of New Zealand and Hawaii.

Though language work is tremendously valuable to Indigenous peoples, the academy has not always valued academic scholarship in this area. For example, my father, Chris Mato Nunpa, for over a decade has been the coordinator of the Dakota-English Dictionary Project, whose major goal has been the badly needed revision of the dictionary completed by white missionary Stephen R. Riggs in 1890. While his project could conceivably be one of the most important Dakota linguistic works for the next century, he was initially denied tenure at Southwest State University in part because many of his white colleagues did not consider his work "scholarly enough." Similarly, even white scholars who have engaged in linguistic work beneficial to tribes do not always receive the recognition they deserve from their white colleagues.[30]

Another aspect of Indigenous knowledge recovery crucial to our survival is in the area of health and diet. The health of Indigenous people in North and South America has been declining since the first germs were unleashed by the disease-carrying men of Columbus' second voyage. But while smallpox and influenza are not taking our lives in the twenty-first century, other diseases that are products of colonialism are still ravishing our nations. Diabetes and heart disease (not to mention alcoholism) have all taken extreme tolls on our communities, and it is rare that an Indigenous family is not touched by at least one, if not all, of these devastating conditions. Certainly diabetes and heart disease are long-term consequences of the poor diet fed and taught in boarding schools and the government commodities program combined with the loss of traditional lands, ecosystems, and way of life. With the highest rates of diabetes in America occurring among Indigenous people (with rates of over fifty percent in the adult populations of some communities), most of us are accustomed to the sight of people with missing limbs from diabetes-caused amputations. As these conditions were nonexistent prior to the invasion of our homelands, it is obvious that knowledge and recovery of our traditional food ways is an important means to restore health among our people. Indigenous scholars can utilize knowledge of precolonization food sources, including planting and harvesting methods. Many of these ways developed after thousands of years of interacting with a specific environment and have much to contribute to Western knowledge.

For example, scientists on the Cornell University campus have examined with interest the agronomically sound planting methods of the Haudenosaunee in seeking agricultural systems that are productive and sustainable over the long term while providing resistance to soil and land degradation. The Haudenosaunee have for over eight hundred years planted corn, beans, and squash together (referred to as the "Three Sisters"), which serves a variety of important functions: the corn provides support for the bean plants to grow, the beans provide nitrogen to the system, and the low-growing squash or pumpkins choke out any competing plant life (weed control). Combined with good soil management and crop rotation, they are assured a consistent and varied diet that is also respectful to the environment.[31]

At a diabetes conference last summer a group of us in attendance committed to the revitalization of our traditional ways discussed the importance of Dakota people returning to our traditional diet. In an experimental language and culture settlement we were brainstorming, we all agreed that in order to build healthy bodies, we need to return to a diet based on the plants and animals also indigenous to our homeland. If we could participate in a lifestyle that would allow us to sustain ourselves on the lean meats of venison, buffalo, and fish, wild rice from our traditional lands, corn, beans, and squash from our gardens, and the numerous berries, nuts, and root vegetables we routinely harvested, diabetes would not be a health concern for future generations. The supposedly "superior" diet and food ways forcefully imposed on us have only served to deteriorate the health of our people.

In addition, because Indigenous people have unsurpassed knowledge of our unique homelands and ecosystems, incredible stores of knowledge remain about medicines and healing practices. While these also could potentially provide invaluable contributions to modern medicine, we also need to be cautious about the extent to which we bring those to the academy. Exploitation of Indigenous knowledge can be profitable to opportunists interested in recognition and fortune. For example, after Loren Miller (director of the International Plant Medicine Corporation) obtained knowledge on a plant (ayahuasca) sacred to the Indigenous people of Ecuador, he successfully applied to the U.S. Patent and Trademark Office for a patent on the medicine, giving him monopoly rights in 1986 to commercialize the product.[32] Indigenous peoples of the Amazon Basin were faced with the biopiracy of their traditional knowledge; to Miller and the PTO it did not matter that it was a medicine Aboriginal peoples had used for centuries. While scientists in particular can use their skills to help us achieve specific goals, we must be cautious of the dangers inherent in publicly researching and publishing on these kinds of traditional knowledge.

As Indigenous academics, we can articulate the need for this recovery of a traditional diet and relationship with the land while also using our research skills to learn how this can be accomplished in the twenty-first century. We need to become active in this aspect immediately, as in many of our nations it is now only the elders who possess such knowledge and they are rapidly leaving this world. The recovery and practice of traditional knowledge, coupled with the political actions to make sure the positive environmental conditions of Indigenous animals and plants are protected, will assist in the physical and spiritual recovery of our people in a very concrete way. As Indigenous scholars, we must not fear this kind of political activism. In fact, if we seclude ourselves in our ivory towers and refrain from involving ourselves in the political aspects of these issues, we become betrayers of our nations.

While I briefly discuss in this essay specific aspects of traditional knowledge that have received some scholarly attention and are important to Indigenous survival (including Indigenous governance, oral history, language, and environmental understandings), these by no means exclusively represent all the areas in need of scholarly attention that are important to Indigenous survival. For example, there have been a variety of excellent recovery projects such as the result of work accomplished for repatriation efforts, historic and sacred site protection and preservation, community health projects, and others. Because it is truly only a recent phenomenon that scholars are asking how their research might benefit tribal communities (rather than what might be extracted from tribal communities), it is an area with wide-open possibilities and much more work to be done.

Reclamation of Indigenous knowledge is more than resistance to colonial domination, it is also a signifier of cultural revitalization and mounting Native nationalism. While the hard work of our internal decolonization remains a project that can only be taken up by people from within our communities, Indigenous scholars have the opportunity and obligation to utilize our research, analytic, writing, and teaching skills to facilitate that process in whatever way we can. In taking up this task the process of Indigenizing the academy has already been put into motion, but this is only the means to an end, not an end in itself. Ultimately, the strength of our Indigenous cultures rests in our ability to exert our humanity through the decolonization of our minds and the transformation of the world around us while recognizing that our truths stem from the eternal nature of our languages, ceremonies, worldviews, and values.

Notes

1. I prefer the term "Indigenous" over "American Indian," "Indian," and "Native American" because of the implicit notion of coming from the land, being of the land, which is an accurate description of our people's origins but also a political declaration about our claims to the land. The concept of Indigenous also challenges the anthropological explanation of how we came to populate this part of the world and thus is an especially important term in the context of academic writing. I also occasionally use "Aboriginal," "First Nation," or "Native" interchangeably with "Indigenous."

2. Paulo Freire, *Pedagogy of the Oppressed* (New York: Continuum International, 2001), 51. Originally published in 1970.

3. See Cynthia Brown, "Literacy in 30 Hours: Paulo Freire's Process in Northeast Brazil," in Ira Shore, ed., *Freire for the Classroom: A Sourcebook for Liberatory Teaching* (Portsmouth NH: Boynton/Cook, 1987), 215–31. Based on Freire's commitment to a liberatory pedagogy, he was the first to invite readers to critically examine his work and point out aspects he had not perceived. See Freire, *Pedagogy of the Oppressed*, 39. Similarly, in her feminist critique of Freire's work, bell hooks described his openness to her interrogation and thus "exemplified by his actions the principles of his work." See bell hooks, *Teaching to Transgress: Education as the Practice of Freedom* (New York: Routledge, 1994), 55.

4. Frantz Fanon, *Wretched of the Earth* (New York: Grove Press, 1963), 99.

5. Fanon, *Wretched of the Earth*, 55–58.

6. Fanon, *Wretched of the Earth*, 99.

7. Winona Lu-Ann Stevenson, *Decolonizing Tribal Histories*, PhD diss., University of California, Berkeley, 2000, 212.

8. Some might argue that poverty was prevalent in Indigenous societies prior to European or American intervention, and indeed, if one were to measure poverty by materialistic standards, this might be true. However, only in extreme circumstances would our ancestors have gone hungry, and most of our "riches" we would measure by nonmaterialistic standards.

9. Taiaiake Alfred, *Peace, Power, Righteousness: An Indigenous Manifesto* (Don Mills, Ontario: Oxford University Press, 1999), 143–44.

10. Haunani-Kay Trask, *From a Native Daughter: Colonialism & Sovereignty in Hawai'i* (Monroe ME: Common Courage Press, 1993), 52.

11. Elizabeth Cook-Lynn, *Anti-Indianism in Modern America: A Voice from Tatekeya's Earth*, (Urbana: University of Illinois Press, 2001), 154.

12. Robert Allen Warrior, *Tribal Secrets: Recovering American Indian Intellectual Traditions* (Minneapolis: University of Minnesota Press, 1995), 30.

13. Warrior, *Tribal Secrets*, 123.

14. Alfred, *Peace, Power, Righteousness*, xv.

15. Anton Treuer, "Building a Foundation for the Next Generation: A Path for Revival of the Ojibwe Language," *Oshkaabewis Native Journal* 3, no. 1 (spring 1996): 3–7.

16. This was during his presentation at the "Symposium on Cultural Sovereignty: Native Rights in the 21st Century," College of Law, Arizona State University, March 2001.

17. While many Indigenous people, including some academics, would argue that identity is not dependent on cultural or linguistic factors, this does not explain the tremendous sense of loss (versus cultural change) felt by many traditional elders. Indeed, I have heard many of my Dakota elders repeatedly lament the loss of our traditions and even suggest that there are no Dakotas left in some of our gaming communities, in spite of any blood-quantum requirements that might be met by its members.

18. Michael Yellow Bird, *A Model of the Effects of Colonialism*, (Lawrence: University of Kansas Office for the Study of Indigenous Social and Cultural Justice, 1998).

19. For an interesting discussion of membership requirements among the Mohawk, see Gerald R. Alfred, *Heeding the Voices of Our Ancestors: Kahnawake Mohawk Politics and the Rise of Native Nationalism* (Toronto: Oxford University Press, 1995), 169–77.

20. For example, in 2000 I was awarded a doctorate from Cornell University in history, partially fulfilled by a dissertation that used Dakota oral histories exclusively as its primary sources. Even a decade or two ago I am not sure this would have been possible.

21. Richard White's book *The Middle Ground: Indians, Empires, and Republics in the Great Lakes Region, 1650–1815)* (New York: Cambridge University Press, 1991) had already achieved marked recognition in the academic world, and White's name seemed to be synonymous with "God" in history departments across the country.

22. For an excellent discussion of the problems with some of these prize-winning scholars in the area of American Indian history, see Susan A. Miller, "Licensed Trafficking and Ethnogenetic Engineering," in Devon A. Mihesuah, ed., *Natives and Academics: Researching and Writing about American Indians* (Lincoln: University of Nebraska Press, 1998), 100–110.

23. Of course there are a few exceptions. For example, I admire the work of David Stannard, *American Holocaust: The Conquest of the New World* (New York: Oxford University Press, 1992), despite his insistence on perpetuating the Bering Strait migration myth; Howard Zinn, *A People's History of the United States* (New York: Harper Perennial, 1980), who has made the commitment to include voices that have been previously ignored or silenced; Robert Venables, who has shown exceptional commitment to Indigenous peoples in offering his expertise to serve tribal needs (particularly for the Haudenosauneee and Dakota); and Peter Iverson, who has given primacy to Indigenous voices in his most recent work on the Navajo.

24. For example, in 1998 we engaged in a lengthy and hostile battle with the Yellow Medicine East School District over the use of the racist *Little House on the Prairie* series in the school curriculum, which openly justifies and celebrates the genocide committed upon Indigenous peoples or at the very least their displacement to make way for white settlers. Two books per year were being taught in the third, fourth,

and fifth grades, so by the time students entered sixth grade they were thoroughly indoctrinated with the myth of Manifest Destiny and the superiority of white settlers over Indigenous inhabitants.

25. See Peter McLaren, *Life in Schools: An Introduction to Critical Pedagogy in the Foundations of Education* (New York: Longman, 1989), 215.

26. Smith, *Decolonizing Methodologies*, 71.

27. Philip J. Deloria, "Historiography," in Philip Deloria and Neal Salisbury, *A Companion to American Indian History* (London: Blackwell, 2002), 21.

28. Stephen Greymorning, "Running the Gauntlet of an Indigenous Language Program," in Jon Reyner, Gina Cantoni, Robert N. St. Clair, and Evangeline Parsons Yazzie, eds., *Revitalizing Indigenous Languages* (Flagstaff: Northern Arizona University, 1999), 6.

29. Darrell R. Kipp, "Encouragement, Guidance, Insights, and Lessons Learned for Native Language Activists Developing Their Own Tribal Language Programs" (St. Paul MN: Piegan Institute, Printed by the Grotto Foundation, 2000), 7–8.

30. For example, I think the linguistic work of Raymond DeMallie and Douglas Parks at Indiana University has been undervalued, though it is vitally important for the survival of the languages with which they work. In addition, they have generously shared their dictionary database software program (as well as the personal training to use it) with Indigenous people involved in similar language projects.

31. Jane Mt. Pleasant, "The Iroquois Sustainers: Practices of a Longterm Agriculture in the Northeast," in Jose Barreiro, ed., *Indian Corn of the Americas: Gift to the World, Northeast Indian Quarterly* Columbus Quincentenary Edition (spring/summer 1989): 33–39.

32. Craig Benjamin, "Amazonian Confrontation: Native Nations Challenge the Patenting of Sacred Plants," *Native Peoples* (winter 1998): 24–33. Thankfully, it is my understanding that in November 1999 the U.S. Patent and Trademark Office rejected the ayahuasca patent in response to a request for reexamination of the patent in March 1999 by the Washington, DC-based Center for International Environmental Law, on behalf of the Coordinating Body of Indigenous Organizations of the Amazon Basin and the Amazon Coalition.

5. WARRIOR SCHOLARSHIP

Seeing the University as a Ground of Contention

Taiaiake Alfred

What is "Indigenizing the academy?" To me, it means that we are working to change universities so that they become places where the values, principles, and modes of organization and behavior of our people are respected in, and hopefully even integrated into, the larger system of structures and processes that make up the university itself. In pursuing this objective, whether as students attempting to integrate traditional views and bring authentic community voices to our work, or as faculty members attempting to abide by a traditional ethic in the conduct of our relations in fulfilling our professional responsibilities, we as Indigenous people immediately come into confrontation with the fact that universities are intolerant of and resistant to any meaningful "Indigenizing."

It is not simply that universities are founded and function on premises that are different from those that underlie Indigenous cultures, which if it were true would imply a somewhat benign posture to our knowledge and ways of interacting with each other and the world. It is that they are adamantly and aggressively opposed to Indigenous ways. Our experiences in universities reflect the tensions and dynamics of our relationships as Indigenous peoples interacting with people and institutions in society as a whole: an existence of constant and pervasive struggle to resist assimilation to the values and culture of the larger society. In this, contrary to what is sometimes naively assumed by us and propagated by universities themselves, universities are not safe ground. In fact, they are not even so special or different in any meaningful way from other institutions; they are microcosms of the larger societal struggle. But they are the places where we as academics work—they are our sites of colonialism. And, they are our responsibility. Like all Indigenous people, if we are accountable to our nations and truly cognizant and respectful of our cultures, we have as a responsibility to do what we can where we are to ensure the survival of our culture and our nations. Being in the university, we as Indigenous academics have the responsibility to work to defeat the operation of colonialism within the university and to reorder academe.

So, let's get to work. If we are to Indigenize the university, we must first come to understand what it is that we are up against. I have used the term "colonialism," but I sense that our common understanding of what that term means is lacking. We understand colonialism as the major historical evil that our people have had to face; and we understand it mainly in material terms, as political injustices, domination, dispossession of lands, or economic oppression. Some understandings of colonialism touch on some of the psychological or spiritual effects of all of the material loss, manifested in dysfunctional or self-destructive behaviors. But I believe that the true meaning of "colonialism" emerges from a consideration of how we as Indigenous peoples have lost the freedom to exist as Indigenous peoples in almost every single sphere of our existence. The thing that must be defeated, colonialism, is far beyond being merely an economic or political problem with psychological manifestations. I think of it like this instead: it is the fundamental denial of our freedom to be Indigenous in a meaningful way, and the unjust occupation of the physical, social, and political spaces we need in order to survive as Indigenous peoples.

Let us see how far this definition of the problem takes us toward our goal of Indigenizing the university. Colonialism is not an historical era, nor is it a theory or merely a political and economic relationship. It is a total existence, a way of thinking about oneself and others always in terms of domination and submission that has come to form the very foundation of our individual and collective lives. It is a vast unnatural and exploiting reality that has been imposed on the world over the past five hundred years. We have been uprooted from a natural existence and angrily torn down the respectful, harmonious, and spiritual relationships that were the foundation of our societies in the past. In their place, we have adopted anti-nature ways of life and constructed coercive regimes of control. Life was an integral whole and had meaning beyond commerce and a purpose higher than acquisition. But we disconnected from that former life. This experience has torn us apart emotionally and psychologically as we have tried to comprehend and reconcile what has happened; we have been separated from ourselves. The colonial order divided our people into politically and economically manageable units; it separated each one of us from the other. It convinced us to live a commercial ethic and to accept a life of material excess; it has separated all of us as human beings from other beings and the earth. The future purported to offer us liberty and human satisfaction, but only in the denial of truthful histories and suppression of organic social and political relationships that emerge from respectful coexistence between human beings and the other beings and elements of the natural world.

In this denial and suppression, "colonialism" is a lie that divides, and it is a lie that conquers. It is the profound lie must be confronted if we are to have any hope of living free and authentic lives; indeed, if we are to survive at all.

More than anything else, colonialism is a way of thinking. It is a way of thinking about something fundamental to who we are as a society: the relationship between the past and the present, between the newcomers and the original people of this land. Five hundred years of physical and psychological warfare have created a culture of fear among both the subdued and dominant peoples. We have all emerged out of a shameful past, a history of racial and religious hatreds, of extreme violence, and of profound injustice. It is impossible to even acknowledge it truthfully. Our modern culture, for both the victims and the perpetrators, consists in a denial of the past and of its moral implications. It is an aversion to the truth about who we really are and where we come from. More than the moneyed privilege of the newcomers, more than the chaotic disadvantage of the original peoples, this is what we have inherited from our shared past: relationships founded on hatred and violence and a culture founded on lies to assuage the guilt or shame of it all. We are afraid of our memories, afraid of what we have become, afraid of each other, and afraid for the future. Fear is the foundation of the way we are in the world and the way we think about the future. It has become normal, and we have grown used to it.

All of what we know as government and law is founded on these fears. The powerful in our society manage the words we hear and the images we see to ensure that we remain afraid. Although the past and its implications are self-evident, we are complicit in their denial because it is too painful or arduous or costly to imagine an existence unbound from the lies. Emotionally and psychologically, we are attached to this mythology of colonialism because it explains the Euroamerican conquest and normalizes it in our lives. The perpetrators know that it is wrong to steal a country, and to deny it is a crime; the victims know that it is shameful to accept defeat lying down. Yet complacency rules over both because the thought of what might come out of transcending the lies is too . . . fearsome.

What kind of culture has this denial of truth and wearing down of authenticity—of rooted, healthy, and meaningful ways of life—in the service of political and economic power produced? This question must be asked not only of the victim but of the oppressor as well. Colonialism is a total relation of power, and it has shaped the existence not only of those who have suffered its effects but also those who have profited from it. The culture we have inherited is thoroughly infused with the values of domination and submission, fear and compliance, and the act of unrestrained and unthinking consumption that is the engine of our economic and political system. It is an artificial culture that is impossible to sustain and an existence that disconnects people from their lands, their communities, their histories, and their languages, the very things that give them strength, health, and happiness in their lives. This is the life we are leading.

What is the alternative that we can think about and promote? What is the path to freedom that we can help our people find? There is a way to transcend the legacy and implications of colonialism and achieve a better society, one founded on principles of justice. The present injustice is founded on lies, and it can be undone with the truth. I am not referring to one or another versions of ideological "truth" that are really only prejudice, religious, racial, or nationalistic. I am speaking of the development of a collective and shared understanding of who we are and where we are headed as a society. The conception of the truth that will liberate us from our colonial past is this: honesty and courage lead to mutual understanding, and understanding creates the crucial connections that generate the sense of community—love—that is needed to overcome the disconnection and division and mutual hatreds that reinforce colonialism.

The Indigenous struggle to find meaning and to create a psychological and social space for freedom in our lives is the struggle of all people in the modern world who seek to transcend the disconnection that five centuries of oppression have bequeathed us, cynically named "culture." Theorists and activists have long sought ways to bring an alternative postcolonial reality to the world, but they have failed to confront colonialism at the root, as a psychological state and a pattern of thinking and a way of seeing the world and other people—put in terms of our current struggle, the absolute destruction of the Indigenous way of thinking and living.

The university is contentious ground. This may seem like an obvious point, given the petty controversies and personal conflicts that are facts of life in any academic institution. But in asserting that the university is a battlefield, I mean this in a different, profound sense, and in a way that should cause Indigenous scholars to refocus their view on the role they are playing and on the battles they are fighting. In the contemporary era, as Vine Deloria Jr. points out in his essay in this volume, Indigenous scholars have for the most part proven unprepared mentally, emotionally, and physically to take on the struggles of their nations. Indigenous scholars have for the most part escaped to the university and insulated themselves from any accountability to the conflicts and challenges being faced by their people in the communities. With Deloria, I too believe that, in our politics in universities and for the most part in tribal politics as well, we are not making a courageous stand for the integrity of our nationhood or pride in our traditional cultures, we are rushing headlong into the enemy's camp. It's becoming clear that in withdrawing from relevancy and immersing ourselves in the battle for personal gain or involving ourselves only in disciplinary and academic fights, we are playing assimilation's endgame. The important struggles are not in the low-stakes squabbling over professional recognition, maneuvering for prestige and status, or scrambling for departmental resources for our programs. These are all at their roots selfish and premised on a value system that is individualist.

The real struggle is to preserve Indigenous regimes of respectful coexistence in the face of ongoing and intensifying imperial presence in our lands and in our lives. Our freedom and independence and the integrity of our traditional cultures have been nearly decimated, and colonialism's newest turn strikes even deeper than land loss and political control ever could. Today they are after our values and our vision of the future, and universities are the front lines. This is a fight for the future, sometimes open and sometimes subtle, but always ongoing.

I see two competing visions of the future: imperial, with juridical homogeneity and accession of the state's power to impose and enforce one ethical standard for values, behavior, and vision; and coexistence, a social balance between independence and interdependence ("independency") of peoples, and a political relationship founded on an ethic of pluralism in a framework of respect. These are issues of fundamental citizenship and identity that are largely ignored in scholarship and teaching by Indigenous people today. Among our people in universities, there is an unspoken yet profound accession to a government-defined notion of citizenship and a corporate-controlled consumer identity undifferentiated in any significant way from the general population (I am discounting folkloric lamentations or tokenistic posturing as meaningful expressions of Indigenous difference).

For those among us who are opposed to assimilation to the North American standard of conformity to possessive individualism, consumer culture, and state patriotism, there are two imperatives in an Indigenous ethical frame. The first is to respect, value, and honor differences (independence); and the second is to organize one's mind and attitudes around the idea of the sharing of space (interdependence). This is "traditional" Indigenous thinking—for all their diversity in expression, Indigenous worldviews are all predicated on these fundamental notions. But Indigenous scholars in universities are not promoting this worldview today. Instead, universities are part of the larger institutional system serving imperial objectives, today called "globalization" when referring to the economic facets of the process or "modernity" in relation to the cultural facets. With very few exceptions, universities are sites of production of imperial values and ethics, and Indigenous academics are unfortunately no different from the other people who populate universities and are characterized by and large by traits of intellectual servitude to the dominant societies' ideas and theories, moral abdication of the responsibility to stand against the injustice being done to their people, and submission to the incentives structured within a capitalist consumer culture.

Given that academe today is such a crucial part of the larger injustice of modernity—and specific injustices against our nations—Indigenous academics have a responsibility to oppose not only the specific acts of aggression and denial of freedom against themselves and their interests, but the whole structure and function of the university itself. Our people are on the verge of losing an entire way of life, as well as their memory of the histories that not only sustain us as unique cultures but which are also the foundation of the political and economic rights and freedoms that we still do have. All of this is being lost.

The question for Indigenous academics is this: are we part of the process of destruction of Indigenous cultures and nations, or are we upholding our responsibility to contend with it? What can we do? And what is the way to transcend this situation and regenerate our communities and cultures so that our peoples may survive into the future? The most common answers to that question come in the form of big political or economic solutions to massive historical injustices: self-government, land claims, economic development, and the legal recognition of our sovereign rights as nations. It must be admitted that these types of solutions are crucial goals. In the long term, it will be absolutely necessary to redefine and fully reconstruct the governmental and economic relationship between the original peoples and settlers in this country. Yet at this point in our history, to the extent that self-government, land claims, and economic development schemes have been successfully negotiated and implemented, there is no evidence that they have done anything to make but a very small minority of our people happier and healthier.

In most cases, these initiatives create new bureaucracies and put in place new levels and forms of government or new relationships with non-Indigenous business partners. These new arrangements benefit a few people within communities; mainly elected leaders, entrepreneurs, lawyers, consultants, and, to a much lesser extent, the people who staff the various structures. There is no denying that self-government, land claims, and economic development are a great thing for this fortunate minority. This is not to begrudge the fact that some of us have gained the education and skills needed to secure jobs or create businesses—these are the just rewards of honest people who have worked hard to create strength for themselves. But in the midst of all of the apparent progress, there is a nagging sense that something is wrong with the path we are on. There is a dawning awareness among those who think outside themselves, those who care for the not-so-fortunate and all-too-easily ignored ninety percent of our people who do not get any benefit at all from the new political and economic order. It is the sinking feeling that political power and money, the things we've worked so hard to achieve, are still not going to be enough to liberate us from the past.

The real reason most of our people endure unhappy and unhealthy lives has nothing to do with governmental powers or money. The lack of these things only contributes to making a bad situation worse. The root of the problem is that we are living a spiritual crisis, a darkness that descended on our people at the time we became disconnected from our lands and from our cultures. We are divided amongst ourselves and confused in our own minds about who we are and what kind of life we should be living. We depend on others to feed us and to teach us how to look, feel, and live. We turn to white men for the answers to our problems. We have started to trust them. There are no more leaders and hardly a place left to go where you can *just be an Indian*. This is a spiritual crisis. We are the prophetic Seventh Generation. If we do not find a way out of the crisis, we will be consumed by the darkness, and whether it is through self-destruction or assimilation, our nations will not survive another generation.

Large-scale governmental "solutions" like self-government and land claims are not so much lies as they are irrelevant to this root problem of spiritual crisis. For generations now, we have been on a quest for political power and money; somewhere along the journey from the past to the future, we seem to have forgotten that when we started out our goal was to reconnect with our lands and to preserve our culture and way of life. It is these things that are the true guarantees of peace, health, strength, and happiness—of survival—for Indigenous peoples. Before we can ever start rebuilding our nations and then achieve meaningful change in the areas of law and government, of economies and development, we must start to remember one important thing: nations are made up of people. Our concern about defining Indigenous rights and developing models of self-government has led to the neglect of the fundamental building blocks of our nationhood: the women and men, youth and elders who make up our communities.

This is where Indigenous academics can serve a most important role: as teachers of an empowering and truthful sense of the past and who we are, and as visionaries of a dignified alternative to the indignity of cultural assimilation and political surrender. The core of our existence as nations is in our traditional cultures. The strongest weapon we have against the power of the state to destroy us at the core is the truth. We need to turn away from defining our purpose and methods by Western academic standards and be accountable to our cultural heritage and to our people. We need to perform self-sacrifice as a warrior places himself or herself between danger and the people. Where the obvious danger today is assimilation, I say this: to be a real Indigenous intellectual, one must be a warrior of the truth. Fulfilling our purpose means engaging in resistance with the moral purpose of contending against imperial and commercial power and its suffusion into the way we live our lives and see the world.

So what, then, is the new "resistance"? I can think of three aspects of contending with imperial power that would manifest in the way we teach, do scholarship, and live our lives if we lived true to a new Warrior Scholarship ethic:

1. Honor knowledges from Indigenous traditional cultures—defend and promote the "independency" view of a relation to the earth and each other in the face of

increasing and nearly hegemonic consumptive materialism and extreme individualism.
2. Defy the unjust notion of juridical unity—fight for political independences in the face of state sovereignty.
3. Subvert the pretensions of coopted Indigenous scholars and imperial or civil servants—denounce and confront false claims of authority and legitimacy.

In a sense, the new resistance should be directed at a new adversary, and this is the current idea of "authority" itself—statist authority, disembodied and disconnected from the people and in the service of corporate objectives. The Warrior Scholar's cause is freedom to exist as an Indigenous person and within an Indigenous community in accord with the traditional natural philosophies.

Some may think that they've heard this all before . . . But this posture—the academic as warrior in resistance mode—is not just talk, it is seriously anti-imperial. The Warrior Scholar's effect on society can be profound because academic institutions create the attitudes and beliefs that sustain imperial relations, in the generation of false memory and artificial values, and they enable injustice by providing innovation on intellectual techniques and training imperial servants in the mechanics of dominion. Universities are, to turn an old anti-imperial phrase, "the heart of whiteness." They accomplish the acceptance and normalization of Western ideas, the glorification of Western societies as the highest form of human organization, and promote the emulation of North American culture to the next generation of citizens (and to Indigenous students as well unless there is some critical intervention). Although, today it must be recognized that the "white man" has been deracialized and reformed as a mentality within colonizers of all colors.

From concept (theory) to experience (strategy): How do we confront this in our work and in our lives on campus? Action is the key—there is enough knowledge, and enough analyses of the situation, but a desperate lack of action on what we have learned. Indigenous insurgency is most needed in cultural and political forms:

> *Solidarity*—We need to disentangle ourselves from state-imposed identities (tribal or patriotic) and reorient ourselves on traditional Indigenous identities, which inherently reflect the "independency" needed for effective political cooperation toward change. The most important aspect of this is the development of a sense of accountability to Indigenous values and community in conscious

opposition to the imperial accountability enforced in academe (academic disciplines, departmental and university committees, tenure processes, etc.).

Organize—We need to develop effective structures to mobilize the power of Indigenous identity and values. This means an association of Indigenous faculty with independent resources (human, cultural, and financial) to apply in contentious situations, and with the ability to represent an authentic Indigenous voice in academe and to shape the public's view on the rights and responsibilities of Indigenous peoples.

Empower—The need for action. There is no change without contention. And for Indigenous peoples today, change (movement off the path of assimilation) is essential to our survival. Power will come from the restoration of connection (among ourselves and to the sources of strength: traditional teachings, land, and community) and the respect that will emerge as we engage imperial power with dignity in a struggle for justice.

I described the need for warriors of the truth: the truth is the antidote to what Albert Memmi called "the colonizer's disease." Indigenous intellectuals in the United States and Canada are living at the center of the global empire, and we are the best-placed people in the world to counter the ongoing production of imperial attitudes and to defy its pretensions. It is our responsibility to reorient our own values and our ways of being away from cooptation into the imperial system.

The first challenge is to regenerate ourselves, and then our societies, and indeed to do our part to transform the powerful and arrogant exploitative mentality that is on the verge of destroying the earth. But to do so, we will need to rediscover the warrior within ourselves and begin to act on the ethic of courage that sustained our ancestors for many generations of struggle.

We will begin to make meaningful change in the lives of our people as a whole only when we first focus on making real change the lives of our people as individuals. It may sound cliché to some by now, but it is still true that the first part of self-determination is the *self*. In our minds and in our souls, we need to reject the settlers' control and authority, their definition of who we are and what our rights are, their definition of what is worthwhile and how one should live, their hypocritical and pacifying morality. We need to rebel against what we've become and start remembering and acting on who are ancestors were, what they were like, and the things they believed in. This is the spiritual revolution that will ensure our survival.

Let us think about the most basic question: what does it mean to be "Indigenous?" Many times I have listened to one of the wisest people I know, my friend Leroy Little Bear from the Blood Tribe in southern Alberta, and retired from the University of Lethbridge, teach on the basic difference between Indigenous and European languages. European languages, he explains, are based on nouns and are concerned with naming things, ascribing traits, and making judgments. Indigenous languages are based on verbs; they communicate through descriptions of movement and activity. Take my own name, for example, Taiaiake. In English it is a proper noun that labels me for identification. In Mohawk, it literally means, "he is crossing over from the other side." Struggling against and negotiating with the descendants of Europeans occupying our homelands for all these years, we have become very skilled, in the European way, at naming everything about ourselves: beliefs, rights, authorities, jurisdictions, land use areas, categories of membership in our communities . . . as if it were enough to speak these things to make them into a reality. In fighting for our future, we have been sucked into thinking that "Indigenous" or "First Nations," "Carrier," "Cree," or "Mohawk" (even if we use Kanien'kehaka, or Innu, or Wet'suwet'en) is something that is attached to us inherently, and not a description of what we do with our lives.

In the European way of seeing the world a name is a title and symbolizes *being*. In the Indigenous way a name is a responsibility and implies *doing*. Apply this insight to our recent struggles to gain recognition and respect, and you start to get a sense of why we have fallen off the good path. We have mistaken the mere renaming of our situation for an actual reconnection to our land and culture in practice. Living an Indigenous life means much more than applying a label to ourselves and saying that we are Indigenous. It means looking at the personal and political choices we make every day and applying an Indigenous logic to them. It means living according to Kanien'kehaka, Innu, and Wet'suwet'en values; thinking and behaving in a way that is consistent with the laws of nature and the teachings of our ancestors. Coming to understand ourselves as Indigenous peoples in terms of both *being* and *doing*, whether as one person or as nations, is the first step in breaking free of the varied and powerful forms of control over our minds and bodies that others now possess. In this way, we can finally transcend colonialism and begin to create a proud and powerful future for the coming generations. In the current environmental, social, and spiritual crisis, our cultures are a last hope for the world to envision a future outside of degradation and self-destruction. As Indigenous scholars and teachers, we have a crucial role to serve. We have a serious responsibility to do what we can to resist the escapist temptations of the standard academic life and the material rewards of assimilation. Instead, we must stand and contend with the sick vision of the future that is guiding our leaders today and embedded within our modern institutions. We must do what we can to change the places we live and work from sites of imperialism into spaces of resistance, of regeneration, and of human freedom. *Taneh Toh!*

6. SEEING (AND READING) RED

Indian Outlaws in the Ivory Tower

Daniel Heath Justice

"You will find the settlement of this land dark and bloody."—Chickamaugan Cherokee war chief Tsiyu Gansini (Dragging Canoe), upon the signing of the Treaty of Sycamore Shoals, 1775

This Is a Ghost Dance

Tsiyu Gansini was one of the Real People's greatest warriors, and one who was greatly feared by *yoneg* land-stealers.[1] He didn't die in battle; instead, he died in his sleep at his birthplace of Running Water, Tennessee, following a victory dance.[2] He died as he had lived: in defiance of Invasion's devastation.

And even in death, Tsiyu Gansini was a terror to the *yoneg* squatters, as told by Cherokee historian Brent Cox: "It has been said that White settlers and soldiers feared that Dragging Canoe had supernatural powers, and even possibly the ability to [resurrect]. When Dragging Canoe was buried in 1792, it was said that white soldiers [stole] his body, and divided it into two halves. One half was left as his burial near Nickajack, and [the] other portion was taken away. This was done to prevent Dragging Canoe from coming back."[3] That Tsiyu Gansini was cut into pieces is no surprise, as it's the standard stereotype for Native peoples throughout the Americas: we're measured by pieces and parts, "torn between worlds," relegated to some romanticized past, never fully of the present. And sometimes, in reality, we're pulled between the ranks and privileges of powerful institutions and the kitchen tables of our families, where life and culture so often gather. Native wholeness is a threat to white dominance, as it evades the allotment of our lives and lands and faces the threat directly. Our fight is that of all Indigenous peoples: to remain whole, unbroken, and adaptive through tradition.

This is a Ghost Dance that raises the fire and makes our uncle whole again.

This Is a Reminder
Tsiyu Gansini's words are worth heeding: "You will find the settlement of this land dark and bloody." He wasn't speaking only to the *yonegs* who came for the land; he was also speaking to his kinsmen who signed away the lands of the People. He knew, better than most, that the ravenous hunger of the Invaders wouldn't be satisfied until not only the land but the very *presence* of the Indigenous inhabitants was consumed.

Native scholars, when focused on decolonization and academic Ghost Dancing, are part of this battle. We can't forget, as Koyangk'auwi Maidu poet Janice Gould reminds us, that "there is not a university in this country that is not built on what was once native land. We should reflect on this over and over, and understand this fact as one fundamental point about the relationship of Indians to academia."[4] The Academy is the privileged center of meaning-making in this hemisphere dominated by imperial nation-states; as such, its primary history is one that has served colonialist cultural interests, both directly and covertly. This reality—the creation of institutions of learning erected on the lands and the literal bodies of Native people—brings me to the central questions of this essay: How, if at all, can we "indigenize the academy"? And in the struggle for Indigenous Nationhood and self-determination, what is the role of the literary critic?

In the Belly of the Beast, at the Edge of the Fire
In considering the first question—how do we "indigenize the academy"?—I have a connected query: Should we even do so? If our definition of the academy is the hierarchical, institutional structure that enforces an understanding of "knowledge" as that body of mores that have emerged more from a clash of ideas than a thoughtful consideration of them, I'm not entirely certain that this goal is even appropriate. Such a goal turns our attention away from lands and cultural traditions and into the inequitable power dynamics of an increasingly corporatized academic world. Such an academy may well be beyond redemption.

Another view of the academy, however, is more conducive to Indigenous thought. Clearly, if the academy were nothing more than an ideological death camp, most of us wouldn't be here. But the academy at its best is a place of intellectual engagement, where the world of ideas can meet action and become lived reality. Many of us have experienced this directly, such as when a student shares a story that opens the heart and spirit to healing, or when we look into the mysteries of the world and catch a glimpse of understanding. The academy can also be a site of significant cultural recovery work, a place where all people who are disconnected from their histories can begin their journeys homeward.[5]

Though not entirely free from the capitalistic directive, this definition of the academy seeks understanding above reactionary prejudice, insightful connection beyond feel-good catchphrases, acknowledgment of our shared responsibilities over blind bigotry. It's within this definition that Native scholars can best aim our work, as these are Indigenous values, too. While there are many useful ways to pursue this sort of Indigenous education, I'd like to provide four broad recommendations, then move directly into specific suggestions for my own area of literary studies.

One: *This is Indian Country*. Many of us have been educated to believe that we don't belong in this place of meaning-making, that we don't have anything worthwhile to contribute as Native peoples, that the intellectual traditions of our families and communities aren't powerful understandings of the world and her ways. But who is better qualified to understand this land than the peoples who have shared life with her for untold ages? We belong to this land; we're not guests of the Invaders, to be given access at their whim. The knowledge of Native peoples is the voice of Turtle Island that speaks closest to all of humanity. This is our inheritance.

Two: *We must not forget to be both responsible and humble*. This inheritance, however, brings with it two vital and connected understandings: responsibility and humility. Most of our traditions hold us accountable to one another and to the world for our behaviors. My own understanding of these responsibilities includes being dedicated to the pursuit of truth in my work, to be supportive of responsible scholarship, and to connect my work and my privilege as much as possible to the lives and experiences of marginalized peoples.

Humility will remind us that we're just part of the community, not the entirety. To ignore this interconnection and our mutual dependence is to harm both ourselves and our communities—no one hurts a family more than one of its own members turned bad. Tsiyu Gansini was a much-honored war chief, but his authority as a leader came from his community's consent, not from a personal declaration of supremacy. He was responsible to his people; in fact, his own responsibilities were heightened because of this public role. While most Native academics are self-ordained, in some way, to speak about our communities—and humility is elusive in an academic world that privileges individual achievement over communal harmony—our responsibilities are no less because of it. If anything, we must be always sensitive to the powers and privileges that come from this role.

Three: *Be generous of spirit, in war as well as in peace.* One value that seems consistent across tribal cultures is that of hospitality to guests of good heart. We're so often faced with raw prejudice that it's easy to retreat into a stance of eternal defiance, but such a movement is counterproductive if it doesn't include a real hope for worthwhile change and understanding. This isn't to say that we shouldn't ever wage war on those ideas and people who seek, either deliberately or inadvertently, to harm our Nations. On the contrary. To be generous of spirit is to be willing to enter a necessary fight with a goal of healing at its end, not destruction. It's never easy, but the elders I most admire all share this quality, and it gives me much hope for the future.

Four: *The world hasn't always been what it is, and it will be something very different in the future. Look backward and forward as you go.* This is the "Seventh Generations" concept that's often given lip service but rarely reflected upon very deeply. My own test is this: How does my work honor my ancestors? And will it help or hinder those to come? It's impossible to know the true answer to either question, but if we push our academic egos to the side, we'll find good guidance here from our families, friends, elders, ancestors, and the spirit worlds.

Ghost Dance movements aren't only about driving away the Invaders and the devastation they brought with them; Ghost Dances are also about bringing a new world into existence, a world of freedom, peace, and reconnection. This is the goal of Indigenous peoples throughout the world: we dance for a new reality.[6]

Texts and Tellings

I've written elsewhere about some of my fundamental concerns for the future of American Indian literary studies.[7] In that essay, I proposed ways to center these studies in Indian lives and realities, rather than keeping the focus on white perceptions and ideas about Indians. I would like to briefly return to some of these suggestions, as I believe they're quite relevant to this discussion as well.

If Nationhood and liberation are our goals, we must truly acknowledge the diversity of Native experiences by avoiding both the traps of "mixed-blood angst" and of "full-blood purity"—if we focus on blood quantum as the indicator of Indian "authenticity," we emphasize a colonialist paradigm that was imposed on Native peoples for the sole purpose of destroying our Nations, traditions, and landbases. Such a focus ignores the wide variety of responses of different communities to colonialism, and it sets up arbitrary ideas of what makes a "real" Indian (writer) that aren't necessarily applicable to each of the hundreds of tribal Nations in the Americas. Similarly, these traps ignore the fact that we aren't just another immigrant ethnic group—we're independent tribal Nations, with governments and distinctive identities of our own that emerge from our spiritual and cultural relationships to this land. I'm not just an American Indian—I'm a *citizen* of the Cherokee *Nation*, and thus have a political relationship to the colonizing nation-state of the United States that is distinct from those of non-Natives.[8] Nationhood combines with kinship relationships in First Nations communities, and this linked relationship is a unique one.

As part of this wide-ranging analysis, we would also do well to acknowledge the powerful place that both gender and Queer or Two-Spirit[9] sensibilities have within the majority of our Nations and within the scholarly and artistic work emerging from Indian Country. Women, particularly Queer women—such as Chrystos (Menominee), Beth Brant Degonwadonti (Bay of Quinte Mohawk), Paula Gunn Allen (Laguna/Sioux), and the aforementioned Janice Gould, among many others—speak to Indian women's concerns and against patriarchy and male privilege and violence. They also acknowledge the reality that there *are* other ways of viewing the world that value all members of the community for our various contributions and gifts.

The growing body of Queer male Native literature, too, addresses absences in a body of male literature that is often aggressively macho and too often heterosexist. The work of Maurice Kenny (Mohawk), Craig Womack (Muskogee Creek/Cherokee), Tomson Highway (Cree), and others gives young Queer Natives, like myself, a richer understanding of our place in the world. We don't have to cut ourselves into pieces to accommodate either racism or homophobia, but can instead "present ourselves"[10] to our Nations and the world as whole, multidimensional, healthy people. We can also bring this sensibility to our research and to our writing as an Indigenous corrective to white-centered discussions of gender and sexuality.

Similarly, in our acknowledgment of the diversity of Indian experience and worldview, we would do well to remember that there are more than a handful of eloquent and insightful writers throughout Indian Country. The privileging of a few Native voices—who I have, with some hesitation, called "The Noble Nine" because of this tokenization—not only erases a wide range of voices from many varied perspectives and tribal backgrounds, but it also reinforces the overculture's assertion that Indians are generally all alike.[11] Honestly, how many more essays on *Ceremony* or *Love Medicine* do we really need? Leslie Marmon Silko (Laguna Pueblo) and Louise Erdrich (Turtle Mountain Chippewa) have written many books, some much more challenging and discomfiting than these pieces, particularly Silko's revolutionary (if highly homophobic) *Almanac of the Dead*. While much of the emphasis on *Ceremony* and *Love Medicine* is clearly admiration, I suspect that for some scholars there's a good degree of laziness, discomfort, or fear regarding the exploration of other texts and traditions, and these aren't particularly useful qualities for the creation of an insightful or representative criticism.[12]

Perhaps the biggest concern I have about Native literary studies is the fact that there are still too many scholars—mostly non-Indians, but some of our own, too—who approach the work as though Indians aren't really even a part of the work at all or, if present, exist only as antiquated museum pieces who should just look exotic and keep quiet. This isn't a turf war issue, as some might simplistically claim. There are many non-Indian scholars in the field who approach it with respect and who bring incredible insight to their readings of the work, and many of these—A. LaVonne Brown Ruoff, Frances W. Kaye, and James H. Cox, David Moore, among others—have demonstrated a significant commitment to decolonization efforts in both their academic work and in personal activism. Yet there are others who treat Indians—by implication or directly—as obstacles to their research *about* Indians.

For example, I've given up reading anything by *yoneg* scholar Arnold Krupat, who has long been a leading critical voice in the field. While he seems to be sincerely concerned about the oppression facing Native peoples, the core of his critical philosophy seems to be an insistence on seeing contemporary Indian writing as an expression more of white influences than as the vibrant artistry emerging from *adaptable* tribal traditions.[13]

For example, in *The Turn to the Native*, Krupat spends much time explaining how "there is no purely indigenous, autonomous, 'Native' mode of criticism for written texts, for reasons that are obvious"[14]—namely, because the texts are generally written in languages of the colonizer and produced in forms derived from European intellectual and aesthetic traditions.

This undercurrent of presumed stasis ignores a simple fact: while the forms of these traditions may have been imported, they have been indigenized by Native peoples through over five hundred years of engagement and either forced or voluntary adoption. While our Mothertongues[15] remain the worldview centers of our cultures, they aren't the only viable means for Indian peoples to express ourselves. Some of us still maintain our languages, but many of us don't, and although linguistically separated from the full measure of understanding our Indigenous tongue we can still "reinvent the enemy's language," as Joy Harjo (Mvskoke/Cherokee) asserts in an introductory conversation with Gloria Bird (Spokane):

> We are coming out of one or two centuries of war, a war that hasn't ended. Many of us at the end of the century are using the "enemy language" with which to tell our truths, to sing, to remember ourselves during these troubled times....
>
> But to speak, at whatever the cost, is to become empowered rather than victimized by destruction. In our tribal cultures the power of language to heal, to regenerate, and to create is understood. These colonizers' languages [English, French, Spanish, etc.], which often usurped our own tribal languages or diminished them, now hand back emblems of our cultures, our own designs: beadwork, quills if you will. We've transformed these enemy languages.[16]

Those of us who don't speak our Mothertongues can do many things: relearn these languages ourselves; work hard for language revitalization and recovery efforts to help ensure the continuity of tradition and Indigenous worldviews; and acknowledge the ability of English and other languages to also carry cultural understandings, though not necessarily the same ones carried by the Mothertongue. We can't underestimate the trauma and violence of the loss of our Mothertongues, but we can work to ensure that those cultural understandings continue into the future.

Or take *yoneg* social anthropologist Charles Hudson, who objects to religious studies and literature scholar Mary Churchill's (Cherokee) review of his book, *The Southeastern Indians*, particularly her assertion that contemporary elders be consulted about work being done about their tribes. He writes:

> Since my concern in *The Southeastern Indians* was principally the beliefs and behaviors of eighteenth- and nineteenth-century Indians, I would like to know how the relevant elders and Native practitioners could be resurrected from the dead. Or does Churchill require that my work be vetted by contemporary Indian "elders" and "Native practitioners"? If so, any self-respecting scholar would find such a requirement repugnant. One would want to know, for example, how such contemporary elders attain their office. Is it that to be an elder a person must (1) pass a racial and/or cultural test and (2) reach a certain age? Is that all? Are no scholarly credentials required? May a contemporary religious practitioner also be a believing Christian, as most contemporary Native Americans are?[17]

Hudson repeatedly betrays his own ethnocentric paternalism in this passage, particularly in his horror of the idea that a tribal community might actually have knowledge to contribute about its own past, or that the tribe might be able to decide for itself who its own experts and elders are, without a white scholar's stamp of approval. A straw man argument, placing his own scholarly "objectivity" (which is transparently absent here) against stereotypes of tribal "bias," rather than engaging fully with the implications and possibilities of Churchill's suggestion.

Rhetoric scholar Malea Powell (Eastern Miami/Shawnee) speaks to this perspective in her own analysis of what it means to be a Native scholar, especially when we're engaging in debate with such scholars:

> When scholars convince themselves that they cannot study Indians (i.e., others) from the basis of Indian experience and existence, that they must make their efforts "scientific" and thus distance their work from Indian "reality," they displace the very voices—those of Indian peoples—that they claim they want to hear. They convince themselves that they are no longer influenced by those imperial American narratives, those media (and mediated) images of "Indian-ness," and that *their* work can be "scientific." To assume that an admiration for Native American culture coupled with a position within the Academy will somehow offer protection from the "smarminess" of American cultural imperialism is to open up room for Indian cultures to be appropriated, distorted, and objectified in increasingly new and approved "scholarly" terms.[18]

It shouldn't be news that Indians aren't just relics of the past, but actual human beings, most of whom have maintained ties to the land and traditions in spite of over five hundred years of terrorism from the Invader populations. Yet Krupat and Hudson, and many scholars in many disciplines, seem to need reminding. In this they're not far different from the ostensibly well-intended but patronizing and, ultimately, destructive "Friends of the Indian" of the nineteenth century, who never listened to the Native peoples of their time, either. The words may change, but the conversation is, regrettably, all too familiar.

Reading Red

I now return to the second central question of this essay, as I think it highlights a number of important issues for both Native scholars and the academy itself: *In the struggle for Indigenous Nationhood and self-determination, what is the role of the literary critic?*

It's difficult to ask this question without defining, to some degree, the complicated nature of literature, as both an art form and as an agent for political and social transformation. In the United States, and in those industrialized nation-states most heavily influenced by European aesthetics, particularly those of the nineteenth- and early twentieth-century Decadents, the purest art is that which speaks to itself: as Oscar Wilde was fond of noting, it's the idea of "art for art's sake." Art transcends petty politics, morality, and even human life; in this view, "great works of art are living things—are, in fact, the only things that live. . . . For life is terribly deficient in form."[19] To the Decadents of old, the only reality was art, and the only beauty to be found in nature was in its transience. The artist's individual personality is central to this aesthetic view, with individual self-expression as the ultimate value of art.

Such a view—while often an appealing balm to those of us who were tormented in school for being bookish, theatrical, or otherwise artistic—frequently brings with it a hypernarcissism and self-centered conceit that contributes to the destabilization of the basic values and kinship ties of tribal communities. If the individual is the only thing that matters, what happens to the tribal community? If we gain nothing of value from those around us, where is the place of a figure like Thomas Darko, the protagonist of Geary Hobson's (Cherokee-Quapaw/Chickasaw) novel, *The Last of the Ofos*?

> But now I come back to them that made me and taught me the most—Mama, Papa, and Grandpapa. All three, but especially Mama and Grandpapa, taught me the ways of being a Ofo. A Indian person jist ain't born a Indian—like a Ofo, or a Tunica, or a Choctaw—and let it go at that. That person need to learn to be a Ofo,

> or a Tunica, and such-like, and it is that learning makes them Ofos and such-like. It's learning comes through the community, even if it's jist a tiny community of three older folks or so, like ours was. We are born, we grow, and we learn—first, that we are in the Ofo world, a place made the good place it is by Sun Father, and the ground we walk on is our Mother. We have to do things right, keep everything on an even keel, don't rock the foundations, do our part to keep the world we live in and on in a good balance with the sky world above and the underworld below. Everything about being Ofo begins with this sense of evenness.[20]

While something of a generalization, I believe it's fair to say that most tribal artists—novelists, poets, singers, painters, dancers, filmmakers, and so on—are creating art not only for themselves, but also for the survival and enduring presence of Native people. Darko speaks of his life as inextricably linked to those of his family, of his very world connected by those tender ties. In most Native literature, art becomes more than just a vehicle for self-expression, although it's certainly that. It becomes, as Cherokee/Appalachian poet Marilou Awiakta has noted, "art for Life's sake, as opposed to art for Art's sake."[21]

This philosophy defines my approach to Nation-building, sovereignty, self-determination, and decolonization: the creation and critique of "art for life's sake" within specific tribal traditions, and the extension of those efforts to broader pan-tribal understandings. While our survival and growth require strong economic and political activism, so too do they require an activism of imagination, a dedication to realizing ourselves outside of colonialist lies and stereotypes. Art that speaks only to itself is of little help in this struggle.

No transcendent "muse" speaks from on high to aid us in this struggle for survival. Permanence of our art doesn't seem particularly important if the living presence of our Nations is erased. Beth Brant reminds us of the taproot of Native aesthetics—absent the "muse"—in her analysis of Native women's texts:

> It is so obvious to me that Native women's writing is a generous sharing of our history and our dreams for the future. That generosity is a collective experience. And perhaps this is the major difference between Aboriginal writing and that of European-based "literature." We do not write as individuals communing with a muse. We write as members of an ancient, cultural consciousness. Our "muse" is *us*. Our "muse" is our ancestors. Our "muse" is our children, our grandchildren, our partners, our lovers. Our "muse" is Earth and the stories She holds in the rocks, the trees, the birds, the fish, the animals, the waters. Our words come from

the very place of all life, the spirits who swirl around us, teaching us, cajoling us, chastising us, loving us.[22]

We needn't look very far—this land and her spirits can provide us with the aesthetic tools we need to best speak to the goal at hand. Perhaps the best place to look is home, to the land, the histories, the family ties and stories, and all the visible and hidden words and ways that define us as Indian people. And as we look homeward for these connections, so too must we look to our own responsibilities as Indigenous scholars and artists. Will the work we do today contribute to the health and well-being of our Nations? If the answer is no, we're not doing our job.

Creating a viable, sustainable web of Indigenous aesthetics is a worthy aim of all Native artists—be they elders, medicine people, writers, artists, activists, political leaders, or scholars—but the task is a difficult one. We are struggling against over five hundred years of pervasive, degrading images, worldviews, and lifeways that were imposed upon us for the sole purpose of *destroying* us. As African Caribbean lesbian poet and essayist Gamba Adisa/Audre Lorde has pointed out, "To survive in the mouth of this dragon we call america, we have had to learn this first and most vital lesson—that we were never meant to survive. Not as human beings."[23] The physical and the material are in no way separate, for just as we fight to preserve and enhance the traditions that tie us to this place, so too do we fight to preserve our lands, our languages, our identities, our bodies, and our relationships to the world and to one another.

While political leaders and activists often center their work on the material conditions and lives of the communities—land rights, housing, care for our elders and children, ending violence against women, opposing the U.S. incarceration machine, feeding the hungry—the artists and writers, poets, and dreamers extend this work into the imaginative, the world of words and images that enrich the spirit and provide a different kind of sustenance. While also examining the work of other Native scholars and writers, my own work is fundamentally an expression of Cherokee intellectual traditions, to contribute to the making of meaning and understanding our place in the world.

Art for life's sake: this is why, in Native literature classes, I don't teach any books that aren't written by First Nations peoples. Some of the additional articles that provide context and, occasionally, explication, are by non-Natives if no First Nations texts are available, but the primary voices are unapologetically Indigenous. Native Hawaiian scholar and activist Haunani-Kay Trask articulates this position: "To Natives, the burst of creative outpouring that accompanies cultural nationalism is self-explanatory: a choice has been made for things Native over non-Native. Politically, the choice is one of decolonization."[24] The first day of class I write on the chalkboard in bold letters, THIS IS INDIAN COUNTRY, and from that day to the last the classroom is an extension of that phrase. We grapple with decolonization, sovereignty and self-determination, the devastation of Invasion, and the anger and joys and hopes of contemporary Native peoples looking to the future.

Art for life's sake: this is why some of the white students complain that they expected to read about quaint Indian myths and legends, not all the Native history and political science texts that are assigned along with the fiction and poetry. They're generally taking the class because they like the romance of *Dances with Wolves* or because they have to fill a diversity requirement and think Native literature will be "easier" (read "less threatening") than African American literature, more "inspirational" (read "more romanticized") than Chicano/a literature. Every semester requires a dual process: first, deconstructing the hackneyed stereotypes they've absorbed in seventeen-plus years of life, then opening students' eyes, minds, and hearts to the artistry and issues emerging from Indian Country. Sixteen weeks isn't much time to reeducate someone who's been miseducated for a lifetime. It's a big task and perhaps more than a little idealistic and arrogant to imagine doing so, but I can't imagine teaching these classes any differently; more, perhaps, than any other literary field, Indigenous literatures are grounded in the cultural survival of the communities from which they emerge. As Elizabeth Cook-Lynn (Crow Creek Sioux) notes, "Indian tribes, of course, are not like any other American landowners. They are sovereign, separate, and distinct peoples, with signed treaty rights, and more work needs to be done to articulate that idea on behalf of the indigenes."[25] If such articulation can't take place in the literature classroom, where *can* it take place?

Art for life's sake: this is why, when Native and other students of color enter a decolonizing classroom, they encounter, perhaps for the first time (particularly at predominantly white institutions), an environment that privileges *their* stories, *their* perspectives, *their* presence in both the classroom and in the world. Whether Native or non-Native, we've been trained by the overculture to see whiteness as normative and eternal; decolonization, in this worldview, is not only portrayed as unrealistic, but even pathological, for it brings into question the very conceptual foundations upon which the colonial estate is built.

Yet teaching is only part of the academician's vocation. The other major aspect is that nebulous idea of the creation and preservation of knowledge, a task that poses great opportunities for Native academics. Yet this terrain is also a tricky one for us, as the institutional mechanisms of the academy often fail to recognize the intellectual work that takes place in our communities; when our own scholarship and critical methods look to our home communities for definition, conflicts are inevitable. For example, when I first decided to go into Native literature as an undergraduate, I was told by a white professor, "I thought you were a better scholar than that." He saw nothing intellectual emerging from Indian Country—his loss, certainly, but indicative of some of the continued bigotry that we face.

Add to this the issue of politicization, which many (generally conservative) scholars fear is a distraction that places polemics above substantive intellectual engagement. Such attitudes don't bode well for Indian outlaws who refuse to be comforted by the myth of objective scholarship, for whom the political realities of this world can be transformed through intellectualism and liberatory aesthetics. At some point we've got to choose which values are most important to us: those of our families and kin, or those of the institution. This doesn't mean that we abandon the institution; indeed, we may find that, given our own individual skills and gifts, we do more good for our people from within the walls of the academy than outside them, that we can undermine the destructive aspects of academia through changing curricula, increasing access to more Natives and other marginalized peoples, and advocating change through substantial and strategic intellectual engagement and publishing. It's not easy, but just as the colonial regime has taken generations to establish itself, so too will it take generations to dismantle it. It's going to happen, though; Ghost Dances are visions, not dreams.

Yet we should always be wary of the seductions of colonialism that reach out to us in this place. The more we become enmeshed in the privileges and power of the academy, the more tempting it is to forget that, for many of us, the reason we entered the academy in the first place was to give voice to the experiences and intellectual traditions of our communities, our families. When we lose sight of this aim, we cease to create art for life's sake and instead become just more agents of colonialism.

Artistry and intellectualism don't belong only to *yonegs*; scholarship doesn't take place only in the academy. The academy is a difficult terrain to negotiate when your work is centered in Indian Country, but we're fortunate to have thoughtful forebears and contemporaries who have opened a place for a Native presence, however small, in most colleges and universities in the United States and Canada. This isn't to say that the battles don't still continue, or that activist scholars aren't targeted in the war of meaning in the academy: Trask's persecution at the University of Hawai'i is perhaps the most public example of just how dangerous a place academia can be for those seeking decolonization: "I was a public person in a little colonial university where public dissent, especially on the side of Natives, is perceived as outrageous and threatening."[26] But we can now draw not only on our own tribal traditions, but also on a rich body of Native intellectualism that has as its goal the liberation of Turtle Island.

These forebears took on the fight at its infancy, when American Indian studies programs were unthinkable to the white intellectual establishment. Our elders—many of whom are still working to see their vision become a reality—stood beside their non-Native allies in a common goal of carving a valued place for Indian experience within the ivory tower. Now, those of us who are coming into the discipline have a chance to go a step further, to make the academy both responsive and responsible to First Nations goals of self-determination and well-being. Yet success on this front isn't ever assured, and we've got to be wary of becoming either careless about the hard-fought victories to date or seduced by the privileges of the academy. Much work remains, and it remains for us to do it. Whether we do so responsibly is up to each of us.

In literary studies we have critics who have engaged with both texts and sociopolitical realities, from Cook-Lynn's repeated assertion that the preservation of our lands and traditions should be central to our work as Native scholars, to Gerald Vizenor's (Anishinaabe) deconstructions of words and language codes that bind Native realities to oppressive stereotypes, to Robert Allen Warrior's (Osage) exploration of Native intellectual sovereignty and Womack's advocacy for a literary separatism that places Native literature at the center rather than the "American" literature of the colonizers. Similarly, artists such as Harjo, Simon Ortiz (Acoma Pueblo), Wendy Rose (Hopi/Miwok), Thomas King (Cherokee), N. Scott Momaday (Kiowa/Cherokee), and many others write of the transformative powers of language and literature, always with Native presence at the center. Decolonization theory isn't limited only to critical essays and textual analyses; it's also deep within the flow of meaning within poetry, fiction, and creative nonfiction.

Together with other Native writers, these voices move toward an awakening of what Shuswap political activist George Manuel has called "The Fourth World," a "vision of the future history of North America and of the Indian peoples,"[27] a vision in which traditional spiritual and cultural values meld with economic self-sufficiency and political self-determination to liberate Native peoples from colonialist shackles placed upon mind and body. Like all such visions, it's ambitious, but it's viable and, perhaps, inevitable. As Manuel notes, "As we view the North American Indian world today, we must keep in mind two things: Indians have not yet left the aboriginal universe in which they have always dwelt emotionally and intellectually, and the Western world is gradually working its way out of its former value system and into the value system of the Aboriginal World."[28] The study of literature provides all of us a rich and varied range of texts that express Native values and perspectives, all of which speak to Indigenous endurance, and most of which move beyond survival of Indian peoples to invoke the *revival* of full Native sovereignty and self-determination.

Sovereignty itself is a tricky issue, though. Political theorist Taiaiake Alfred (Kahnawake Mohawk) has written quite convincingly of the ironic dangers to Native self-determination that arise from adopting a European concept of "sovereignty," which places Indigenous autonomy under the definition and control of European political paradigms. In its place he advocates an unbending return to decolonized traditional values and sociopolitical structures.[29] For those who don't embrace Alfred's critique of sovereignty, there are other complications, particularly when moving across disciplines. Vine Deloria Jr. (Standing Rock Sioux), recently noted: "I fear we have raised a generation of sell-outs who have no commitment to the Indian Community. . . . this generation is doing nothing for the people that come. They keep themselves in a little intellectual ghetto and throw around big words like 'sovereignty' and think they are doing something. Not likely. If Clyde Warrior were alive today he would puke at what is happening."[30] Deloria, a stalwart elder who has long been a champion of political sovereignty for Native peoples, makes a good point, albeit a limited one. Sovereignty isn't an easy issue, and it's a word that's all too often thrown around breezily without a significant engagement with the profound implications of such a concept. Few in academia who discuss sovereignty have fully grappled with the full implications of what sovereignty really means to tribal communities. Will sovereignty emerge from traditional values and the circle of kinship responsibilities, enhancing the health, growth, and vitality of our communities? Or will sovereignty, as Alfred fears, merely result in our nations being coopted by the Invader settler states, with the assimilated tribal leaders mere toadies to their colonial masters, exploiting their communities for their own benefit? These are profound questions that deserve substantive engagement, if for no other reason than because the futures of our peoples will depend on how we approach these issues and questions.

Yet Deloria's critique, apparently directed at the "intellectual sovereignty" discussion emerging from Warrior's work and subsequently embraced by many Indian literature scholars, ignores the profound and transformative vitality of examining sovereignty through the literatures we write today and those that have come before us. Sovereignty isn't just a legal concept. As Warrior asserts,

> If our struggle is anything, it is the struggle for sovereignty, and if sovereignty is anything, it is a way of life. That way of life is not a matter of defining a political ideology or having a detached discussion about the unifying structures and essences of American Indian traditions. It is a decision—a decision we make in our minds, in our hearts, and in our bodies—to be sovereign and to find out what that means in the process. . . . the struggle for sovereignty is not a struggle to be free from the influence of anything outside ourselves, but a process of asserting the power we possess as communities and individuals to make decisions that affect our lives.[31]

Sovereignty and self-determination require more than just a redefinition of political and legal relationships between Indigenous nations and the nation-states of the Invaders; they also require a reimagining of ourselves beyond the antiquated artifacts that the Invaders insist we become. Our traditions, families, and nations all contribute to that reimagining, and so too do the literatures we craft in response to this challenge. With each poem or story or novel or song or other text that emerges from Indian Country, we assert the enduring Indigenous presence in this hemisphere. As Queer Chicana writer Cherríe Moraga has written, "Revolution is not won only by numbers, but by visionaries, and if artists aren't visionaries, then we have no business doing what we do."[32]

Words matter. Perhaps more than anyone else in academe, literature scholars and writers of the literary arts grapple with the dangerous power of words and their meanings. For many of us art is an essential mechanism for the liberation of our Nations. And while we're responsible (and responsive) to our communities, we're engaged in more than the mere repetition of ideas—we're also active participants in the community's making of meaning. We're not outsiders looking in; we're insiders looking in *and* out. It's important to remember that Sequoyah, who is today regarded by most Cherokees as both a dedicated traditionalist and a visionary intellectual, battled with many of his traditionalist kinfolk over his creation (or revelation) [33] of the syllabary. There were many who believed he was involved with witchery—a crime punishable by death—and some, including his wife and neighbors, set fire to the first materials he had spent years developing as a result of this fear. Sequoyah understood the importance of his work, but it was always grounded in his knowledge of and love for his people, and after the syllabary became public it quickly became the primary vehicle for informing exclusively Cherokee speakers about issues affecting the Nation.

The point isn't to abandon either our cultural roots or our academic training, but to bring them together in service to the People. Brant gives voice to this purpose: "Story is meant to be spoken—that has not changed. The written becomes the spoken whether by hands or mouth, the spoken enters the heart, the heart turns over, Earth is renewed. In the end, this is what matters to me. 'I write because not to write is a breach of faith.' I believe that now as surely as I did in 1984 when I wrote those words."[34]

And yet, this battle for our words, for our own aesthetic principles that not only emerge *from* our Nations but also return *to* them, will be long and painful. Tsiyu Gansini's words reach from the past: "You will find the settlement of this land dark and bloody." It's a struggle that has endured for over five hundred years, and it will continue long after our individual deaths. The Invaders still think we'll vanish into a bloody sunset; they've worked hard to ensure that our words will end, the only reminders the disembodied names used to sell third-rate vehicles (Jeep Cherokees, Winnebagos), shoddy clothes (Cherokee and Crazy Horse brands), and weapons of slaughter (Apache helicopters). Gros Ventres literary scholar Sidner Larson has written: "American Indian people have recently experienced the end of the world. . . . [We] are a postapocalypse people who, as such, have tremendous experience to offer all other people who must, in their own time, experience their own cultural death as part of the natural cycle. The ways in which American Indian people have suffered, survived, and managed to go on, communicated through storytelling, have tremendous potential to affect the future of all mankind."[35] This "going on" is more than simple survival. It is what Vizenor calls "survivance"—"survival" plus "resistance"—that moves beyond the daily quest for sustenance and shelter toward a rebuilding of healthy lives and the recovery of lifeways that promote such healing. We work toward a common goal: the return of the Fourth World.

Autonomy of community and self-within-community—as opposed to postmodern individualism—requires at least two things to sustain it: a community from which memory is spoken, and a sovereignty of mind and body, both the body politic and the physical body. Womack makes the connections between our literatures and our sovereignty explicit:

> Native literature, and Native literary criticism, written by Native authors, is part of sovereignty: Indian people exercising the right to present images of themselves and to discuss those images. Tribes recognizing their own extant literatures, writing new ones, and asserting the right to explicate them constitute a move toward nationhood.... A key component of nationhood is a people's idea of themselves, their imaginings of who they are. The ongoing expression of a tribal voice, through imagination, language, and literature, contributes to keeping sovereignty alive in the citizens of a nation and gives sovereignty a meaning that is defined within the tribe rather than by external sources.[36]

Womack's work reflects the interwoven connections between community, sovereignty, and Indigenous aesthetics. While drawing from the People, such work also becomes part of the intellectual heritage of the community—a respectful reciprocal exchange, and one that is certainly a worthy model for other Native scholars, both within literary studies and in other disciplines.

This Is a Reminder

What do we bring back to the People, to the well-being of future generations and the honor of the ancestors? How do we create art for life's sake? I believe that the taproot of this art, our Indigenous aesthetic, has been here all along. Yet we don't always listen. It may speak differently to us today than in the past, but it's still here. It's our stories—those of ages past and the ones that are given voice today. It's our families, our lands, our ancestors, ceremonies, languages. It's the Fourth World made manifest. Native literary scholars bring important skills with us to discussions about nationhood and decolonization, and we can engage the issues through the power of metaphor, of poetry, of symbolism, and of the transformative powers of language.

We must emphasize the living, breathing relevance of Indian Country today as well as in the past, and we can do this by engaging with many Indigenous voices and perspectives, as well as with political realities facing contemporary Native peoples. Perhaps the nineteenth-century writings of Pequot minister William Apess can speak across the ages to challenge the racist journalism of Jeff Benedict's *Without Reservation*, in which Benedict claims that modern Pequots are just a fabrication created to enrich a small group of opportunists. Or perhaps the contemporary fiction and poetry of Adrian Louis (Lovelock Paiute) or Ray Young Bear (Mesquakie) can undermine white writer Ian Frazier's search for romanticized Indian playthings in his book *On the Rez*. And maybe Jeannette Armstrong's (Okanagan) fiction, or Drew Hayden Taylor's (Ojibway) plays, can make clear how vital First Nationhood is to the survival of Native Canadians, Thomas Flanagan's reactionary *First Nations? Second Thoughts* notwithstanding. We must move ourselves and our students out of the classroom and into the world. Above all, we must never forget that, as Native artists and critics, we're part of a much larger web of reality, one that brings with it not only distinctive responsibilities to home and kin, but also distinctive joys that emerge from our relationship to this land and its many peoples.

Awiakta has noted that "All people have poetry in them. Some can't write it, but the poet can listen intently to what people say and send it out into the world. It's a process of translation for the people."[37] "Art for life's sake" is an interpretive strategy as well. The interpretation isn't between the community and the colonizers; instead, it's between the community and its past, its present, and its potential. It's both the exercise and the development of our understandings of sovereignty, community, and Indigenous intellectualism and aesthetics that draw deeply from the collected wisdom and endurance of our communities.

This Is a Ghost Dance

Turtle Island is more than an ancient land to which we have ancient ties; it's also an idea, a wordscape of contested meanings. Understanding art for life's sake aids all Indigenous peoples, including the literary scholars among us, to decolonize our world in mind as well as body, to dismantle the ideas and forces that tear us into pieces. In this way, we're not just surviving in this postapocalyptic world of today—we're returning it to the People.

Notes

1. Many thanks to Devon Abbott Mihesuah, Angela Cavender Wilson, Barbara Tracy, Qwo-Li Driskill, Ahimsa Timoteo Bodhrán, James Cox, and Jeremy Patrick for their thoughtful comments and responses to various versions of this essay. I don't pretend to speak for anyone other than myself, but it's my hope that my words are responsible to the teachings and guidance of my family and friends, my mentors, and my elders. Any errors, omissions, or misrepresentations in the text are my own. I welcome engaged feedback at outlandcherokee@hotmail.com. *Wado!*

2. Pat Alderman, *Nancy Ward, Cherokee Chieftainess/Dragging Canoe, Cherokee-Chickamaugan War Chief* (Johnson City TN: Overmountain Press, 1978), 73. The victory dance was in honor of Tsiyu Gansini's brother, The Badger, who had returned with a war party from the November 1791 battle against U.S. General St. Clair—one of the most decisive defeats of U.S. troops ever. The Chickamaugan warriors had joined the Native confederacy led by Miami chief Little Turtle.

3. Brent Alan (Yanusdi) Cox, *Heart of the Eagle: Dragging Canoe and the Emergence of the Chickamauga Confederacy* (Milan TN: Chenanee, 1999), ix–x.

4. Quoted in Malea Powell, "Blood and Scholarship: One Mixed-Blood's Story," in *Race, Rhetoric, and Composition*, ed. Keith Gilyard (Portsmouth NH: Heinemann, Boynton/Cook, 1999), 1.

5. There are still far too few of these programs, and they too often struggle for basic funding, but one developing example is the Native American studies program at the University of Nebraska-Omaha, which views cultural recovery and the service of Nebraska's urban Indian population as two guiding principles.

6. In a conversation with poet/activist/scholar Qwo-Li Driskill (Cherokee Two-Spirit/Queer, also of African, Irish, Lenape, and Lumbee *ascent*), about this issue, s/he noted hir belief that the vibrant decolonization work being done throughout Indian Country today is a fulfillment of the prayers of many generations of our various peoples.

7. See Daniel Heath Justice, "We're Not There Yet, Kemo Sabe: Positing a Future for American Indian Literary Studies," *American Indian Quarterly* 25, no. 2 (spring 2001): 256–69.

8. I'd like to note here, though, that I don't believe enrollment (in the United States) or status (in Canada) to be the only defining characteristic of this political relationship. While important, enrollment and status are policies imposed by the Invader nation-states to define tribal communities out of existence by undermining traditional definitions of community. Bureau of Indian Affairs governments are not necessarily the sole arbiter of Indian identity, and I resist placing more emphasis on

their policies than on those of our communities themselves. Similarly, numerous smaller Nations in the United States were "terminated" by the colonialist government when its agents attempted to disavow their treaty responsibilities to the indigenous population; as such, members of those Nations are "unenrolled" in the political landscape of Indian Country, even if fully immersed in the traditions and histories of their communities. While citizenship in a Nation "recognized" by one of the settler-states does bring with it a distinctive political relationship to those states, it isn't the only relationship of significance for Native peoples, and I would hesitate to emphasize it as the defining characteristic of Native identity.

9. I use these terms with the understanding that not all First Nations communities have a Two-Spirit social role within their traditions, and with the knowledge that some people prefer other terms for self-identification; for example, I don't use the term "Two-Spirit" to describe myself, preferring either "Queer" or "gay," as I'm hesitant to adopt a term that has very tribally specific histories and traditions for certain communities. Other Native people take a different approach. At any rate, "Queer" and "Two-Spirit" are deliberately political as well as descriptive, and they move outside of the gay/lesbian binary to include multiple sexual and gender realities.

10. Beth Brant provides "presenting ourselves" as a Native alternative to "coming out," the terminology most often used in popular Western culture, in *Writing as Witness: Essay and Talk* (Toronto: Women's Press, 1994):

> Presenting ourselves to Creator means realigning ourselves within our communities and within our spiritual selves to create balance. Balance will keep us whole. To be a First Nations Two-Spirit means to be on a path that won't be blocked by anyone or anything.... There will be no cover-up in this recovery—by white imperialism or by my own people....
>
> Recovery means that we transform ourselves. Presenting ourselves means that we transform our world. (45–46)

11. My own list includes N. Scott Momaday, Leslie Marmon Silko, Louise Erdrich, Sherman Alexie, Diane Glancy, Gerald Vizenor, Joy Harjo, the late James Welch, and Paula Gunn Allen, although others might include Joseph Bruchac, Linda Hogan, and the late Louis Owens and Michael Dorris. These writers are all powerful artists and thinkers, and they are deservedly acknowledged as among the best writers in North America today, but there are many voices that are silenced when our syllabi, our essays, our journals, and our critical analyses are focused only on the celebrities of the moment and their most famous texts. What about the richly textured works of Eden Robinson (Haisla), William Sanders (Cherokee), Ray Young Bear (Mesquakie), Richard Van Camp (Dogrib), and Luci Tapahonso (Navajo)?

12. When I discussed this issue with Melungeon/Cherokee scholar Barbara Tracy, she noted that the devotion of a critic to one author is also very much a part of Euroamerican scholarly traditions—we're trained to focus on (or to discover) a single writer and thus become *the* expert and authoritative voice (or at least one of the few) in studies of that author. While this has long been the tradition in the academy, it

might not be the best way for Native scholars to go, particularly as it still marginalizes other significant Native voices. Perhaps focusing on broader patterns, themes, or on specific tribal traditions is more responsive to tribal worldviews than a myopic dedication to a single individual.

13. For example, in his recent review of three Native-themed books in *College English* ("Review: Red Matters," vol. 63, no. 5, May 2001), Krupat reviews Craig Womack's *Red on Red: Native American Literary Separatism* (Minneapolis: University of Minnesota Press, 1999), stating that Womack "makes the claim that the 'primary culture' out of which the stories arise is the only legitimate source for analyses of them" (660). Krupat's critique hinges on this loose assertion when, in fact, Womack states precisely the *opposite*:

> My argument is not that this is the *only* way to understand Creek writing but an important one given that literatures bear some kind of relationship to communities, both writing communities and the community of the primary culture, from which they originate.
>
> In arguing, then, that one viable approach is to examine Creek authors to understand Creek texts, or, more generally, Native authors to understand Native textual production, this study assumes that there *is* such a thing as a Native perspective and that seeking it out is a worthwhile endeavor. (*Red on Red* 4; emphasis in original)

Womack's approach is unapologetically Native-centered, but he nowhere claims that his is the only or authoritative perspective; his assertion of a separate literary criticism implies within it an acknowledgment of multiple readings, with his own focus on Creek-centered analysis of Creek texts. Krupat's misreading thus sets up a straw man argument, against which his own reading can be seen as both reasoned and reasonable and Womack's misrepresented as blindly ethnocentric. This doesn't give me much hope for Krupat's newest book, *Red Matters*.

14. Arnold Krupat, *The Turn to the Native* (Lincoln: University of Nebraska Press, 1996), 62. See also the first chapter of the book, "Criticism and Native American Literature," for an extended explication of this perspective.

15. *Wado* to Qwo-Li (note 6 above) for the following way of understanding "Mothertongue": "I have decided to use this term, rather than 'mother tongue,' to point out the specific relationship First Nations people have with our languages, regardless of whether or not we speak them as our first language. Though our Native languages may not be, in a linguistic sense, our mother tongues, they are nevertheless the languages from which we originate. In addition, I use this term to draw attention to the vital roles mothers play in carrying language from one generation to the next." (From "Mothertongue: Incorporating Theatre of the Oppressed into Language Restoration Movements," unpublished essay, 2002.)

16. Joy Harjo and Gloria Bird, eds., "Introduction," in *Reinventing the Enemy's Language: Contemporary Native Women's Writings of North America* (New York: Norton, 1997), 21–22.

17. Charles Hudson, "Reply to Mary Churchill," *American Indian Quarterly* 24, no. 3 (summer 2000): 499.

18. Powell, *Blood and Scholarship*, 5.

19. Oscar Wilde, "From 'The Critic as Artist,'" in *The Picture of Dorian Gray*, Norton Critical Edition, ed. Donald L. Lawler (New York: Norton, 1988), 315.

20. Geary Hobson, *The Last of the Ofos* (Tucson: University of Arizona Press, 2000), 18.

21. Thomas Rain Crowe, "Marilou Awiakta: Reweaving the Future." *appalj* (fall 1990), 43. I was reminded of other ways art can be an expression of healing by Ahimsa Timoteo Bodhrán, a queer mixed-race writer, dancer, performance artist, activist, and scholar of Moroccan Sefardí and other bloods, in an e-mail commentary on an earlier draft of this piece: "What about art as activism, art for change sake, art for transformación?" (personal correspondence).

22. Brant, *Writing as Witness*, 10.

23. Audre Lorde, "The Transformation of Silence into Language and Action," *Sister Outsider* (Trumansburg NY: Crossing Press, 1984), 42.

24. Haunani-Kay Trask, *From a Native Daughter: Colonialism and Sovereignty in Hawai'i*, revised edition (Honolulu: University of Hawai'i Press, 1999), 43.

25. Elizabeth Cook-Lynn, *Why I Can't Read Wallace Stegner and Other Essays: A Tribal Voice* (Madison: University of Wisconsin Press, 1996), 25.

26. Trask, *From a Native Daughter*, 162. Trask's battle for tenure at the University of Hawai'i was a grueling experience complicated by a state media more dedicated to colonialist hype than thoughtful engagement of Native Hawaiian concerns and the racism of white students and faculty at the university. As Trask notes: "I had won, but I had also spent nearly five years under terrible employment conditions because I was both a Hawaiian nationalist and a critic of the United States. No victory, no matter how sweet, could repay those lost five years" (165).

27. George Manuel with Michael Posluns, *The Fourth World: An Indian Reality* (New York: The Free Press, 1974), 12.

28. Manuel and Posluns, *The Fourth World*, 11.

29. See Taiaiake Alfred, *Peace, Power, Righteousness: An Indigenous Manifesto* (Don Mills, Ontario: Oxford University Press, 1999).

30. Vine Deloria Jr., "Wisdom of the Elders," *Paradoxa* 15 (2001): 287.

31. Robert Allen Warrior, *Tribal Secrets: Recovering American Indian Intellectual Traditions* (Minneapolis: University of Minnesota Press), 124.

32. Cherríe Moraga, *The Last Generation: Prose and Poetry* (Boston: South End Press, 1993), 56.

33. See Grant Foreman's *Sequoyah* (Norman: University of Oklahoma Press, 1938) for the most commonly held view of Sequoyah's life. There is, however, another view. Traveler Bird's *Tell Them They Lie: The Sequoyah Myth* (Los Angeles: Westernlore, 1971) challenges every single popular and widely accepted notion of who Sequoyah really was, including the assertion that the syllabary had existed for many years, a secret code used by traditionalists to maintain traditions during times of great chaos as well as a method of exchanging information between resistance war leaders. That

Bird's account is still viewed as a viable account among some Cherokees is evidenced in Robert Conley's (Keetoowah Cherokee) note at the end of his 1992 novel, *The Way of the Priests* (New York: Quality Paperback Book Club, 1995): "I believe that the Cherokee syllabary *may* be an old system, and therefore it exists in *The Way of the Priests*. (I am not, by the way, the first to make this claim. Traveller Bird, a Cherokee, did so earlier in a book about Sequoyah called *Tell Them They Lie*)" (171–72).

34. Brant, *Writing as Witness*, 82.

35. Sidner Larson, *Captured in the Middle: Tradition and Experience in Contemporary Native American Writing* (Seattle: University of Washington Press, 2000), 18.

36. Womack, *Red on Red*, 14.

37. Rain Crowe, "Marilou Awiakta," 52.

7. KEEPING CULTURE IN MIND

Transforming Academic Training in Professional Psychology for Indian Country

Joseph P. Gone

Some years ago during a visit home to the Fort Belknap Indian reservation in Montana, I was approached in an uncharacteristically serious manner by a close family member who confided with evident desperation that he needed to talk with me at once. We found a quiet space near the woodstove and settled into stuffed chairs across from one another. I sat silently and waited for my relative to speak. After mustering his courage, he whispered determinedly, "I'm going through a really tough time and I need your help. Will you do therapy with me?" I was stunned into silence, quickly reviewing my years of doctoral training in clinical psychology in search of an adequate response. After several seconds passed, I mumbled something about the impropriety of conducting psychotherapy with a close relative and haltingly suggested that he could pursue therapy with an Indian Health Service clinician or substance abuse counselor. He winced almost imperceptibly, and then his voice hardened: "What makes you think I would trust anyone outside of this family with my problems?" A moment later, he was gone. And he has not entrusted me with his problems since.

Such encounters are not unfamiliar to most American Indian or Alaska Native psychologists who live or work in Indian country, where the tools of our trade often seem woefully inadequate. Not surprisingly, Native American people are relative newcomers to the ranks of academic and professional psychology.[1] Although precise numbers are difficult to obtain, there can be no more than 150 Native persons to have earned doctorates in psychology during the past half-century in the United States.[2] Furthermore, if the participants at the annual convention of American Indian Psychologists are at all representative of our professional population, the vast majority—particularly among the more senior cohorts—found their graduate training in psychology perplexing, alienating, and even infuriating.[3] As a result, the majority of Native psychologists have steered clear of the academy—indeed, the number of Indian psychologists actively employed as full-time faculty in academic institutions must surely number less than one-sixth of the trained population. If one further reduces this academic population to those Native psychologists who serve on faculties in professional psychology training programs, while actively publishing scholarly research in peer-reviewed journals and books about topics and issues directly related to the well-being of American Indian or Alaska Native communities, the persons so designated can be counted on one's fingers.

Those of us who remain in the Western academy as faculty in professional psychology training programs (especially the clinical and counseling psychology subfields) seek to render our research, teaching, and service relevant to Indian country. In my mind, such dedication entails two distinct (but related) goals, including transforming the conventions of mental health service delivery in Native communities on the one hand, and transforming the conventions of academic training in psychology on the other hand. The first goal is designed to ensure that mental health services within Native communities are fundamentally responsive to the local cultural constituents of "mental" health and well-being, while the second goal is designed to ensure that cross-cultural proficiency and sophistication characterize the preparation of all psychologists in the multicultural twenty-first century. Since the doctorate is required for licensure to practice psychology in the United States and Canada, both goals converge in the training of graduate students in professional psychology—especially American Indian and Alaska Native students—who must profit from the latter if they are to accomplish the former. Indeed, it would seem that similar commitments must characterize any professional psychology training program dedicated to facilitating competency in research, teaching, and professional service with the "culturally different."[4] But in the case of contemporary indigenous America, where "Indians into Psychology" training programs have proliferated at several universities over the past decade, we are in serious danger of placing the cart before the horse. That is, in our enthusiasm to recruit, retain, graduate, and credential Native psychologists, we must not forget that *substantive transformations* are in order, for conventional training in professional psychology is suited *neither* for reconfiguring mental health services in terms of local cultural practice *nor* for preparing mental health professionals who are proficient in sophisticated cultural analysis.

This, then, is the curricular conundrum that threatens to confound even our most affirmative efforts within academic psychology to provide Indian country with more effective psychological researchers and service providers.

In the remainder of this chapter, I will first elucidate the (post)colonial[5] predicament of professional psychologists who aspire to relevance for Native American communities, namely that the conventions of professional practice in psychology are Western in origin and frequently diverge in profound and problematic ways from the cultural concepts and practices of contemporary Native communities. Then I will illustrate the character and significance of such cultural divergences with summary analysis of the career of a famous nineteenth-century Gros Ventre medicine person, Bull Lodge, whose preparation and performance as an unusually effective healer is situated in a complex web of cultural meanings and practices that contrast markedly with those of the modern psychotherapies. Finally, I will attempt to resolve the (post)colonial predicament by outlining a strategy for "indigenizing" academic training in professional psychology toward the preparation of professionals who are proficient in the kinds of cultural analysis necessary for ultimately grounding innovative mental health service delivery in the local concepts and practices of Native American communities. Throughout this essay, I use the terms "American Indian," "Indian," "Native American," "Native," and "indigenous" to refer to the contemporary descendants of the aboriginal communities of North America—since each of these terms may be found in both academic and colloquial discourse by Native individuals, I will use them more or less interchangeably.

The (Post)colonial Predicament of Professional Psychology

That the "elders" of American Indian psychology would consistently voice great ambivalence regarding the value of their graduate training over the course of their lengthy careers is testament to a deep incommensurability between the tenets of academic psychology and the practices of indigenous lifeways. The signs of such discordance are usually immediately evident to Native students pursuing psychology doctorates in graduate school. During my own graduate student years, for example, I was frequently asked about my studies whenever I traveled home. On various occasions when I explained to a community member that I was pursuing a degree in psychology, someone would inevitably joke (with evident anxiety) that he hoped I was not reading his mind. Although much has changed culturally at Fort Belknap during the past century, this concern can be traced historically to complex understandings regarding the power of thought and its use by others, sometimes even for harmful purposes. Of interest here is the simple fact that such responses depend upon an extant (but, in most instances, a deeply implicit) indigenous "ethno-" (or culturally local, emergent, or emic) psychology of mind, self, and personhood. This local ethnopsychology is fundamentally dependent upon an ancient Gros Ventre cosmology detailing (in part) the supernatural properties of thought. Indeed, one Gros Ventre name for the Supreme Being is loosely translated as "He Who Controls All by the Power of Thought." The notion occurred to me in the aftermath of these encounters that if modern professional psychologists are implicitly suspected by some community members of using such power for intrusive and controlling purposes, then extreme reluctance to consult a mental health professional—especially in vulnerable times of distress—seems perfectly reasonable.

In the realm of clinical research, the long pursuit by psychological clinical scientists for effective therapies, treatments, and interventions has generated a variety of techniques that are proven to reduce suffering, impairment, and distress in the lives of individuals struggling with psychological problems.[6] In fact, mental health professionals now command an arsenal of approaches specifically developed to assist people suffering from nearly every major category of disorder classified in the American Psychiatric Association's fourth edition of its *Diagnostic and Statistical Manual of Mental Disorders*.[7] Nevertheless, when it comes to this country's small population of American Indians and Alaska Natives, there is not a single, rigorously controlled outcome study that has assessed the efficacy or effectiveness of a conventional psychological intervention with Native clients. It remains an empirical question as to whether—and under what conditions—state-of-the-art mental health interventions are likely to benefit Native persons in distress. Nevertheless, there are clear reasons to suspect that conventional psychological interventions might in fact be detrimental to American Indian "mental health" *even if* they could be proven to reduce symptoms and improve functioning for particular individuals, owing to the thorny (post)colonial context in which mental health professionals find themselves vis-à-vis Native people. More specifically, the history of Euro-American colonization renders the provision of conventional psychological interventions to Native people a potentially detrimental encounter, resulting from the fundamental cultural incongruence of such interventions with the extant healing traditions of many tribal nations.

In the context of cross-cultural mental health service delivery, the dominant treatment paradigms typically employed by Western psychologists are suffused with concepts and categories, principles and practices that are culturally alien to most indigenous ways of being in the world. Consider the Freudian legacy of the tripartite mind, defense mechanisms, or the alleged role of unconscious emotion in the etiology of psychopathology that shapes both public and professional discourse on human psychology in the West despite its inherent unsuitability for scientific refutation.[8] These influential (albeit often untested and untestable) concepts, models, and orientations comprise a Western ethnopsychology with all manner of implications for the construction of Western minds, selves, and persons, as well as for the pathologies that afflict them and the interventions that heal them. The problem is that these influential Western ethnopsychologies—which quite naturally inhabit conventional mental health practices owing to the their Western origins—are discordant with most tribal ethnopsychologies with regard to emotional experience and expression; norms governing kinds and qualities of acceptable communication; the nature of distress, disorder, and its treatment; and the meanings of personhood, social relations, and spirituality.

Western ethnopsychologies of the person typically embrace the traditions of dualism, individualism, and modernity, conceptually separating mind from body, prioritizing the individual self over social relationships, and typically excluding attention to spirituality. One implication of these formative cultural assumptions is the organizational segregation of "mental health" from the rest of biomedicine within Western health care systems. In contrast, it is routinely observed that most Native cultures conceptualize the person in holistic terms without fragmenting selves into physical, mental, and spiritual components. Furthermore, illness is frequently understood in Native cultures to result from disrupted spiritual and social relationships. Finally, and perhaps most important, healing in Native communities is modally understood to require access to sacred power.[9]

In considering similar comparisons and contrasts, we must never forget that the Western cultural assumptions embedded within conventional psychotherapeutic practices are not merely mundane ideological alternatives—instead, they emerged historically in the context of a brutal U.S. colonialism. Any particular instance of an American Indian "client" or "patient" seeking assistance from a Western mental health professional is inherently shaped by a colonial tradition of power relationships, the troubling implications of which have been widely unexamined within academic and professional psychology. Given the fundamental cultural incongruence of Western psychological interventions with American Indian and Alaska Native cultural practices in the historical context of U.S. conquest and colonialism, the disturbing possibility arises that conventional mental health practices may actively undermine the stated commitment of most contemporary tribal communities to cultural preservation and revitalization by surreptitiously displacing key facets of the local ethnopsychology with those of Western ethnopsychology. In this regard, it may be that professional psychologists (and mental health practitioners of all stripes) have become the secular missionaries for a new millennium, unwittingly proselytizing Native clients through psychotherapy and related interventions by facilitating a "conversion" to Western forms of personhood. And it is the contemporary (post)colonial context specifically—emerging from long histories of asymmetrical power relationships—that renders this ongoing cultural proselytization and conversion distinct from otherwise similar cross-cultural encounters.

For instance, I well remember a fascinating family interaction that first impressed this point upon me. In the midst of an otherwise pleasant afternoon visit, my grandmother paused to recount an incident involving her favorite sister, who died while both of them were still adolescents. As she talked of her sister, Grandma was momentarily overcome with grief and wept quietly for a minute or two before resuming her account. Shortly after my grandmother departed for home, a relative from my mother's generation confided (with evident frustration) that Grandma needed to "confront her unresolved grief" because crying over a lost loved one several decades later could only lead to emotional problems. What impressed me most vividly about this exchange was the striking generational difference in terms of ethnopsychology. I knew that my grandmother would have considered the failure to intermittently express her feelings of loss for her favorite sister (no matter how many years had passed) as a morally inappropriate abdication of her kinship obligations. In contrast, however, my middle-aged relative considered the expression of this particular form of kinship obligation as certainly dysfunctional if not actually pathological. To what did I attribute this contradiction? Although I may never know for sure in this particular instance, I reasoned that my relative's perspective originated from her previous participation in substance abuse treatment and psychotherapy that quite probably socialized her into the view that "unresolved" emotional experiences are necessarily harmful in psychological terms. As psychologists we must directly confront the distinct possibility that Western clinical interventions represent a nearly invisible (but ongoing) "cultural proselytization" of distressed American Indian clients in their most vulnerable hour.

Incongruent Healing Traditions: The Career of Bull Lodge

If the provision of conventional psychological interventions within Native American communities truly represents the potential for neocolonial cultural proselytization, the implications for professional training in psychology are both disturbing and profound. As a result, it seems appropriate here to illustrate the relevant cultural incommensurabilities more concretely. There are undoubtedly numerous facets of the modern health care system that could be examined with regard to deep cultural incongruence with indigenous communal traditions, but the focus here will simply encompass the incompatibility of psychotherapeutic practices with extant Gros Ventre healing tradition. In order to canvass the relevant issues as concisely as possible it will be instructive to consider briefly the career of Bull Lodge, the most renowned healer in Gros Ventre history.[10]

Bull Lodge (ca. 1802–86) was widely revered throughout the northern Plains for his prowess in war and success in healing, both of which earned him uncommon distinction among the Gros Ventre people. In order to comprehend his remarkable place in Gros Ventre life, one must understand that historically, leadership and recognition in the community depended on valor and generosity.[11] Honors in war, including ferocity in the face of life-threatening odds, merited the highest regard, and every young Gros Ventre man aspired to an illustrious career in horse raiding and battle. Additionally, political and economic influence for both men and women was earned through obtaining supernatural powers for healing. The formal pursuit of supernatural powers, however, was less esteemed than cultivating and relying on one's own personal resources for success—in fact, Gros Ventres believed that the ritual use of sacred powers actually shortened one's life. The preferred means to success and recognition thus depended principally on individual talent, initiative, and tenacity, including personal religious devotion and prayer.

Bull Lodge came to exemplify such valor and generosity—augmented by unusual healing powers—following a series of impressive supernatural encounters that commenced when he was merely a boy. Bull Lodge was born to a poor family but, even as a youngster, nurtured his ambitions to become a prominent person by praying devoutly to the community's sacred Feathered Pipe to pity him and help him "to be a man." At the age of twelve, he had a vision in which the spirit of the Feathered Pipe told him, "Your cries have moved me with compassion—I pity you, my child." The Pipe promised Bull Lodge that he would be "powerful on this earth" and promised a series of subsequent experiences in which the requisite sacred knowledge would be conveyed. In one subsequent vision, for example, a Spirit Being displayed a war shield to Bull Lodge and taught him how to construct it. This sacred shield was understood to have supernaturally protected Bull Lodge on numerous war parties throughout his life. Still later, Bull Lodge was instructed to fast and pray on seven buttes throughout present-day north-central Montana. On each butte, Bull Lodge received additional spiritual instruction regarding the procurement, construction, and use of a wide range of objects endowed with supernatural powers for help in healing and war. For instance, Bull Lodge was known to "operate" with a woodpecker tail feather during his healing ceremonies. Near the end of a very prominent career, he was bestowed with perhaps the greatest honor a valorous and generous man could receive: he was selected as a ceremonial Keeper of the sacred Feathered Pipe medicine bundle. This Pipe provided the Keepers (husband and wife) with additional supernatural abilities necessary to fulfill their roles as intermediaries with the Thunder Being (who was accountable to the One Above) on behalf of the community.[12]

Now, it turns out that even this briefest of accounts is actually quite fertile with regard to the comparison of Gros Ventre healing tradition and psychotherapeutic practice and the contradictory implications of each for personhood. In the interest of space, I will identify only two principal incompatibilities or incongruities. First, Bull Lodge exemplified the path to prominence through uncommon valor. Indeed, the "ferocity"[13] required in such circumstances to compellingly demonstrate the personal ambition, energetic agency, and unyielding tenacity that Gros Ventres have esteemed for centuries characterizes not just Bull Lodge's most famous war exploits, but the narrative arc of his career as well (as recounted by his daughter, Snake Woman, to my great-grandfather, Fred Gone, in the 1940s). This pronounced esteem for tenacious agency is grounded in the Gros Ventre ethos of self-sufficiency in which persons should not need to depend upon other people (outside of the appropriate kinship relations) for material assistance, support, or other kinds of resources toward success in life. Such was evident in the case of Bull Lodge, in which his ambitions were ultimately realized because of unusual religious devotion and resultant supernatural favor—in fact, the narrative of Bull Lodge's life does not recount even one instance of his seeking guidance or resources from other community members.

This regard for *tenacious agency* and *self-sufficiency* persists among contemporary Gros Ventres and leads to a dilemma when it comes to psychological intervention of the kind familiar to mental health professionals. Gros Ventres are culturally committed to a view of personhood that celebrates forbearance, emotional reserve, and strength of mind in the face of hardship, suffering, or distress. As a result, to this day many modern Gros Ventres interpret the explicit pursuit of "counseling" or "mental health" services in times of distress as a serious moral failure, a sign of weakness, impotence, and dependency in a world that requires uncommon stamina and personal resourcefulness in the pursuit of one's ambitions. This is why it was so difficult for my close relative to approach me for "therapy" and why he was so easily alienated by my blundering response. Such a view of personhood stands in sharp contrast to the cultural assumptions embedded within the most prevalent contemporary psychotherapies, in which confessional acknowledgements of weakness, fragility, or dependency are explicitly encouraged and unvarnished expressions of illicit thought or troubling emotion are directly solicited. Gros Ventres today who commence psychotherapy are immediately confronted with the jangling psychological discordance that results from deep incongruence in conceptions of personhood.

A second incongruity or incompatibility with obvious relevance pertains to the significance of suffering for Gros Ventre personhood. More specifically, sacrifice and suffering are understood by modern Gros Ventres as the necessary prerequisites for supernatural intervention (which is why fasting, the Sweatlodge, and especially the Sacrifice Lodge all involve hardship and endurance). That suffering in the context of personal religious devotion was crucial to Bull Lodge's success as a healer and leader cannot be overemphasized. His unique boyhood relationship to the sacred Feathered Pipe during which he prayed in anguish to the Pipe to "have pity on me" inaugurated a healer's training that depended directly on an impressive series of supernatural encounters providing the requisite "professional" knowledge to perform supernatural acts of healing. This is an essential point: among the Gros Ventres it was historically meaningless to conceive of healing practices in the absence of ritual smudging, singing, smoking, and supplicating that was understood to result finally in access to sacred power. To elaborate further, this power was obtained from Spirit Beings by evoking their pity through ritual. The operative phenomenon here is *pity*, and in order to interpersonally evoke pity from powerful Spirit Beings, it is necessary for humans to become pitiable through sacrifice and suffering. This is why Bull Lodge fasted and prayed (or "cried") on seven buttes for days at a time in order to obtain pity and thereby win divine favor—sometimes, he sacrificed strips of his own flesh in order to become even more pitiable. In sum, Bull Lodge's sojourns of suffering were the necessary prerequisite for him to later become a powerful healer—otherwise he would have had no means to access the sacred knowledge that allowed him to harness supernatural power for beneficial healing purposes.

The regard for suffering, pity, sacred knowledge, and supernatural power in Gros Ventre healing persists among contemporary Gros Ventres, and it leads to a second dilemma when it comes to conventional psychological interventions. Gros Ventres are culturally committed to a view of personhood that encompasses interpersonal relations with a wide variety of Spirit Beings and the resultant potential for accessing sacred power for the purposes of sustaining life "in a good way." As a result, to this day many modern Gros Ventres expect that bona fide healers have endured numerous experiences of ritual hardship and sacrifice to garner the favor of Spirit Beings who directly instructed them in the ceremonial practices designed to access sacred power for curative purposes. Such a view of personhood stands in sharp contrast to the cultural assumptions embedded within the most prevalent contemporary psychotherapies, in which therapeutic efficacy is understood to result from extensive training in the theory and techniques of psychological intervention within the secular context of graduate study in the Western academy. This represents another instance of psychological discordance resulting from the deep incongruence in conceptions of personhood as experienced by contemporary Gros Ventres who commence psychotherapy.

These fundamental incommensurabilities reveal the crucible of mental health service delivery in indigenous cultural contexts, namely, that professional psychologists—using the conventional therapeutic techniques of our trade—may unwittingly enculturate our suffering patients into the ways of Western personhood through the subtle negotiations and transformations of self that occur in the psychotherapeutic encounter. In the end, considering just two facets of the complex divergence in concepts of personhood embedded within Gros Ventre healing traditions and contemporary psychotherapeutic practice, respectively, leaves psychologists with a single pressing question: In the face of such cultural divergences and the resultant potential for implicit cultural proselytization, what is the appropriate and acceptable response of faculty (Native or otherwise) in professional psychology training programs who are committed to the well-being of indigenous individuals and communities?

Indigenizing Academic Training in Professional Psychology

The commitment to "indigenizing" North American colleges and universities is shared by each of the essayists in this collection. In order to envision more concretely what this commitment might entail for doctoral training in professional psychology, three brief observations related to this endeavor are in order. First, contemporary American Indian and Alaska Native people continue to struggle with the historical legacy of Euro-American conquest and colonialism, including the bereaved pursuit of viable (post)colonial sources of coherence, connectedness, and historical continuity in the face of rapid and cataclysmic disruptions in our aboriginal ways of life. Second, Native American experiences of Euro-American colonialism have always inspired acts of resistance, discourses of critique, movements of agentic negotiation, and moments of alternative possibility, though always in the context of asymmetrical power relations. Finally, those of us who pursue doctorates and subsequent careers in the university professoriate inevitably negotiate these processes of (post)colonial meaning-making and counnstercolonial critique with specific regard to the institutions and traditions of the Western academy. To the extent that we are committed to refashioning, reenvisioning, or reforming the Western academy with recourse to indigenous thought and practice, we are inevitably prescribing (whether implicitly or explicitly) what we are willing to adopt from the Western university tradition, what we are willing to adapt of our own indigenous epistemological traditions, and which aspects of these disparate traditions we are prepared to omit from the transaction altogether. The intrinsic complexity here involves an infinite array of strategies for deciding what to adopt, what to adapt, and what to omit from these divergent ways of knowing and learning within our visions for transforming the academy. It is essential to acknowledge at the outset that my recommendations for indigenizing doctoral training in professional psychology reflect my own proclivities as an American Indian psychologist for adopting, adapting, and omitting as I attempt to hurdle the colonial abyss, and I offer them with all humility.

There can be no doubt, however, that my willingness to seriously consider what it means to indigenize psychology reveals my own commitment to the discipline: while I worry about the cultural dangers of practicing psychology-as-usual in Native communities, I also believe that the profession harbors the potential to contribute something of value for modern indigenous lives. This is so for at least four reasons. First, the doctoral degree in professional psychology is one distinctive and influential pathway to mental health service provision within the contemporary U.S. health care system. As such, psychologists lay claim to expertise, access, prestige, and resources in their efforts to assist persons in distress in ways that are distinct from other kinds of health care professionals—in fact, virtually every federally recognized Native American community receives services from a professional psychologist through the Indian Health Service. Second, doctoral training in psychology—even in professional psychology—emphasizes familiarity and facility with complex variable-analytic methodologies for conducting psychological research. In short, psychologists are routinely trained in relatively sophisticated strategies of inquiry that prepare them to investigate a wide range of psychological phenomena, including those of potential interest to Native communities. Third, the traditions of empirical inquiry that predominate within mainstream psychology have reinforced the discipline's claim to "scientific" status within American society. As a result, psychological findings wield concrete influence in contemporary U.S. policy and decision making (albeit not nearly as extensively as most psychologists would prefer). Certainly, most tribal governments would appreciate similar opportunities to influence the particular governmental policies and practices that directly affect their communities. Finally, psychology is a diverse discipline with a wide range of subfields typically organized by phenomena of interest, including clinical, community, cognitive, developmental, personality, social, biological, industrial-organizational, and quantitative psychology, to name the most prevalent branches within typical psychology departments. This diversity testifies further to the wide variety of domains addressed by the discipline. More important, it speaks to the potential of the field to accommodate novel areas of inquiry either within, between, or across subfields, a characteristic seemingly necessary to the viability of an indigenized psychology.

In response to the question regarding the appropriate and acceptable response of faculty in professional psychology training programs who are committed to the well-being of indigenous individuals and communities, my view is that the opportunity to indigenize psychology basically entails a transformation of professional training in the discipline so as to render the field *pragmatically beneficial* (as opposed to irresponsibly irrelevant or actively detrimental) for Native communities. This transformation should minimally result in *the preparation of professional psychologists for innovative "mental health" service delivery that attends substantively to the co-constitution of indigenous cultural practice and psychological wellness.* Two facets of this explicit objective warrant explanation and comment. First, in contrast to typical psychologists whose professional training consists of an extended apprenticeship guaranteed to reproduce existing clinical approaches, technologies, and techniques, the next generation of professionals who aspire to relevance for indigenous lives must be prepared for reflective and systematic innovation in their psychological theories of wellness and disorder, in their therapeutic practices of assessment and intervention, and in their institutional conventions for providing helping services. Since it is often impossible to predict in advance what these innovations might look like in the context of any particular indigenous community, such professionals cannot be instructed in detailed approaches and procedures that have yet to be devised. Instead, they must be trained broadly in the conceptual, methodological, cultural, political, and interpersonal principles and orientations that will equip them *not* with the concrete knowledge of what to do in a given indigenous setting (e.g., burn angelica root before talking of serious personal matters within certain California tribal communities), but will equip them instead with the tools and skills to actively formulate such concrete knowledge as part of their negotiated entrée into one of any number of indigenous communities with widely variant practices and traditions.

One significant tradition for equipping innovative professional psychologists with the necessary tools, skills, and approaches to undertake more open-ended (and open-minded) service in Indian country can be found within community psychology. Established in the 1960s as a critical alternative to conventional clinical psychology, community psychology has sought to integrate its professional commitments with rigorous psychological science, human resource development, and progressive political activity in the context of explicitly embracing cultural relativity, diversity, and ecology.[14] With regard to the conventions of mental health service delivery, community psychologists have long advocated community-based education and consultation (as opposed to clinic-based psychotherapeutic services) emphasizing collaborative and empowering relationships with community stakeholders (as opposed to expert-client relationships with patients) toward the development of strengths-focused (as opposed to deficit-focused), preventive (as opposed to rehabilitative) interventions.[15] More concretely, a community psychologist might take the following steps in her efforts to assist Native communities in a mutually beneficial collaboration targeted at promoting psychological wellness: (1) identify and engage a variety of local community members, agencies, and institutions in order to forge relationships that will sustain the development, implementation, and assessment of the intervention; (2) determine with involved community members what the focus of the intervention should be (e.g., to promote prosocial behavior among troubled community youth, to facilitate effective support and advocacy by individuals on behalf of distressed family members, to consolidate and extend treatment or healing resources within the community, etc.); (3) consult with community members to design a specific intervention with careful attention to targeted participants, required resources, desired outcomes, and assessment methodology; (4) pursue extramural funding from private foundations or government agencies to fund the project; (5) implement the intervention in close collaboration with community members; (6) assess intervention outcomes; and (7) disseminate results, revisions, and modifications of the program within the community itself as well as to other scientific and grass-roots circles. The emphasis here is clearly on the development of a demonstrably effective intervention that directly addresses the pressing "mental health" concerns of the community of interest.

If preparing psychologists for more innovative work in American Indian and Alaska Native communities is essential to indigenizing academic training in professional psychology, then ensuring that such innovation is thoroughly responsive to the cultural foundations of health and wellness in indigenous communities guarantees that novel efforts and interventions will actually remedy the dangers of Western cultural proselytization. Thus, a second important facet of indigenizing professional psychology is the requirement that the next generation of professionals who aspire to relevance for indigenous lives must be prepared for sophisticated analysis and inquiry related to the mutually constituting aspects of culture and mind. For it is only by respectfully engaging tribal conceptualizations of health and wellness, disorder and dysfunction, ceremony and healing that professional psychologists might come to understand the local ethnopsychology within particular indigenous communities with enough sophistication to formulate alternative kinds of helping interventions that reinforce and extend (rather than subverting and displacing) endangered cultural practices related to tribal notions of self, personhood, emotion, social relations, and spirituality. Once again, it is quite difficult to equip professional psychologists in advance for service in specific indigenous communities with adequate knowledge regarding the cultural practices related to wellness and healing; rather, such professionals require more general conceptual and methodological preparation for studying culture and mind that they can later apply in the particular settings in which they work.

In this regard, academic training in professional psychology would recommend a great deal more for Indian country if it were less methodologically parochial. That is, psychology's longstanding "physics envy" has yielded the canonization of analytic tools and strategies that reinforce the field's status as "scientific." As a result, credible methodology in psychology is almost always statistical and variable-analytic, as applied to experimental or correlational studies of psychological phenomena.[16] Such approaches retain clear advantages for investigating many kinds of psychological phenomena, but scientific psychology's hegemonic celebration of these methods in the construction of disciplinary knowledge renders many other kinds of inquiry into a variety of legitimate psychological phenomena extremely difficult. Moreover, these privileged methods are best suited for testing a priori (i.e., hypothesized in advance) explanations of phenomena as opposed to developing a posteriori (i.e., following empirical discovery) explanations in the first place.[17] The implications of these divergent modes of inquiry are readily apparent if one considers, for example, the contrasting ways in which social psychologists (within the variable-analytic traditions of social science research that privilege standardized surveys and statistical analysis of coded responses) and sociocultural anthropologists (within the interpretive traditions of social science research that privilege participant-observation and qualitative analysis of meaning-full phenomena) undertake the study of cross-cultural differences in human behavior. With regard to indigenizing academic training in professional psychology, the former must be augmented with the later.

It is absolutely essential that academic training in professional psychology incorporate additional (as opposed to displacing existing) methods of inquiry that are specifically tailored to the sophisticated study of cultural meaning and practice. More specifically, the adoption of interpretive or qualitative methods—methods that are patently nonscientific to most psychologists' way of thinking—is a necessary prerequisite for ensuring professional psychology's viability in American Indian and Alaska Native communities. Absent facility with such methods—especially ethnographic methods—it is unclear precisely how psychology might ever substantively formulate local ethnopsychologies in the effort to systematically guide clinical innovation so as to develop alternative, culturally appropriate helping interventions.

Psychology must diversify methodologically if it is to keep culture in mind—that is, if it is to attend seriously to the cultural construction of mind, self, and personhood in Native communities. An increasingly influential interdisciplinary tradition with clear relevance here is the reemerging field of cultural psychology.[18] Cultural psychology takes as its conceptual point of departure the co-constitution of culture and mind.[19] Its central locus of inquiry therefore concerns the semiotic (i.e., symbolically mediated) nature of human experience. The resultant formulation of local ethnopsychologies within the framework of cultural psychology will encompass multiple relevant content areas, including culture, language, and mind; self and personhood; emotional experience and expression; concepts of health, illness, and healing; and research reflexivity (i.e., attention to how the knower constructs the known). Each of these phenomena harbors important implications for the transformation of conventional psychological intervention within Native communities, and each requires alternative methodological tools for its appropriate investigation. Therefore, it would seem that the investigation and analysis of each would be necessary and appropriate between steps (1) and (2) in the development of a community-based intervention as detailed above. In any case, without proper training in the sophisticated study of such phenomena, professional psychologists will never be able to circumvent the dangers of invisible cultural proselytization that remain inherent to our work.[20]

Conclusion

My vision for indigenizing academic training in professional psychology is thus complete: drawing on the extant traditions of community and cultural psychology respectively, new generations of professional psychologists who aspire to relevance for Indian country will be equipped conceptually and methodologically through their training to re-envision mental health service delivery in Native American communities so as to facilitate and enhance cultural preservation rather than unknowingly subverting it. Indigenizing psychology will challenge both the dominant conventions of clinical intervention as well as the dominant conventions of conceptual and methodological training within the discipline, thereby allowing it to overcome a formidable (post)colonial predicament. This is, of course, an extremely modest proposal: I harbor no fantasies of integrating indigenous epistemologies with psychological training because I concede that the essence of professional psychology is fundamentally dependent on the Western rationalist and empiricist epistemologies that are largely incommensurate with Native ways of knowing. Instead, my vision for a pragmatically beneficial professional psychology assumes that it will remain Western in essence, albeit tailored to appreciate and engage the local epistemologies and ethnopsychologies of Native communities in substantive, supportive, respectful, and constructive ways.

The actual prospects are promising for establishing a handful of training sites within professional psychology that adequately equip future psychologists with the necessary conceptual and methodological tools for apprehending the subtle nuances of cultural meaning and practice in Native (and other non-Western) communities. Even though psychology remains a relatively conservative discipline in the generally traditionalist social sciences, its breadth and diversity—combined with the realities of an increasingly multicultural U.S. population desiring or requiring professional services—suggests that current tolerance and (perhaps) eventual regard for the adoptions, adaptations, and omissions of indigenous psychologists pursuing viable (post)colonial alternatives to psychology-as-usual will characterize at least some of the most reputable psychology departments in the country.

Notes

1. For an origin story, see T. D. LaFromboise and C. Fleming, "Keeper of the Fire: A Profile of Carolyn Attneave," *Journal of Counseling and Development* 68 (1990): 537–47.

2. The American Psychological Association (*The Directory of Ethnic Minority Professionals in Psychology*, 4th ed. [Washington DC: APA, 2001]) currently lists 106 Native American psychologists among its membership of roughly 150,000 professionals.

3. For a personal account, see J. E. Trimble, "Bridging Spiritual Sojourns and Social Science Research in Native Communities," in M. H. Bond, ed., *Working at the Interface of Cultures: Eighteen Lives in Social Science* (London: Routledge, 1997), 166–78.

4. D. W. Sue and D. Sue, *Counseling the Culturally Different: Theory and Practice*, 3rd ed. (New York: Wiley, 1999).

5. In considering the colonial experience of the indigenous peoples of the United States, the issue of appropriate terminology becomes tantamount. Despite its currency in contemporary literary circles, the term "postcolonial" seems inappropriate to the contemporary indigenous circumstance because the colonizers (or their descendants) retain dominance over the domestic, political, and economic affairs of tribal communities—indeed, the U.S. Congress might well exercise its plenary power to terminate tribal communities at any time. At the same time, the term "colonial" also seems inappropriate because U.S. policies of military conquest, occupation, and resource theft ended a few short generations ago. In fact, since the era of self-determination commenced in the 1970s wherein tribal governments exercise a degree of authority and autonomy uncharacteristic of colonial subjects in other parts of the world, the term "colonial" seems even less appropriate. Furthermore, for several generations now many American Indian peoples have found innovative sources of meaning and coherence within established Euro-American symbols and institutions (e.g., sovereignty, literacy, legal claims, military service, blood quantum, IRA governance, Christianity, star quilting, cattle ranching, casino operation, tribal college administration, etc.), effectively rendering them distinctively our own (in the "postcolonial" sense). In order to capture this extremely complex state of affairs, I have chosen to adopt the ambiguous term "(post)colonial" from Chadwick Allen (*Blood Narrative: Indigenous Identity in American Indian and Maori Literary and Activist Texts* [Durham NC: Duke University Press, 2002]), albeit with slightly different connotations.

6. For example, see D. L. Chambless and T. H. Ollendick, "Empirically Supported Psychological Interventions: Controversies and Evidence," *Annual Review of Psychology* 52 (2001): 685–716.

7. American Psychiatric Association, *Diagnostic and Statistical Manual of Mental Disorders*, 4th ed. (Washington DC: APA, 2001).

8. F. C. Crews, ed., *Unauthorized Freud: Doubters Confront a Legend* (New York: Viking, 1998).

9. For more detailed reviews of such cultural contrasts, see: T. D. LaFromboise, J. E. Trimble, and G. V. Mohatt, "Counseling Intervention and American Indian Tradition," *The Counseling Psychologist* 18, no. 4 (1990): 628–54; S. M. Manson, J. H. Shore, and J. D. Bloom, "The Depressive Experience in American Indian Communities: A Challenge for Psychiatric Theory and Diagnosis," in A. Kleinman and B. Good, eds., *Culture and Depression: Studies in the Anthropology and Cross-cultural Psychiatry of Affect and Disorder* (Berkeley: University of California Press, 1985), 331–68; J. E. Trimble, S. M. Manson, N. G. Dinges, and B. Medicine, "American Indian Concepts

of Mental Health: Reflections and Directions," in P. B. Pedersen, N. Sartorius, and A. J. Marsella, eds., *Mental Health Services: The Cross-cultural Context* (Beverly Hills CA: Sage, 1984), 199–220.

10. See F. P. Gone, *The Seven Visions of Bull Lodge as Told by His Daughter, Garter Snake*, G. P. Horse Capture, ed. (Lincoln: University of Nebraska Press, 1980).

11. For much more detail see R. Flannery, *The Gros Ventres of Montana: Part I. Social Life* (Washington DC: Catholic University of America, 1953); L. Fowler, *Shared Symbols, Contested Meanings: Gros Ventre Culture and History, 1778–1984* (Ithaca: Cornell University Press, 1987).

12. Gone, *Seven Visions of Bull Lodge*, 30, 32.

13. Fowler, *Shared Symbols*.

14. J. Rappaport, *Community Psychology: Values, Research, and Action* (Fort Worth TX: Holt, Rinehart, and Winston, 1977).

15. See J. Rappaport and E. Seidman, "Social and Community Interventions," in C. E. Walker, ed., *The Handbook of Clinical Psychology: Theory, Research, and Practice* (Homewood IL: Dow Jones-Irvin, 1983), 1089–123.

16. L. J. Cronbach, "The Two Disciplines of Scientific Psychology," *American Psychologist* 12, no. 5 (1957): 671–84.

17. Drawing on the distinction between the contexts of discovery and justification in H. Reichenbach, *Experience and Prediction* (Chicago: University of Chicago Press, 1938).

18. See J. S. Bruner, *Acts of Meaning* (Cambridge MA: Harvard University Press, 1990); M. Cole, "Cultural Psychology: A Once and Future Discipline?" in J. J. Berman, ed., *Nebraska Symposium on Motivation* 37 (1990): 279–336; R. A. Shweder, "Cultural Psychology—What Is It?" in J. W. Stigler, R. A. Shweder, and G. Herdt, eds., *Cultural Psychology: Essays on Comparative Human Development* (New York: Cambridge University Press, 1990), 1–43.

19. See R. A. Shweder, *Thinking Through Cultures: Expeditions in Cultural Psychology* (Cambridge MA: Harvard University Press, 1991); R. A. Shweder and M. A. Sullivan, "Cultural Psychology: Who Needs It?" *Annual Review of Psychology* 44 (1993): 497–523.

20. For a more detailed discussion, see J. P. Gone, "American Indian Mental Health Service Delivery: Persistent Challenges and Future Prospects," in J. S. Mio and G. Y. Iwamasa, eds., *Culturally Diverse Mental Health: The Challenge of Research and Resistance* (New York: Brunner-Routledge, 2003).

8. SHOULD AMERICAN INDIAN HISTORY REMAIN A FIELD OF STUDY?

Devon Abbott Mihesuah

Why do we write American Indian history? What is the point of attempting to reconstruct the past? Historians usually say they study and write Native history because they are curious about long-ago happenings. Something—a specific event, a person, a chain of happenings—has caught their interest. Perhaps they are interested in their ancestors, human nature, or discovering stories of those who are often ignored in U.S. history texts. These are among the reasons I entered graduate school in 1984.

Thousands of books and essays have been written about Native peoples and Indigenous-white relations, so obviously, there is a great deal of interest in historic Natives among scholars and readers. However, there is a great deal of difference between historians who are concerned about present-day realities Natives face and historians—both non-Native and Native—who pursue their armchair interests while vehemently supporting academic freedom and claiming to be inclusive in their writings, yet simultaneously appearing to have no concern for the people they write about.

Most humanities scholars argue that acquiring knowledge of the world's cultures and their histories is important to understanding ourselves and is the mark of an educated person. Even many individuals who are not formally educated watch *National Geographic Explorer*, The Discovery Channel, or read *Biography* because they are curious about humanity. While curiosity about Others is not a problem in itself, it becomes a moral problem when scholars write colonialist histories about Others for distribution only among themselves in the ivory tower and only for their benefit.

Grants, fellowships, and awards have been bestowed upon hundreds of historians who write about Natives, and there is no question that many historians of "Indian history" have prospered from creating versions of the past. Contrary to the lifestyles of historians in academia, conditions for many Natives remain stark. Standing Rock Sioux Vine Deloria Jr. stated in 1991 that "We need to eliminate useless or repetitive research and focus on actual community needs; it is both unethical and wasteful to plow familiar ground continually."[1] Indeed, poverty, racism, disease, frustration, and depression are common throughout many tribal nations. How many works of history actually analyze the perpetrators of colonialism in an attempt to ascertain how we have arrived at this point? How many history books and essays have tried to find solutions to these problems? What can we say is the usefulness of all these history books that focus on Natives? If essays are going to continue to be reprinted in anthologies, then why can't we see more collections of papers devoted to the historical reasons why Natives are in their current situations, in addition to proposed solutions to the problems? Ironically, many of the "powerhouse" scholars have never met an Indian or visited tribal lands, illustrating the actuality that "highly educated" people can simultaneously be insulated from many of the realities of life. As a historian who has read hundreds of history works in my eighteen years of seriously studying "Indian history," and who also knows quite a few historians, I can think of only a few non-Native or Native historians who study past events truly with tribes' benefits in mind.

Native intellectual activists and our non-Native allies are growing in number, and most of us are concerned about this issue, much to the discomfort of established historians who have maintained their power base in Native history and in Native studies as a whole. Indigenous intellectuals are also becoming increasingly vocal in their objections to the way their ancestors have been portrayed or ignored in works of history and how those images and absences in stories about this country's past translate in the present. We are impatient with scholars who continue to profit from editing anthologies of essays focusing on familiar topics we've seen repeatedly and composing stories that are useless as tools of decolonization. Our impatience also stems from facing gatekeepers determined to keep Native intellectuals who have much to say out of the picture and from being denied tenure or promotion (or at least receiving it only after resorting to formal complaints or legal action) and funding for projects, in addition to receiving poor evaluations from patriotic students who don't want to hear about colonialism in the United States.

Many scholars understand that how history is written can directly impact modern Native people for good and bad. Like Wahpetunwan Dakota historian Angela Cavender Wilson asserts, "American Indian history is a field dominated by white, male historians who rarely ask or care what the Indians they study have to say about their work."[2] Many Natives argue that they possess viable versions of their pasts, and Native scholars know that their theories and methodologies have been ignored, while the majority of works focusing on Natives do not contribute to tribes' well-being.

Kanien'kehaka scholar Taiaiake Alfred writes that "the state attempts to rewrite history in order to legitimize its exercise of power (sovereignty) over Indigenous peoples."[3] Similarly, Foucault states in his *Power/Knowledge* that writing history is often used for social and political reasons and that writing history can be an instrument of power;[4] historian Alan Munslow argues that "written history is always more than innocent storytelling, precisely because it is the primary vehicle for the distribution and use of power."[5] Although Natives can also invent versions of the past for their benefit, the reality is that Natives are rarely in authoritative positions, while many white historians have created history using their entrenched methodological standards to maintain and justify their power base and privileged positions.

History philosopher Hayden White asserts that "For any effort to comprehend that politics of interpretation in historical studies that instructs us to recognize 'the war is over' and to forgo the attractions of a desire for revenge, it seems obvious to me that such instruction is the kind that always emanates from centers of established political power and social authority and that this kind of tolerance is a luxury only devotees of dominant groups can afford."[6]

I am not stating that all non-Native historians are bourgeois colonialists bent on keeping Natives in subservient positions. On the contrary, through my tumultuous years in academia some of my strongest supporters, good friends, and most knowledgeable mentors have been non-Natives. What I am saying is that there are many historians, and some are Native, who have little interest in decolonization efforts, balanced narratives, and political activism. They are content to focus only on creating biased stories about the past and would be happy if modern Native people would stop dwelling on the transgressions committed by long-dead colonists and get on with life. And herein lies the problem: life today for many Natives is lived as colonized peoples who continue to be stereotyped, discriminated against and kept impoverished by subtle and blatant policies and behaviors that also occurred historically. To argue that everyone has equal shots at success is either ignorant or racist, and to continue to write similar history stories and to reprint the same stuff with no concern for the descendants of the ancestors we generate stories about is selfish.

Nietzsche asserted that "the unhistorical and the historical are necessary in equal measure for the health of an individual, of a people, and of a culture."[7] For Indigenous people, knowledge of the past is crucial for their identity growth and development, pride, problem-solving strategies, and cultural survival. Nietzsche also claims that being "unhistorical"—able to forget the past—is one way to find happiness. In some circumstances, the advice to "forget it and move on" is useful, especially for trivial day-to-day events and confrontations. But the strategy of becoming unhistorical is simply not possible for tribal people with complex histories and cultures and devastating past (and present) relations with non-Natives that have shaped their modern realities.

Without question, writing and teaching Indigenous history are political acts. There can be many versions created of the same historic event depending on the author's bias, political beliefs, social pressures, and major professors' and publishers' demands. Because of the growing number of concerned Indigenous scholars and their allies in the academy, all historians, Native and non-Native, are becoming more conscientious about presentation, whether they side with Native people or not. There are obvious strategies (apparent to Indigenous scholars and our allies, at least) that writers of Native history use in order to appear "politically correct," such as claiming in their book's introduction that they use "Indian voices," and do not, or thanking Native writers in the acknowledgments even though that person had nothing to do with the creation of the work, or claiming that he or she writes from the "Indian perspective." Many historians identify themselves as "ethnohistorians," another ploy they use to appear as if they are really doing thorough research. Although ethnohistory is supposed to be a melding of historical and anthropological methodologies (for example, archival research and oral accounts that would in theory be a more inclusive way of finding information), few ethnohistorians actually bother to talk with Natives and instead depend on theories formulated by white thinkers to create stories of what may have happened in the past.

Another example is asserting in their introductions that a Native scholar's theories provided inspiration for their work. In Deloria and

Salisbury's *A Companion to American Indian History* (2000), for example, Angela Cavender Wilson is thanked in the introduction for helping to "form some of the understandings that underpin this book," but nowhere in the anthology do we see evidence of Wilson's influence, and only a brief discussion of her ideologies appear at the end of Deloria's essay "Historiography," which reveals Deloria's misunderstanding of what Wilson says.[8]

Empiricist scholars argue that as long as one thoroughly scours the archives and remains objective while analyzing the data, then accurate history can be written. But consider the events in a day in the life of one modern person. Conversations take place all day. Phone calls are made, meals are consumed, goods are purchased, newspapers and chapters of books are read, television shows are watched and children are disciplined. Weights are lifted, miles are run, and appointments are kept. We drive back and forth across town, breathe thousands of breaths, listen to dozens of songs on the radio and try to tune out even more commercials. White lies, embellishments, gossip, and racist comments emerge as a result of wishful thinking, patriotism, blind faith, racism, and suspicion. Countless thoughts, visions, and nighttime dreams fill our consciousness and unconscious, all meshing together to form motivations and physical acts. Each day every person performs countless chores, thinks millions of thoughts, and makes decisions, and most of those actions and thoughts result in counteractions by either ourselves or someone else. The vast majority of everyday actions are not recorded or even remembered. And, we tend to forget the things we did the day before. If we don't document much of what happens today—and we have computers and dictaphones—how can anyone seriously state that we can reconstruct events of the long-ago past (populated by millions of people) with accuracy?

We can't. Even those Natives who argue the necessity of using oral testimonies agree with historian Norman J. Wilson's comment, "History is best defined as a continual, open-ended process of argument, which is constantly changing. No question is closed because any problem can be reopened by finding new evidence or by taking a new look at old evidence. Thus there are no final answers, only good, coherent arguments: history is not some irreducible list of 'the facts' but continually changing bodies of evidence."[9]

Although we still try to do the best we can by including archival data along with oral testimonies, that is often not enough. It is usually a no-win situation for Native historians: we get hung up by gatekeepers who insist that the only "real Indians" lived in the past[10] and therefore modern Natives possess only "mythological" stories.[11] Real Natives (who, according to gatekeepers, aren't "really real") want to empower themselves and their tribes. They try to accomplish this by talking with elders in order to acquire traditional knowledge, but that information is not considered viable by influential gatekeepers such as Richard White, who refers to such data as "privileged information" that should not be used because it cannot be proved.[12] It seems fair to say that work containing analysis based on oral stories is seen by many historians as inferior and not worthy of attention or citation.

Historians often create their historical stories in the same fashion as fiction writers, with imagination and creativity. A historian who wrote a Pulitzer Prize–nominated book once said to me that it took him days to compose the artful introductions to each chapter, paragraphs describing colorful sunrises, the weather, and emotions that he hoped had taken place in those days almost three hundred years ago. Was this fiction, or by coincidence, really real? It depends on how you define "fact." As Alan Munslow says, "The evidence is turned into 'facts' through the narrative interpretations of historians."[13] Names, dates and places are only a part of the picture. The narrative (organization and creation of the story) gives the stories their substance and direction. Narrative is also the reflection of the author's bias, political agendas, and patriotic fervor. If one needs to prove a point, any history is possible. And if the history written agrees with and is accepted by the reader, then it is "fact," at least to that person.

Some historians argue that tribal stories are embellished and formulated to serve the purposes of the tribe, which may be true enough in some instances. But this brings up two important points about Native history. The first is that most Natives believe that the tribal stories held by those obligated to the task are more accurate than stories created by outsiders. This is a political, social, and religious statement that will not change just because some historians see Natives' interpretations as subjective. Second, mainstream historians are going to continue to write the way they do; therefore, Native historians and our allies should have the right to identify histories that are helpful to the tribes, accurate in their tribe's eyes, racist, or incomplete. Wilson proposed it first by entitling one of her essays "American Indian History or Non-Indian Perceptions of American Indian History?" and by suggesting that authors admit what they are attempting to accomplish.

A useful model in understanding why historians write the way they do is the "patterns" of history put forth by Grob and Billias, in which they argue that writers analyze the past according to the standards and political and social climate of the generation in which the historians live. "Every generation of American scholars seems to have reinterpreted the past in terms of its own age," they write. "Thus, each succeeding generation of Americans seems to have rewritten the history of the nation in such a way as to suit its own image."[14] The late historian R. G. Collingwood concurs: "The historian . . . is not God, looking at the world from above and outside. He is a man, and a man of his own time and place. He looks at the past from the point of view of the present: he looks at other countries and civilizations from the point of view of his own."[15]

Space does not allow exploring here the cycles of American Indian history beginning with Spanish missionaries or Adair's *History of the American Indians* (1775) and moving through cycles of histories to the present. But what we can clearly see today in the realm of Native history are at least two distinct types of writing: one is a patriotic form that eschews Native voices and theories in favor of non-Native versions of the past, and the other emanates from the Indigenous intellectual camp and our allies who demand a more thorough story of the tribal past that tells the story of not just confrontation and resistance, but also of the colonialism that continues to the present and how Natives can recover traditional knowledge to empower themselves.

Numerous essays discuss specific periods of Native studies or the historiography of certain fields (such as military encounters, boarding schools, missionaries, or specific tribes), but many of those serve little purpose other than to make lists of what has been written. An exception (and an example of fence-sitting in regards to how history should be written) is Phil Deloria's essay "Historiography" that appears in his *A Companion to American Indian History*, in which he categorizes the periods of Native storytelling: "(1) an 'oral/traditional' period in which people used and recalled significant events as temporal markers imbued with historical and cultural significance; (2) a period shaped by Christianization, in which mergings of the ideologies and tropes of the Bible with those of oral traditions became relatively common, shaping the nature of historical discourse among Indian people; (3) a period shaped by academic and non-academic scholarship, in which detailed ethnographic and historical inquiry into Indian history helped reshape native conceptions and narrations of the past."[16]

Deloria's grouping illustrates one of the problems with categorizing how "Indian history" has been written and how it is a misunderstanding of past and present tribal values. For example, this "oral/traditional period" is still in effect for many Indigenous peoples who depend on oral storytelling for cultural knowledge and identity. Second, not all Indigenous peoples became Christians. They rejected the overtures of missionaries and would not have been influenced by the Bible; many still are not. Finally, the last listing does not actually exist because few scholars have reshaped anything, and, even if there is a revolution in academia, it will take quite a while before it affects tribal communities.

What good does all this historiographical listing serve? So far, none, really. We must be courageous enough to step on some toes and analyze the "important works" that are authored by the people who say hello to us in the hallways and at conferences (and who evaluate our promotion, merit, and grant applications). We must identify investigations of the past that can assist people in the present, and we must identify books that are not helpful. This does not mean students should not read the lesser studies; but they and their professors should be informed of the purposes their required readings serve. Awareness of Native history scholarship is crucial because the book list is growing and harm is done by many histories.

A common thread that runs through most stories of Natives' pasts is that authors tell stories in a vacuum and do not attempt to figure out how past events helped create the present. According to Natives who are concerned about their present-day situations, this is a critical methodological oversight. Some historians and philosophers, however, doubt that this should be done. Reconstructionist G. R. Elton, for example, dislikes this approach of "present-centered" history, which he argues is incomplete and "entails selecting from the past those details that seem to take the story along to today's concerns."[17] This is not the methodology of Native intellectuals; they know from experience that the portrayal of peoples and events in the past directly impacts how their descendants are viewed and treated. Considering the dismal situation of many tribal people and their cultures, in addition to the privileged positions of descendants of the colonizers, most Native people would argue that an honest view of the past that is as thorough as we can muster does indeed tell the stories of how we arrived to where we are today. But what happens if inclusive stories are not told?

Since most Americans are ignorant of all things "Indian," they tend to believe what they see in movies, and most of what appears in movies came from information supplied from books. Historians who do not include Native voices and perspectives about their versions of the past tell readers that Native voices are not important or necessary. Many works on Native history attempt to justify colonialism, that it truly was (and continues to be) God's will that Natives are subsumed and inferior. And, on an ethical level that all of us can understand, the writers prosper while the objects of their writings often live in misery. Another problem is that many writers of history simply refuse to incorporate the perspectives of Native peoples about their past, which results in exclusive history and tragic perceptions of the present.

For example, many tribes, especially those of the Plains, are often portrayed as historic noble savages. Tribes that were victorious at the Battle of the Little Big Horn are usually described dramatically as organized and powerful adversaries. To Custer supporters (and modern Custer fans worldwide), they were without question strong, otherwise they could not have overwhelmed Hero Custer. Telling tales about Comanche Quanah Parker also serves this purpose. Parker was never chief of Comanches, yet historians continue to portray the war leader as "Chief" and Comanche men as monolithically warlike and aggressive in order to make U.S. victories over the powerful Comanche tribe appear more impressive.

Many Natives might say these descriptions are not problematic because they portray them heroically and in winning situations. But how do you suppose Allen Lee Hamilton's *Sentinel of the Southern Plains: Fort Richardson and the Northwest Texas Frontier, 1866–1878* (1988) comes across to my living, breathing full-blood Comanche father-in-law, in which Hamilton describes the "lurking" (p. 127) Comanches as living in "lairs" (p. 126), refers to Indian females as "squaws" (p. 132), and takes delight in describing Comanche atrocities without mentioning those committed by whites?

One obvious problem with these stories is stereotyping, and another is when storytellers and readers decide to turn against those "warlike" tribes because of fighting abilities that came into play while defending themselves. For example, even though countless Americans and Europeans adore the movie *Dances with Wolves* because it depicts Plains tribes exactly the way fans prefer to think of them—handsome, buffalo-hunting, and tipi-living (and didn't address the messier reservation period that makes them feel guilty)—many other reviewers feel the need to educate us about the "real" Lakotas, who were barbaric and committed to perpetrating atrocities upon hapless whites and powerless neighboring tribes.[18] Much further south and even farther away in time, the Mexicas of Tenochtitlan engaged in behavior distasteful to many historians, and therefore, the same analytical strategy is used to evaluate them: they are often viewed as murderers who, in the words of historian Keith Windschuttle, "practiced incessant, ritualistic murder" because of "their whole bloodthirsty regime organized to gorge the appetites of their imaginary gods."[19]

Not content to wail just about the Aztecs, Windschuttle asserts that "Human sacrifice was practiced by the Aztecs of Mexico, Mayas of Yucatan, Incas of Peru, the Tupinambas and the Caytes of Brazil, the natives of Guyana and the Pawnees and Huron tribes of North America."[20] I know few Natives who will argue that some tribespeople were not violent and quite imaginative when it came to destroying their enemies and placating the Creator. But like those critics who refuse to consider the barbarism committed by European invaders who utterly devastated Native North and South America and are still doing it today, Windschuttle also is compelled to chastise those who sympathize with the Natives: "In taking the high moral ground on behalf of the indigenous dead of five centuries ago they are making a transparently insincere gesture."[21] So what are they supposed to do? Unequivocally take the side of the colonizers because some Natives might display shocking behavior?

Considering the number of repetitive books that cite each other about historic Comanches, Sioux, and Iroquois tribes, non-Natives apparently find the dead ones more interesting than the live ones. Modern tribespeople are viewed much differently than those come and gone. Sadly, as my father-in-law can attest, Comanches in modern Oklahoma are often viewed with disdain by ignorant citizens. As with other plains tribes, the "military period" is quite popular, but intricacies of how and why they lost traditions (that is, the racism, policies, and subtle but effective behavior of neighboring whites) are usually skipped over. Now Comanches are collectively portrayed as pathetic drunks or freeloaders on welfare who are mere shadows of their former proud selves.[22] One example of the latter interpretations of Plains tribes is the nonhistorian (but history fan) Ian Frazier, who wrote *On the Rez* (2000), which perpetuates the idea that the Sioux on Pine Ridge are all alcoholics wallowing in poverty and won't do anything about it.[23] A cursory look through web listings that admire Frazier found a typical fan review: "If every textbook in every school were written with the style and grace—the sheer readability—of

Ian Frazier's *On the Rez*, all the schoolchildren in America would clamor for more, anxious to read about our great land, eager to discuss what they have learned, and ready to move beyond folklore and stereotyping."[24]

One cannot find many books more full of folklore and stereotyping than *On the Rez*, and to say that this book might inspire one to read more about the "great land" after learning the unfortunate situation on Pine Ridge is stunning to say the least. So, why do instructors prefer to use Ian Frazier's *On the Rez* instead of works about how tribes can empower themselves? Perhaps a look at Frederick Jackson Turner's stance can reveal part of the answer. Turner's thesis emphasizes this theme of Natives serving as obstacles for the intrepid migrating Americans to overcome, but after being confined to reservations the tribespeople became useless since they were no longer character-shaping obstacles.[25] Maybe these stories are what many Americans need to read in order to maintain their sense of superiority and to justify the subjugation of Indigenous people.

Another example of how history storytelling impacts the present is that Indigenous women are invisible entities until they emerged in the past few decades, when historians began focusing on their important tribal roles. Until the 1960s and the advent of the women's movement, discussion of Native women was usually limited to Pocohontas and Sacajawea, who were exalted as heroines for assisting non-Native men in the westward movement. Despite the call from the 1960s onward for histories that include women and their tribal-stabilizing economic, religious, political, and social roles, a survey of the "Indian" section in any library reveals that the most prominent books about Natives (many authored by award-winning writers) do not mention women in their lengthy tribal narratives. Even authors, and some are Native, of recent publications who should know better also choose to exclude gender as topics in their works.

Their exclusions (which render their stories incomplete) would please G. R. Elton, who says that historians should not use modern standards of morality to assess the past and that "partial and uneven evidence must be read in the context of the day that produced it."[26] Historians who ignore gender in their studies, or who place women in unimportant positions, apparently do not understand that women were excluded from historical documents for a reason: they were written by white men with no understanding of tribal gender roles, and who therefore produced biased, sexist, and incomplete diaries, letters, and reports. How do these incomplete stories impress young readers and scholars of Native histories who read these works and find that women did not exist? This does indeed impact Native women today, for unless students are cognizant of the powerful roles women held in their tribal societies and in their tribes' cosmologies (and that usually means being taught by sensitive professors concerned about women's issues, which, as we all know, makes a good many students and professors shudder), and unless Natives are taught of the important female tribal legacies, then women will continue to be abused and seen as second-class citizens, even among their own people.

There are numerous other examples of incomplete history: historians retain an intense interest in Andrew Jackson, although his Indian removal policy proved devastating to Natives and to their cultures. And Natives still feel the impact. Historians who prefer to focus on Jackson as a rugged individualist who epitomizes the American character either downplay or ignore the tragic results of his actions. In addition, Cherokees are also favorites of historians, and one cannot overestimate the influence historians of Cherokee history and culture have on modern Americans. Despite the large numbers of traditional, full-blood, and phenotypical-looking Cherokees in Oklahoma (at least), historians prefer to dwell on the mixed-blood, Christianized, "white Cherokees" who support colonialism, giving the impression to the modern U. S. public that all Cherokees look and act like their colonizers and they are an acceptable enough tribe to claim as part of their exotic, yet civilized, heritage.

With all these exclusions and biased histories on the shelves and in the works, why then, should "Indian history" continue to exist as a field of study? One answer is that if the works of Native historians are not respected or accepted because of the methodologies used to garner information, then neither should the work of historians who maintain the status quo. But that is not a pleasant response. There are some rationales that should allow the field to flourish, but they also mean that historians must reevaluate their motives for writing. Certainly, a lot of history written about Natives is useful because it supplies tribes with information such as names, dates, and places that may be missing in the tribal narratives. Sometimes scholars have the training and money to find information that has been lost to tribes. Some works are joint efforts, so both scholars and nonscholar Natives can learn and benefit. In fact, some of the scholars whom Native intellectuals take to task have uncovered much important information, and I, for one, am not hesitant to cite and credit useful data, regardless of who found it. The key word here is "some," however, and just because a publisher touts a work as "cutting edge" does not necessarily mean that the book or essay as a whole is useful.

A major reason for the field to continue is to revise stories that have already been told by not only including Native perspectives but also by honestly considering the impact of colonialism. Granted, many historians have already done much of the work, but what they omit is how these policies and ideologies have persisted to the present day and how the descendants of the Native people they discuss are alive and suffering the consequences of contact. Historians could spend the next few decades rewriting incomplete history.

Studying the Native past offers solutions to current problems. Taiaiake Alfred argues in his *Peace, Power, Righteousness* that an understanding of traditional political processes and values will enable tribes to "restore pride in our traditions, achieve economic self-sufficiency, develop independence of mind, and display courage in defense of our lands and rights."[27] Knowledge of the past is crucial for understanding treaty rights and land claims and ultimately is indispensable to keeping Native cultures alive. As noted elsewhere in this volume, the study of traditional diets and the correlations between diet change (especially the overuse of sugar, fats, carbohydrates, and alcohol) and health deterioration could motivate Natives to change their eating habits.[28]

Abuse of women and children within tribal communities has escalated, and so have murder, rape and substance abuse. Many argue that among the reasons for self-destructive behavior and abuse of females is the poor self-esteem that stems from ignorance of tribal traditions. Learning tribal traditions, which includes women's respected places in tribal traditions, can help modern Natives cope with the impersonal world by offering them foundations to form their identities, self-confidence, and strategies for dealing with adversity.[29] The academy is not the place for Natives to learn intimate tribal customs such as religion (that is the responsibility of the tribes), but the academy is an influential source of information for Native intellectuals who desire to work for their communities after graduation. Armed with tribal management, communication, and research skills, in addition to respect for Indigenous cultures, traditions, and concerns, the empowered academy-trained Native scholars can return to their families, communities, and tribes and hopefully inspire them to try to recover Indigenous knowledge from tribal elders who in many cases are waiting patiently for their descendants to engage them.

An inclusive view of the past can educate readers about the contributions of Natives to the world. Discovering their contributions to the world's diets, to the arts and sciences, and to the U.S. political system is empowering to Natives and can help establish pride and self-esteem. Because the portrayals of peoples and historical events directly impact how their descendants are viewed and treated today, more accurate presentations of the past help to counteract movies, television shows, literature, and cartoons that often portray Natives as savages, buffoons, teary environmentalists, or enthusiastic supporters of colonialism.

The key to this type of "contribution history" is to allow it to happen. All of these histories require Native perspectives, meaning that writers of history must talk with tribal people, not just rummage through archives, and they must respect tribes' privacy and not write about sensitive topics. Search, merit, and promotion committees, as well as publishing houses and book reviewers, must be supportive of these types of histories that are actually stories with specific purpose and are often political and subjective, as are all histories.

We know this is a difficult task. "Successful" historians are not about to change what they are doing and give up their fan base. In fact, a recently formed group, The Historical Society, is bent on silencing those with political agendas. The Historical Society is a group that purports not to be conservative, but according to one of its supporters, who is concerned that not enough attention is devoted to political, economic, social, or military questions, "This is not to suggest that panels on race, ethnicity, or gender should be excluded. It is time, however, to address more serious concerns."[30] It is interesting to note that race, ethnicity, and gender are relatively new historical topics, and the University of Arkansas' Evan B. Bukey's suggestion reveals the underlying agenda of the group that possesses a very strong, exclusive political agenda and hundreds of dues-paying members.

Native intellectual activists are interdisciplinary in their studies, meaning that they not only utilize a variety of methodologies to arrive at their conclusions, they also include Native voices and perspectives, question historians who do not appreciate Native versions of the past, and are concerned about their tribes and communities. Almost without exception, however, they face adversarial gatekeeping in their departments because of their nonmainstream approach to research and writing, in addition to their focus on what tribes need instead of what colleagues think they should write and how they must write it. Gatekeeping is a stark reality, and it is particularly stunning that Phil Deloria states that in regards to Indians and the Other, the "boundaries have disintegrated." He asserts that "one can see it in the most recent census data . . . in aesthetics . . . politics and the media . . . and in the telling of history."[31] Indigenes suffering from racism, stereotyping, poverty, discrimination, and patronization, in addition to disrespect in academia for our ideologies, concerns, and work are pleased to read that. When, then, shall we expect to see respect and equality?

Considering that this is a country founded by colonizers whose policies and behaviors disrupted and almost destroyed Indigenous cultures, historians of the Indigenous past have a responsibility to examine critically the effects of their historical narratives on the well-being of Natives and to also examine their stories' influence on the retention and maintenance of the colonial power structure. Some historians feel so strongly about this ideology that we have shifted from being discipline-specific to interdisciplinary studies in order to write about a host of issues that concern Natives. Personally, I side with history philosopher Hayden White, who argues that "any science of society should be launched in the service of some conception of social justice, equity, freedom, and progress—that is to say, some idea of what a good society might be."[32]

And what is wrong with that?

Notes

1. Vine Deloria Jr., "Commentary: Research, Redskins, and Reality," *American Indian Quarterly* 15, no. 4 (fall 1991): 467. I have used Vine's quote in numerous publications, and it is interesting to note how this truthful statement continues to be ignored. As we were editing this anthology, yet another repetitive anthology published in 2001 by Routledge was brought to our attention, edited by Federick Hoxie, Peter C. Mancall, and James H. Merrell: *American Nations: Encounters in Indian Country, 1850-Present*. *American Nations* contains Vine's essay but does not take his advice. Not only is Vine the only Native voice in the collection, the expensive and expansive anthology consists of previously published essays, and only a few of those even hint at decolonization strategies. This is not too surprising considering that the volume prior to this one, *American Encounters: Natives and Newcomers from European Contact to Indian Removal, 1500–1850* (New York: Routledge, 2000) is organized and written in the same way. The only Native person contributing to that volume is a coauthor.

2. Angela Cavender Wilson, "American Indian History or Non-Indian Perceptions of American Indian History?" in D. Mihesuah, ed., *Natives and Academics: Researching and Writing About American Indians* (Lincoln: University of Nebraska Press, 1998), 23.

3. Taiaiake Alfred, *Peace, Power, Righteousness: An Indigenous Manifesto* (Don Mills, Ontario: Oxford University Press, 1999), p. xii.

4. Michel Foucault, *Power/Knowledge* (Brighton: Harvester Press, 1981), 130–33.

5. Alun Munslow, *Deconstructing History* (New York: Routledge, 1997), 13.

6. Hayden White, *The Content of the Form: Narrative Discourse and Historical Representation* (Baltimore: Johns Hopkins University Press, 1987), 81.

7. Daniel Breazeale, ed., *Nietzsche: Untimely Meditations* (New York: Cambridge University Press, 1997), 62.

8. Philip Deloria and Neal Salisbury, *A Companion to American Indian History* (Oxford, England: Blackwell, 2002), 16, 20–21.

9. Norman J. Wilson, *History in Crisis? Recent Directions in Historiography* (Upper Saddle River NJ: Prentice Hall, 1999), 3.

10. For examples, see James A. Clifton, *The Invented Indian: Cultural Fictions and Government Policies* (New Brunswick: Transaction Publishers, 1990).

11. William H. Lyon asserts that "the Navajo and other tribes are ahistorical and do not have a memory of their past except as it is mysteriously extrapolated into myth" in "Anthropology and History: Can the Two Sister Disciplines Communicate?" *American Indian Culture and Research Journal* 18, no. 2 (1994): 171.

12. See A. C. Wilson's essay, this volume.

13. Munslow, *Deconstructing History*, p. 6.

14. Gerald N. Grob and George A. Bilias, *Interpretations of American History: Patterns and Perspectives* (New York: The Free Press, 1972), 1.

15. R. G. Collingwood, *The Idea of History* (Oxford: Clarendon Press, 1993), 108.

16. Deloria and Salisbury, *Companion to American Indian History*, 17.

17. G. R. Elton, *Return to Essentials* (Cambridge: Cambridge University Press, 1991), 65.

18. See for example, W. M. Sarf, "Oscar Eaten by Wolves," *Film Comment* 27, no. 6 (Nov.–Dec. 91): 62–64, 67–70.

19. Keith Windschuttle, *The Killing of History: How Literary Critics and Social Theorists are Murdering Our Past* (New York: The Fress Press, 1997), 62, 66. In this particular essay, "The Omnipotence of Signs: Semiotics and the Conquest of America," Windschuttle takes issue with Tzvetan Todorov's sympathetic view of the Aztecs' downfall in Todorov's *The Conquest of America: The Question of the Other* (New York: HarperCollins, 1985). He also states that with the exception of Inga Clendinnen's work—which he admires very much because she describes Aztec sacrifice in great, gory detail and therefore, in his eyes, has given reason for their comeuppance—other scholars are negligent for not discussing the sacrifices and not making it clear that the millions of Natives killed by smallpox was not the fault of the Spanish who brought it to them, because "it would make their moral outrage appear ludicrous" (p. 66).

20. Todorov, *Conquest of America*, 62.

21. Todorov, *Conquest of America*, 67.

22. See D. Mihesuah, *First to Fight: The Story of Henry Mihesuah*, (Lincoln: University of Nebraska Press, 2002).

23. For critical discussions of *On the Rez*, see the series of commentaries in *American Indian Quarterly* 24, no. 2 (spring 2000): 279–306.

24. http://www.pifmagazine.com/2000/05/b_i_frazier.php3.

25. Frederick Jackson Turner, "The Significance of the Frontier in American History" (microform) (Madison: State Historical Society of Wisconsin, 1894).

26. Geoffrey Rudolph Elton, *Return to Essentials: Some Reflections on the Present State of Historical Study* (New York: Cambridge University Press, 1991), 9.

27. Alfred, *Peace, Power, Righteousness*, 48. See also Robert Young, *White Mythologies: Writing History and the West* (New York: Routledge, 1990).

28. I discuss this further in *American Indigenous Women: Decolonization, Empowerment, Activism* (Lincoln: University of Nebraska Press, 2003).

29. Also see Gary Paul Nabhan, *Enduring Seeds: Native American Agriculture and Wild Plant Conservation* (San Francisco: North Point Press), 1989.

30. Evan B. Bukey, letter, in "Letters to the Editor," *The Chronicle of Higher Education*, June 12, 1998, B3.

31. Deloria and Salisbury, *Companion to American Indian History*, 18.

32. Hayden White, "Afterward," in Victoria E. Bonnell and Lynn Hunt, eds., *Beyond the Cultural Turn: New Directions in the Study of Society and Culture* (Berkeley: University of California Press, 1999), 316.

9. TEACHING INDIGENOUS CULTURAL RESOURCE MANAGEMENT
Andrea A. Hunter

Throughout the last century, American archaeology witnessed many changes in its professional mandate, and it has continued to expand in the methods practiced, technology used, and theories applied. For the most part, the discipline has been grounded in the paradigms of Western science in an effort to explain and understand humans' past. Recently, Native Americans have challenged this single, scientific approach to studying past cultures. Native Americans contend that their perspectives and knowledge of the past are valid and should be acknowledged by the scientific community. Communication and amicable work relations between Native Americans and archaeologists are fairly recent phenomena.

Since the 1960s, Native American and archaeology communities have been brought into contact through divergent and common interests in the preservation, management, and study of Native American ancestral sites, material remains, and human remains. The issues between these two communities center on various aspects of cultural heritage, that is, who owns the past, who manages the past, and who has the right to tell the stories about the past. Imbedded within these questions, particularly the question of who owns the past, is the concept of repatriation and protection of sacred ancestral sites and objects. The repatriation of human remains and sacred objects in the United States is a critical issue that has brought about a much-needed change in the methods and ethics in the discipline of anthropology. This change has resulted in our Native American communities having the legal right to prohibit excavation, analysis, and in some cases the destruction of their ancestor's remains, sacred sites, and sacred objects.

In 1989 and 1990, two landmark repatriation bills were passed by Congress: the National Museum of the American Indian (NMAI) Act (20 USC

§§ 80q-80q-15), which pertains to the Smithsonian Institution, and the Native American Graves Protection and Repatriation Act (NAGPRA, 25 USC §§ 3001–3013), which pertains to all federal agencies and institutions that receive federal monies. With the 1996 amendment to the NMAI Act, both laws outlined procedures for the return of all Native American human remains, funerary objects, sacred objects, and objects of cultural patrimony. When the NMAI Act was originally passed in 1989, there were no deadlines for the completion of the inventories of human remains and associated funerary objects. Instead, the law mandated a five-member review committee to monitor the process at the Smithsonian. In 1990, I was appointed to this committee from a nomination submitted by an Indian organization in Oklahoma. In this chapter I will discuss how my involvement in the Smithsonian's repatriation process set the foundation for my participation in an international Indigenous cultural resource management project, and I will also investigate how these roles have affected the curriculum I teach as an anthropology professor of undergraduate and graduate students at Northern Arizona University (NAU). I will also discuss what "Indigenizing the academy" means for archaeology and cultural resource management.

Incorporating Indigenous Cultural Heritage and Cultural Resource Management Studies into the University Curriculum

My role as a member on the Smithsonian's Native American Repatriation Review Committee for over a decade, and as chair of the committee since 2001, has afforded me the opportunity to participate in the repatriation process on a national and international level. As an anthropology professor, I see it as my responsibility to teach students about federal and state repatriation law and how we must change our research agendas to operate in a more ethical manner by working with Indigenous communities and respecting Indigenous perspectives in cultural heritage preservation and management.

Over the past decade, I have tremendously expanded class lectures in the undergraduate introductory and proseminar archaeology courses that relate to state and federal repatriation law and Indigenous cultural resource management. Liberal arts students, and particularly our anthropology majors, are exposed to these critical issues and changes in our discipline at the undergraduate level. It soon became apparent, however, that the time allotted in these archaeology courses did not allow for an all-encompassing review of the history, law, and practice of repatriation and Indigenous cultural resource management. Fortuitously, an opportunity arose that would lay the foundation for the development of courses specifically focused on these issues.

In 1995, anthropologists and Indigenous studies scholars from Northern Arizona University and the University of South Australia (UniSA) wrote a grant proposal to develop a cooperative educational and research program for Native American, Australian Aboriginal, and Pacific Islander cultures. The purpose of the program was to promote Indigenous cultural and natural resource preservation and management. Serving on the Smithsonian's Native American Repatriation Review Committee, and being an enrolled member of the Osage Nation, I was invited to participate in the project. The three-year project, funded by the United States Information Agency (USIA), was a great success, and the programs that were created continue to inspire new directions in our undergraduate and graduate curriculum.

During the course of the USIA project, a multidisciplinary Indigenous program developed among the three universities. These included the Department of Anthropology and the Department of Criminal Justice at Northern Arizona University (Flagstaff), the faculty of Aboriginal and Torres Islander Studies at the University of South Australia (Adelaide), and the School of Maori and Pacific Development at the University of Waikato (Hamilton, New Zealand). A formal partnership agreement was created among the three universities to participate in joint teaching, research, and developmental programs that involved faculty, staff, students, and administrators. An infrastructure was established to conduct a cooperative program for Native American, Australian Aboriginal, and Maori exchange on international Indigenous cultures and on Indigenous perspectives in cultural and natural resource management and preservation issues. To date, the program resulted in: (1) two international Indigenous undergraduate courses taught at all three universities; (2) reciprocal Native American, Australian Aboriginal, and Maori educational resources being sent to the three universities; (3) an International Indigenous People's Resource Center at Northern Arizona University; (4) the cooperative development of an internet website called "Indigenet" that was used for the international courses; (5) undergraduate and graduate student exchange; (6) cooperative archaeological research projects between NAU and the University of South Australia; (7) undergraduate and graduate Indigenous cultural resource management courses at NAU; (8) a new undergraduate anthropology major option at NAU, the International Cultural Immersion Program; and (9) the current development of a cooperative anthropology department and Applied Indigenous Studies Department program at NAU for Indigenous cultural resource management.

1. Two international Indigenous undergraduate courses taught at all three universities

The two international university courses developed by the USIA project were designed and staffed by Indigenous faculty from each of the three universities. Both of the courses were senior-level undergraduate courses that were taught simultaneously at all three universities, with the Indigenous faculty rotating to the other two universities in midsemester. Each Indigenous faculty member was a visiting lecturer for three weeks at the other two institutions. The visits included both teaching and initiating discussions with faculty and students about potential cooperative research projects. At the end of the six weeks, the three faculty members returned to their home institutions, where they concluded their courses with capstone lectures and student presentations and papers. Students from all three universities had the opportunity to learn directly from and interact with representatives of each of the cultures they studied, and they had the opportunity for a cumulative experience with an Indigenous faculty member from their own institution.

The first course taught was "International Perspectives in Indigenous Studies." This course provided cross-cultural instruction on the three Indigenous peoples affiliated with each institution. The course, taught simultaneously at each university, included common introductory and concluding sessions, plus the three, three-week sessions taught by the Native American, Aboriginal, and Maori faculty rotating to each institution during the semester. The topics discussed by each Indigenous faculty were broken down into three sections. The first section included an introduction to the belief system of the specific culture, the history of contact with the dominating culture with emphasis on colonization and assimilation, and an overview of cultural continuity by examining the current socioeconomic and political status of each Indigenous group. The second section included issues concerning land rights, sovereignty, health care, legal and justice issues, environmental issues, and demographics. The last section provided information on Indigenous self-determination, governance and administration, state and community development, political movements, and enterprises.

The second course taught was "International Indigenous Perspectives on Cultural and Natural Resource Management." This course also began with a common introductory section that outlined the historic and prehistoric foundations for the issues to be discussed by first giving an overview of the archaeological and scientific view of the past, then proceeding with a discussion of Indigenous views of the past. From this point the individual modules were taught by the three rotating faculty. The first section discussed legal issues, specifically the laws regarding the legal definition of archaeological sites, cultural objects, and historic and prehistoric human remains. The administration and implementation of cultural resource management and repatriation laws were covered in detail. In the second section, Indigenous ownership and traditional management issues were emphasized. This included cultural heritage centers, Indigenous museums, and the programs they offer, such as language reintroduction and retention programs. In addition, issues regarding native land management, preservation of prehistoric and traditional cultural properties, repatriation and reburial, and natural resource utilization (e.g., sacred and medicinal plant collecting areas, mineral rights, water rights, timber rights, and native hunting and fishing rights) were presented. The last section discussed Indigenous peoples' participation at the community level and at the professional level in cultural and natural resource ownership, management, research, and interpretation. When all three faculty returned to their home institutions, the courses were concluded with the students comparing and contrasting the three Indigenous groups to provide a global perspective.

At Northern Arizona University, I taught the "International Indigenous Perspectives on Cultural and Natural Resource Management" course, and Dr. Linda Robyn from the Department of Criminal Justice taught the "International Perspectives in Indigenous Studies" course. At the University of South Australia, the two courses were taught by instructors from the faculty of Aboriginal and Torres Islander Studies, Dr. Mary Ann Bin-Sallik, who is a member of the Djaru Aboriginal group of Western Australia, and E. J. April Blair, from the Werriagkia Aboriginal group of Southern Australia. At the University of Waikato, the courses were taught by instructors from the School of Maori and Pacific Development, Tom Roa, (Waikato-Maniapoto Maori), Martin Mikaere, and Hoturoa Barclay-Kerr.

During our stay at each foreign university, each visiting faculty member also participated in public lectures and guest lectures in other courses and also worked with the host institution to explore joint research and additional course development possibilities.

These courses provided an excellent opportunity for an international cross-cultural dialogue, and they could be a model for teaching and learning about diversity within global systems and learning about Indigenous cultures from the viewpoint of the individuals who are part of those cultures. We hope that others will use this program as a template for expanding into the areas of joint curriculum models, shared teaching programs, and cooperative research programs in Indigenous studies, natural resource management, and cultural preservation.

> 2. *Native American, Australian Aboriginal, and Maori exchange of educational resources*
>
> 3. *International Indigenous People's Resource Center at Northern Arizona University*

As the Indigenous faculty prepared to teach their international courses for the USIA project, it became apparent that as each traveled to the other host universities, students at each location, as well as the visiting faculty themselves, would need access to cultural education resources. This need prompted the Indigenous faculty to exchange lists of Native American, Australian Aboriginal, and Maori books, articles, and videos for use at each institution. Each institution assembled collections of the resources that were available in their country, and the exchange faculty added to those collections during their stays at each location. At Northern Arizona University, the anthropology department established the International Indigenous People's Resource Center to house the rich accumulation of cultural education resources.

> 4. *Cooperative development of the website "Indigenet" for the international courses*

Another important aspect of the USIA project was the development of Internet resources for use by the students and faculty. The University of South Australia obtained an independent grant to develop a website called "Indigenet." NAU and the University of Waikato also developed links within the Indigenet website that provided support for the USIA courses. The information on the websites included Indigenous bibliographies, paths to all three universities' libraries, video listings, listings of faculty working in Indigenous studies, Indigenous resource centers, and course-specific information.

We considered the use of the Internet and the university websites an indispensable part of the project. We wanted the students from all three universities to communicate with each other, meet each other, and to share ideas about what they were learning. Our objective was to provide an open door for the students to develop an international cohort that would evolve into a professional network of scholars.

5. Undergraduate and graduate student exchange

Another objective of the USIA project was to promote student exchange among NAU, University of South Australia, and the University of Waikato. The three participating Indigenous groups represent a set of cultures that present an excellent cross-cultural opportunity for study in terms of similarities in cultural history and present social and political situations. All three cultures have been impacted by European contact. All are facing crucial issues of cultural survival, historic preservation, land rights, language change, social and economic pressures, and a need to maintain traditional values within the context of our rapidly globalizing world. These three cultures also present an array of different cultural patterns, both at contact and in the present. Undergraduate and graduate exchange between the universities would encourage learning about diversity within global systems and also learning about Indigenous cultures from the viewpoint of the individuals who are part of those cultures.

To date, the cooperative international partnership has resulted in eleven aboriginal students from Australia studying at NAU, ten undergraduate students and one graduate student from NAU studying and doing field research in Australia, and three undergraduates from NAU studying in New Zealand. The primary obstacle, of course, for students to study abroad is the cost of international travel. A secondary issue for students is the need to stay on track with their undergraduate or graduate program hours and course requirements when attending a foreign university. To aid in this regard, the anthropology department at NAU has developed a new international program (see section 8 of this chapter).

6. Cooperative archaeological research projects between NAU and South Australia

The faculty from the Department of Anthropology at NAU and the School of Aboriginal and Torres Islander Studies at the University of South Australia conducted two cooperative archaeological research projects in South Australia. One project focused on documenting prehistoric aboriginal pictographs (rock art) in Chambers Gorge in the Flinders Range north of Adelaide. The other research project focused on documenting ethnographic uses of plants recovered from prehistoric archaeological sites in the area of Lake Hindmarsh and Lake Albacutya in Victoria and creating a database for paleoethnobotany scholars. Besides faculty from each university codirecting and participating in the projects, the pictograph research involved a graduate student from NAU, and the plant use project was conducted by an undergraduate student from NAU and a graduate student from UniSA.

7. NAU undergraduate and graduate Indigenous cultural resource management courses

At NAU, I have taken the design of the USIA project course and developed two classes focused specifically on North American tribes. The Department of Anthropology now offers an upper-level undergraduate course and a graduate level course entitled "Indigenous Perspectives in Cultural Resource Management." In both courses, students gain an understanding about the treatment of Native Americans by our government and the scientific community; archaeological views of the past and Native American views of the past; legal and government descriptions and legislation regarding archaeological sites, cultural objects, and humans remains in the United States; Native American ownership and management of cultural resources; and Native peoples' participation at all levels (community and professional) in cultural and natural resource ownership, management, preservation, research, and interpretation. The underlying questions addressed in the courses are: Who owns the past? Who manages the past? Who tells the stories about the past? Every semester I teach these courses, both undergraduate and graduate students comment that the courses should be core requirements in our curriculum for all anthropology students. At some point in the near future that recommendation will be presented to the Department of Anthropology.

8. Undergraduate anthropology major option, International Cultural Immersion Program

To further the concept of international exchange for our students, I, along with other faculty members, developed a new degree option for the anthropology undergraduate program. Traditionally, students had the option of selecting a minor or an extended major in anthropology as part of their core curriculum. Students now have the option of selecting the

International Cultural Immersion (ICI) Program. When students select this option for their B.A. in anthropology, the undergraduate completes either one or two semesters in a foreign country. The program is different than the typical study abroad program in that our students work closely with the International Cultural Immersion Program coordinator in selecting their courses. Their courses at the foreign university focus on anthropology and the host country's Indigenous population. One semester prior to studying abroad, students are required to enroll in the International Cultural Immersion Workshop.

The International Cultural Immersion Workshop is a course designed to prepare students for their program abroad. The workshop covers a wide range of topics, from the basics of how to apply for a passport and visa, attain required vaccinations, negotiate long-distance travel, secure housing and transportation, exchange money, and enroll and schedule courses abroad to proper social protocol and health issues. The course also provides an introduction to the Indigenous population's social, cultural, historical, political, and economic setting. During the course of the workshop, students work with the ICI Program coordinator to establish a faculty and an Indigenous sponsor at the host institution. The purpose of the faculty sponsor is to ensure the student's course enrollment, to advise if there are changes in their course schedule once the student is at the university, and to give general guidance for study. The purpose of the Indigenous sponsor, who may be the faculty sponsor as well, is to aid the student in their immersion experience into the Indigenous culture in off-campus activities, such as attending local cultural events, visiting cultural heritage sites, museums, etc.

Since NAU has developed a formal cooperative relationship with the University of South Australia and the University of Waikato, these are the current two choices for the anthropology undergraduates at NAU. We intend to expand our host countries over the next few years.

9. Cooperative Anthropology and Applied Indigenous Studies Program at NAU for Indigenous cultural resource management

Currently, I am working with the Applied Indigenous Studies faculty at NAU and we have developed a multidisciplinary Indigenous cultural resource management program. The program is designed to prepare Indigenous and non-Indigenous students to work in the field of national or international Indigenous cultural resource management. The curriculum includes anthropological and archaeological method and theory, basic cultural resource management training, Native American history, Native American contemporary cultures and associated issues, and cross-cultural communication and consultation. In the near future the program will include an Indigenous cultural resource management internship or field school component. The intent is to give Indigenous and non-Indigenous students the hands-on experience of consulting with and working closely with Indigenous groups to develop cooperative research designs, carry out fieldwork, and promote cultural heritage preservation. We hope to set up the internships and field schools so they would be jointly offered by NAU and UniSA and be held in alternate years in Australia and the United States.

Indigenizing the Academy

If there has ever been a discipline in the academy that needed to be Indigenized, it is certainly anthropology, and archaeology in particular. The history of archaeology's neglect of the descendants of the Indigenous populations that are studied is disappointing. The mandate for Native American consultations in cultural resource management laws in the 1970s and in the federal and state repatriation laws of the 1980s and 1990s set in motion a much-needed change in relations between the scientific and Native American communities. The change has come about slowly, however. One reason for such slow progress is that a percentage of those in the discipline had, and some still have, a negative view of the federal and state laws that require archaeologists to consult with Native Americans in the management of cultural resources. At the outset, many archaeologists, physical anthropologists, and museum professionals asserted that these laws prohibited them from conducting research on past cultures.[1] The repatriation laws were criticized extensively as well. For instance, some believe that cultural affiliation for repatriation cannot be established between present-day Native American tribes or Native Hawaiian organizations and prehistoric cultures.[2] According to Meighan,[3] establishing such a link for a "familial relationship spanning 20 or more generations of unrecorded history" was an "obvious impossibility." There are others from the scientific community, however, who have rallied behind the human rights legislation and have been supportive in these efforts.[4]

The slow change in relations between the scientific and Native American communities is reflected in the academy as well. Across the country, only minimal progress has been made toward incorporating a strong

Indigenous voice into archaeology classrooms.[5] A major impediment to Indigenizing archaeology centers on pedagogical differences. Traditionally, American archaeology has adhered stringently to a Western, scientific worldview for studying and understanding past cultures and teaching about the past. Incorporating tribal knowledge, oral histories, and particularly migration and origin histories into archaeological research of past cultures is viewed by some as an inappropriate course of study because such resources are considered objectionable. It would be a professional breach of scientific standards to bring these uncorroborated accounts into archaeologists' research strategies and into the classroom.[6]

The two new courses outlined above, the undergraduate and graduate "Indigenous Perspectives in Cultural Resource Management," are officially listed in our catalog of courses offered by the anthropology department at Northern Arizona University. Initially, I did not receive overwhelming support from the anthropology department to develop and teach these courses. This was disappointing to me given the recent national movement to incorporate the Indigenous voice in archaeology. It seems that the department would have seized the opportunity to capitalize on a national trend. Before the university approved the courses, I taught the courses listed under the shared university course lines. Initially, there were several semesters that the courses were offered, however, in which they were dropped during preregistration due to low enrollment. This was frustrating to me because the courses were new and I was looking forward to sharing innovative perspectives with the students. After I submitted the courses to the department and curriculum committee and the courses were approved, I did receive confirmation that the department thought the courses were a good idea. The next year, the anthropology department held a series of meetings on new directions for the archaeology program, and it was decided that an Indigenous cultural resource management program was an area of focus for development.

From my perspective, Indigenizing the academy is a complex process that must be engaged in if we are to successfully meet the challenge of delivering multicultural education and preventing the perpetuation of racist ideas, traditions, and practices.[7] For me, Indigenizing the academy means to reform the curriculum in American archaeology. At the outset, we must infuse in the curriculum morally sound ethics in archaeological methods and practices. Students must recognize and understand that there are many perspectives to studying the past. The Western scientific view is not the only view. There are other ways of knowing the past, and archaeologists must respect the views of others, particularly since anthropology is a holistic discipline where the objective is to explain cultural behavior. In other words, anthropology's ultimate goal is to understand cultures and other cultures' worldviews.

We need to teach the "true" history of archaeological practices in the past. For instance, students need to know that in the past there were archaeologists, following the tenets of Western science, who dug up Native American graves, desecrated graves, and sold the skeletons and artifacts to museums. We need to explain how archaeologists are trying to rectify that history by instituting federal and state repatriation laws. We need to teach the ethical importance of the repatriation laws and how significant the laws are to Indigenous communities. Even though the deadlines stipulated in NAGPRA for the inventories and summaries have passed, repatriation is not over, as some archaeologists contend. The process of Native American burial protection will continue into the future, and the return of Native American human remains, sacred objects, funerary objects, and cultural patrimony objects will continue for many decades to come.

The curriculum in archaeology also needs to include cross-cultural communication courses. Archaeologists are mandated by law to consult with Indigenous communities in matters concerning tribal cultural resources. We need to teach archaeology students how to communicate with Native Americans. The importance of developing relationships cannot be understated. It is critical for archaeologists to understand that, by federally mandated law, if they intend to conduct research on federal lands or Indian reservation lands, they must consult with all affected tribes. Research designs must be developed in consultation with the tribes. Both parties must benefit from the research, not just the scientific community. Cross-cultural communication is a skill that for many must be learned.

Setting up this reform in the archaeology curriculum does not necessarily require Indigenous faculty. But to impart Indigenous perspectives, experience, and knowledge, having Indigenous faculty is essential.

Conclusion

When I was nominated to the Native American Repatriation Review Committee in 1990, I had no idea that my national involvement in the repatriation process would evolve into a direct movement for promoting Indigenous cultural resource management. Over the past decade my attention became focused on Indigenous cultural heritage rights and ensuring that Indigenous voices were heard in the classroom, where future anthropologists and archaeologists were receiving their academic training. The peer support for Indigenous perspectives being incorporated into the curriculum has been slow in coming, yet the student support has been and continues to be overwhelming.

We want students to communicate with each other and to share ideas about Indigenous cultural heritage management and preservation. Ideally, we hope these projects will provide an opportunity for students to develop a local, national, and international cohort that will evolve into a professional network to promote future global sharing of ideas and research. If we want to make headway on the issues that are facing Indigenous groups today, education is one of the keys. The sooner students begin to think about the diverse problems facing Indigenous peoples globally, the sooner they will arrive at solutions.

Notes

1. Anita S. Grossman, "Digging the Grave of Archaeology," *Heterodoxy* (spring 1993): 9–12.

2. Clement W. Meighan, "The Burial of American Archaeology," *Academic Questions* 6, no. 3 (1993): 9–19.

3. Clement W. Meighan, "Burying American Archaeology," in *Archaeological Ethics*, Karen D. Vitelli, ed. (Walnut Creek CA: AltaMira Press, 1996), 210.

4. See Roger Anyon, T. J. Ferguson, Loretta Jackson, Lillie Lane, and Philip Vicenti, "Native American Oral Tradition and Archaeology: Issues of Structure, Relevance, and Respect," in *Native Americans and Archaeologists*, Nina Swidler, Kurt E. Dongoske, Roger Anyon, and Alan S. Downer, eds. (Walnut Creek CA: AltaMira Press, 1997), 77–87; Thomas Biolsi and Larry Zimmerman, eds., *Indians and Anthropologists: Vine Deloria Jr., and the Critique of Anthropology* (Tucson: University of Arizona Press, 1997); Anthony L. Klesert and Shirley Powell, "A Perspective on Ethics and the Reburial Controversy," *American Antiquity* 58 (1993): 348–54; Larry J. Zimmerman, "Sharing Control of the Past," in *Archaeological Ethics*, Karen D. Vitelli, ed., 214–20; Larry J. Zimmerman, "Remythologizing the Relationship Between Indians and Archaeologists," in *Native Americans and Archaeologists*, Nina Swidler et al., eds., 44–56; Larry J. Zimmerman, "Usurping American Indian Voice," in *The Future of the Past: Archaeologists, Native Americans, and Repatriation*, Tamara Bray, ed. (New York: Garland Press, 2001), 169–84.

5. See Desireé Reneé Martinez, "Making My Way in Archaeology," SAA *Archaeological Record* 2, no. 4 (2002): 29–31; Miranda Warburton, "Ethnic Equity in Archaeology:

A View from the Navajo Nation Archaeology Department," SAA *Archaeological Record* 2, no. 4 (2002): 20–23.

6. Ronald J. Mason, "Archaeology and Native North American Oral Traditions," *American Antiquity* 65 (2000): 239–66.

7. See Joe Watkins, *Indigenous Archaeology* (Walnut Creek CA: AltaMira Press, 2000); Joe Watkins, "Native, Marginal Archaeologist: Ethnic Disparity in American Archaeology," SAA *Archaeological Record* 2, no. 4 (2002): 36–37.

10. IN THE TRENCHES

A Critical Look at the Isolation of American Indian Political Practices in the Nonempirical Social Science of Political Science

Joely De La Torre

The field of political science invokes in most an understanding of the study of political systems, institutions, theories, and persons. As a nonempirical discipline it exclusively investigated Western European practices during much of the last century. Political science examines how to study liberal democracy and the modern state, but more recently it has been on a quest to develop into an empirical science. In spite of this, it has often ignored, and even dismissed, the contributions of other voices. For example, Indigenous knowledge in particular, as well as American Indian political practices, have been historically ignored by the discipline, and until very recently they could not be detected in the field. Only in the last few years have there been attempts to incorporate studies on American Indians. In spite of the problematic current status of the discipline, political science offers a valuable potential to assist tribal nations by providing a framework for analyzing contemporary political structures and issues. Reciprocally, Indigenous nations provide opportunities to greatly broaden and enrich the field, which will only serve to strengthen it as an academic discipline.

My concerns regarding the discipline of political science stem from the reality that not only have American Indian political practices been isolated from other areas within the social sciences, they have successfully been driven into the humanities. This is not to suggest that the humanities should not incorporate Indigenous knowledge, but rather to point out that the social sciences have often restricted the dialogue of American Indians to cultural expressions. Because political science is only now beginning to examine American Indians, as American Indian academics we must diligently exert our voices in this area. We have an opportunity to avoid repeating the mistakes made by other disciplines such as anthropology, history, and sociology, which have often decreed to American Indians who, how, when, and why research should take place.

Political science is dominated by white males who are not concerned with Indigenous knowledge, American Indian political practices, or empowering Indigenous people. Instead, they hide behind terms like "academic," "empirical," "quantitative," and "evidence" to avoid any meaningful analysis. The field has limited and isolated those of us who choose to include American Indian political practices in the discourse. Methods of gatekeeping by those invested in maintaining control over the parameters of the discipline are apparent in the first seminar one takes as a graduate student.

I can remember all too vividly how in my second year of my doctoral program in political science I wanted to transfer to a different program to be closer to home and to attend a more prestigious university, which I presumed would offer more resources and opportunities to American Indians. Having proven myself in the two years of my doctoral program, earning a grade point of 4.0 and having participated in empirical research and publication, I felt that I had a good chance of acceptance at the institution. However, I was denied entrance and was told that the reason for denial was that my Graduate Record Examination record (of three years earlier) showed weak numbers in the mathematical section and that my undergraduate record was also weak in this area. Although an "ethnic" member of the enrollment committee fought diligently on my behalf and encouraged me to appeal, the other two members persisted in their dissent on the grounds that no one in the department was interested in American Indian political practices. When I inquired as to the number of American Indians in the program, I was told that there were none, but that a few years earlier two had applied: one individual was from a reservation community in the Southwest and the other claimed to have American Indian ancestry. A decision was made to allow for the entrance of only one individual, and the one selected was the individual who claimed to have American Indian ancestry. That student had a much stronger quantitative background with interests similar to the faculty and did not focus solely on American Indians. He eventually declined acceptance, and the other individual was not invited in his place. I tell this story not to suggest that I should have received entrance into the program, but to point out that those who dominate the discipline work to maintain the status quo.

When they do allow for change, it is on their terms. Therefore, at present I caution those expecting this field to incorporate American Indian political practices. Inclusion of Native concerns, analysis of tribal policies, and finding empowerment strategies will be accomplished only with considerable work. Moving beyond being pawns in their game will be difficult in a field with a firmly established mode of operation with little flexibility or allowance for transitions.

This becomes clear when examining the current status of American Indian involvement in the American Political Science Association (APSA). The APSA's annual meeting has in very recent years offered panel discussions that examine American Indian topics. But these panels are usually held under the "race and ethnic politics" divisions and are sponsored by an organization comprised mainly of non-Indians within the discipline, the Native American Studies Association (NASA). For further evidence of how Indigenous peoples and our knowledge are subsumed in the field, one need only examine the centennial edition of the book published by the APSA, entitled *Political Science State of the Discipline*, which contains twenty-nine essays intended to examine current scholarship and the future of the discipline. Although the book attempts to "demonstrate the field's substantive breadth, normative range, analytical heterogeneity, and methodological diversity,"[1] it is still fails to mention American Indians (the only sovereign "political" group in the United States), even under a section that focuses on the politics of race. In fact, of the twenty-nine essays the majority of contributors represent only a handful of Ivy League academic institutions, demonstrating the conceptual limits and the effective gatekeeping of the field. As the paradigms already established in political science are ill equipped to accommodate American Indian political practices and knowledge, we must create new paradigms based on our practices and knowledge. Having made that assertion, however, I do feel that political science is situated to offer American Indian political practices a location in which to display their contribution to the academy. After all, American Indians first and foremost are sovereign political entities and should be considered as such when our affairs are discussed.

An American Indian Perspective on the State of the Discipline

Political science addresses four conventional subfields (American politics, comparative, international relations, and political theory) and additional fields such as public policy, methods, and public administration. Many of the subfields share substantive themes such as liberalism and democracy, the power of institutions, the nature of the state, and concerns of political participation, identity, and citizenship, which often blend into one another. However, scholars in the field may choose different methodologies in approaching these topics. According to Ira Katznelson and Helen V. Milner in their introduction to *American Political Science: The Discipline's State and the State of the Discipline*, the purpose of the discipline is "to understand liberal institutionalism under democratic conditions, while comparing the U.S. experience to those of others and seeking knowledge about the liberal polity in a dangerous global environment."[2]

The field of political science has long been struggling to be viewed as an empirical social science. World War II stimulated the development of the behavioral approach in political science in the United States. The behavioral approach is the study of individuals rather than larger political units—studies of voting behavior are prime examples of the behavioral approach. This approach seemed to protest the conventional historical, philosophical, and descriptive institutional approaches of the past. The Social Science Research Council had a significant impact on this new direction. E. Pendleton Herring, president of the council in 1948, sought a realism outside of the library and a desire to seek out the individual and group influences on politics. In 1944–45 the council decided to work on a new approach to the study of political behavior: political relationships of men as citizens, administrators, legislators, and so on. In 1945, the council created a committee on political behavior. In 1950, the committee had a new chair, V. O. Key Jr., who held that the committee should be concerned with developing theory and improving methods. The result was a move toward survey data, which the field saw as giving direct access to the characteristics and behavior of individuals. Survey research centers were established at University of Michigan and at Columbia. Additionally, foundations such as the Carnegie, Ford, and Rockefeller were very supportive of this new behavioral approach. By 1950, the behavioral approach went from a minor sect of the discipline to a major influence. Before behavioralism, students studied political systems, but after behavioralism, they studied individuals. Political science now looks to what is—rather than what ought to be—and argues that empirical studies and data collection should be the way in which the direction of the field is influenced.

The need to be viewed as empirical by so many in the field has led researchers to focus on quantitative studies. My review of papers presented at the APSA annual conference in recent years shows a consistent pattern of quantitative methodologies in the study of American politics. This approach is not conducive to effective analysis of American Indian political systems because it does not allow for incorporation of Indigenous knowledge and political practices. Instead, American Indians have been examined and analyzed using the already-existent theoretical approaches of the discipline, such as cost-benefit analysis, rational choice theory, and voting behavior patterns. Missing are concepts central to Indigenous knowledge. One would have to look to the periphery for a platform to discuss American Indian political practices in the policy arena.

Contributions in the area of American Indian politics have primarily been made in two major areas. The first area of research has focused on American federal policies and the impact on American Indians. The second area has focused on categorizing American Indians into a racial paradigm by examining the attitude and political behaviors of American Indians as a racial minority.

Alternative Approaches to Including American Indians in the Discipline

Encouraging new approaches in addressing the study of politics can be found by looking at the theories used in other social sciences. Because a combination of theoretical and empirical analysis along with Indigenous knowledge is central to improving the study of American Indian political practices, we need to step outside the discipline. Cross-disciplinary appreciation can be observed in a review of power studies, which offers an interesting way to combine the various approaches. Positivism is the primary approach used in political science to examine power. However, positivism fails at times to reflect on or respond to the needs of the people and organizations involved, and so it remains only marginally useful. Positivist approaches, by their very assumptive and limiting nature, have been used to justify government actions toward indigenous people. While some aspects of positivist approaches to power might be helpful, other aspects should be disregarded in favor of a postpositivist approach, especially as relating to understanding American Indian political practices.

Postpositivism, or Value-Based, Approaches

Postpositivism differs significantly from positivism in that it does not approach politics from a rational decision-making and economic reasoning approach. Instead, postpositivism tends to use what Deborah

Stone refers to in *Policy Paradox: The Art of Political Decision Making* as political reasoning: "Political reasoning is reasoning by metaphor and analogy. It is trying to get others to see a situation as one thing rather than another . . . Political reasoning is metaphor-making and category-making, but not just for beauty's sake or for insight's sake. It is strategic portrayal for persuasion's sake, and ultimately for policy's sake."[3] This includes approaching the study of politics through values, belief systems, and assumptions. David V. J. Bell contends that "what one sees as a political problem (and its solution) depends largely on one's political values, beliefs, and assumptions."[4] This approach is in contrast with rational decision making and furthermore suggests that values act as presuppositions in policy decisions.

Postpositivism rejects the assumptions of traditional analytic approaches and instead uses practical reasoning based on language, values, and beliefs. Stone contends that political analysis should value politics and community. This approach can be more valuable than an analytic approach because it does not attempt to pass itself off as scientific truth. Stone argues that each of the analytic standards used to set goals, define problems, and critique policy solutions are politically constructed. Postpositivism assumes that political reality is constructed through symbols such as the "War on Poverty" of the 1960s or the "Just Say No" campaign of the 1980s, in which those who supported something packaged it in a symbolic way. Postpositivism serves to deconstruct and interpret. Burnier DyLsa, in her article "Constructing Political Reality, Language, Symbols and Meaning in Politics," argues that political decisions, actions, and policies can all be interpretive to the perspectives employed.[5]

Interpretive Approach to Understanding Power

Interpretive arguments are constructed from theories about social interactions that become symbolically meaningful for human actors.[6] A combination of theoretical assumptions about the social construction of meaning and empirical evidence drawn from ethnographic fieldwork or participant observation is the normal raw material for an interpretive argument.[7] Other kinds of evidence, including texts, surveys, documents, interviews, and even experiments, can be used to construct the symbolic meanings of social worlds or the cultural significance of discourse or ideology. In many interpretive arguments the reader is shown the world of the actors so that he or she can understand their life "from within." Arguments within an interpretive paradigm are explained by reconstructing the social processes of interaction that constitute the detailed texture of social life. All these aspects of human experience can be interpreted from an identical stream of reported events. The methodological issues that arise provide a means for the observer to determine whether "what is going on" is a dream, joke, or a real conversation. Foreground interpretive arguments may take into account multivariate relations and historical processes and reinterpret them. By taking on the actor's perspective, the researchers assume that the actors have an understanding of the factors affecting their actions, whether personal conflicts, economic interests, or the possibility of arrest.[8]

Power and politics analyzed under an interpretive approach become expressions of meanings and an understanding of experiences and shared values; political reality is created or constituted symbolically through language. This differs from the positivist approach, which looks at who gets what, how, and when. Rather than focusing on explaining behavior through scientific or "rational" approaches, interpretivism examines intention and purpose through meanings, language, and symbols.

Positivist approaches based on rational and economic reasoning are consistently used to understand political power and policy. However, these approaches are restrictive, especially in dealing with American Indians and their unique historical, cultural, and political status. Positivist approaches have a tendency to view situations in economic or market situations. This narrow approach often fails to adequately address the policy or situation. Not all situations can be quantified or related to a zero-sum game, but they have been often manipulated by positivist approaches to do so. Although positivist models appear to be value-neutral and objective, they cannot predict outcomes, and they are not as value-neutral as their proponents would argue.

Government policies imposed on American Indians have been informed by positivist influences, even though they are far from value-neutral and objective. The government of the United States has presented American Indian federal policy as being in the best interest of American Indians, non-Indian Americans, and the United States as a whole. The government has argued that their policies benefit American Indians culturally, economically, and politically. However, these policies, such as the Allotment Act, the reservation system, and the Indian Reorganization Act, to name just a few, primarily benefited the colonizer—the federal government, state and local governments, homesteaders, and entrepreneurs, who held a shared belief in market-based principles—when they were implemented and continue to do so today. Under these shared economic values, federal Indian policies were often presented as the most economically efficient and effective solution in dealing with the "Indian problem." Government officials and other supporters of these policies often limited the discussion of the policies to the economic benefits, and the policies were shaped to particularly benefit the U.S. government and its citizens. There was little or no discussion about the negative consequences for the Indigenous populations as they faced genocide and ethnocide, nor was there discussion of the severe losses and injustices inflicted as these policies were implemented. As a result, American Indians have confronted hundreds of years of wholesale destruction of their communities, with incessant indignity to their persons, land, culture, health, and future. In fact, many of the current problems plaguing tribal governments today are a direct result of these policies and their negative effects on Native peoples.

Problems within the Discipline
While applying established political science theories to American Indians and relegating Native peoples to racial or ethnic categories, the field of political science has denied focus on Indigenous practices. Distinguishing between ethnic minority and sovereign nation status is absent in the discipline. The common belief that tribes are political in nature merely precedes the dialogue of Western legal thought and the role of the American Indian in that legal thought. In fact, this discipline along with others has done so well in isolating American Indians into racial and ethnic subfields that many American Indian researchers have supported this principle by writing from that point of view. This concern was raised many years ago by Native scholar Vine Deloria Jr., who challenges this notion of authority and encourages other American Indians do the same:

> All groups must come to understand themselves as their situation defines them and not as other groups see them. By accepting ourselves and defining the values within which we can be most comfortable, we can find peace. In essence, we must all create social isolates, which have economic bases that support creative and innovative efforts to customize values we need. Myths must be re-examined and clarified. Where they are detrimental, sharp and necessary distinctions must be made. The fear of the unknown must be eliminated. The white mythologizes the racial minorities because of his lack of knowledge of them. These myths then create barriers for communication between various segments of society.[9]

The discipline not only omits Indigenous knowledge but also attempts to alter Indigenous knowledge to fit into the theoretical paradigms of the discipline. Such is the case with the constant examination of how tribes vote, or the quantification of political participation, or the debates over minority and individual rights. How is Indigenous knowledge included in this research? The definitions used in the field often collide with tribal definitions, and nowhere is this more apparent than in the numerous papers involving "sovereignty." This word is transformed by how and who is interpreting it and for what purpose. The ideal in political science is to contain sovereignty within a Western European legal critique. Contrary to this restricted understanding of sovereignty, Vine Deloria Jr. contends that American Indians should not be limited to this political-legal understanding of sovereignty if Indigenous empowerment is to persevere and grow. "If sovereignty is restricted to a legal-political context, then it becomes a limiting concept, which serves to prevent solutions. The legal-political context is structured in an adversary situation, which precludes both understanding and satisfactory resolution of difficulties and should be considered as a last resort . . . in which human problems and relationships are seen."[10] Native scholars such as Deloria argue that cultural integrity moves from defining sovereignty as a political power or a legal concept to a value-based approach. In other words, he defines cultural integrity as follows: "Commitment to a central and easily understood purpose that motivates a group of people, enables them to form efficient, albeit informal social institutions, and provides for them clear identity which cannot be eroded by the passage of time. It involves most of all a strong sense of community, a degree of self-containment, a pride that transcends all objective codes, rules and regulations."[11]

Thus, tribal sovereignty encompasses a tribe's cultural identity and is represented in the daily activities and interactions of tribal peoples. It is through tribal culture and values that tribes communicate their political existence to others. Tribes are a distinct people held together primarily by culture that includes shared values, not primarily by political and legal institutions, as is the case in the dominant society. Ultimately, what makes a tribe is its people and their ability to commit to a central purpose. Unlike the dominant society, most tribes are not motivated by individuals, but by a vision of the whole group.

Those in political science who want to incorporate American Indian political practices into the discipline must push the discipline to move beyond the black-white paradigm. Too often, research agendas are established with the black-white paradigm serving as the model for examining other groups. Thus, much of the political behavior research involving American Indians is simply borrowed from that African American models. Again, the powerful alternative is for Native scholars and our allies to structure research agendas that focus on examining American Indians as they really are: sovereign political entities.

The problems within political science are not so different from many of the problems plaguing other disciplines. Angela Wilson argues the point well in her 1998 essay "American Indian History or Non-Indian Perceptions of American Indian History." She begins by asking several questions: "Who is doing the writing? Why? And what do the subjects have to say about this?"[12] These questions are appropriate when examining the isolation of American Indian political practices in political science. Unfortunately, those asking most of the questions about Natives approach their topic from an outsider position and bring with them problematic biases and assumptions. Their subsequent research is subjective and laden with Western European assumptions regarding Indigenous people, culture, and knowledge. Although students of the discipline may study American Indians with noble intentions, their research methodologies and resulting books and essays can cause much discord among Indian communities.

This reminds me of my experience at the APSA annual meeting in August 2001 in San Francisco. I attended the meeting with an American Indian former student who would be leaving soon to enter a PhD political science program at the University of Chicago. We did not register for the conference but wanted to attend the Native studies panels and visit with a fellow Native American political scientist, Professor David Wilkins. To my surprise, the panel consisted of primarily non-Indians who were examining Indians. I was quite disturbed, along with my student, by the research, the questions, the findings, and the assumptions. When it came time for questions, I raised my hand and began to ask about the methodology and encouraged inclusion of tribal voices and Indigenous knowledge in their research and analysis. Before I could finish my questions and comments, I heard sighs and comments all around the room. Then an individual stood and proclaimed his personal understanding and knowledge of the material and proceeded to lecture us on his intimate understanding of the information stemming from him serving as a consultant to the Las Vegas gaming industry. Because he was referring to my tribal nation and several tribes I had served (I was selected by a coalition of over eighty tribes to serve as a spokesperson for the Proposition 5 and Proposition 1a California gaming initiatives), I then informed him of my own first-hand knowledge. Then a woman from behind said vehemently, "I guess only Indians can write about Indians." The purpose of my comments and questions was not necessarily to challenge the non-Native researchers but to inquire why certain questions were being asked, whether American Indians were included in the research, and what the purpose of the research was. I also encouraged collaboration with the very people they were purporting to study.

What was most shocking was the level of emotion in the room. As an American Indian political scientist, I felt both a sense of responsibility to my people and a responsibility as a scholar to address this academic research. Instead, I was challenged (they were shocked when Indians showed up who also had earned PhDs), and an individual attempted to minimize my presence by suggesting that the discussion had moved from analytical to emotional. The rest of the day we attended other sections and receptions that focused on people of color and felt very detached from what we saw and heard. I also began to wonder why there were so few Indians in the Indian studies section and why non-Indians direct this section when all of the other racial and ethnic groups in APSA are coordinated by individuals representative of those groups.

Quality of Research—Why Do You Want To Know?

I am concerned with the quality of research, the type of questions, and purpose of American Indian–centered research. My review of the last few years of panel presentations at the APSA on American Indian topics suggests the ongoing quandary of the overrepresentation of the "outsider" perspective. This is not to suggest that only American Indians can conduct research on American Indians. But what is missing is the Indigenous knowledge from a tribal community approach. This requires much more involved research into the subject matter and demands the development of a trusted and reciprocal relationship between the researched and researcher. I must ask, then, about the recent American Indian panels: are they truly including American Indians in the general dialogue or are they included only to satisfy the ethnic segment of APSA? Or do some in the discipline merely want to carve out a niche of specialization or expertise for the prosperity of their own careers? Given the nature of some of the panels, I do feel that they have crossed the line of assaulting tribal sovereignty by their constant reproach of tribal decision-making without thorough inquiry and understanding of tribal perspectives, history, culture, and people.

For example, many of the questions now focus on tribal gaming, a result of the socioeconomic gains made by American Indians in the last few decades, which has spawned increased interest from and interaction with the dominant society. This in turn has created increased recognition by various sectors of the population, including academic social scientists who now want to focus on questions from a political economy perspective. But the researchers who might be well versed in political economy are often unacquainted with the issues surrounding the tribal nations, including the customs and traditions of the communities, that they so eagerly wish to quantify. Profound misunderstandings then manifest themselves in the discipline and make it difficult for decolonization and recovery of Indigenous knowledge.

In spite of these problems, some positive steps toward awareness of and inclusion of American Indian political practices into the discipline are being developed, and we are now feeling the growing pains. We also exist in a time when Native scholars such as Taiaiake Alfred can offer insightful and beneficial Indigenous knowledge. These scholars and their work should not be ignored or marginalized at the perimeters of the discipline.

Moving Forward

We must ask ourselves, Are we are moving forward judiciously? If political science is to be inclusive of American Indian practices, how do we shift the guidelines and standards of the discipline to include American Indian political practices? We American Indians need to meet the charges of ethnocentricism thrown our way and vigorously defend the need to focus on American Indian topics. We must ask who is conducting research and what is their reason for inquiry. Most important, we must define the terms of our involvement within the discipline and the direction we want to take in it. Rather than have our issues fragmented into the arena of cultural studies versus political status, as is often the case with so much attention being paid to mixed-raced identity and individual issues, a paradigm shift needs to take place. We need to move from focusing solely on the individual or on American Indians as a collective, homogenous group to understanding tribal governments and tribal nations as they exist: complex and diverse sovereign political entities. The shift needs to move Indigenous peoples from the humanities to an increased importance within the social science disciplines through an articulate defense and promotion of Indigenous knowledge. Indigenous scholars must be at the forefront of this movement.

We must also examine who is behind the voice on American Indians in political science, including their backgrounds and experience. Researchers outside of American Indian communities focus on the infringement of the individual rather than on the tribal government as a collective political unit. This is clearly seen with the number of analyses that *Santa Clara v. Pueblo* has spawned within the field of political science. Apparent also is the constant analogy of individual freedoms and individual rights versus group rights without any understanding of tribal culture, history, customs, and issues. If scholars pursue analyses of tribal peoples, customs, histories, governance, and traditions with an emphasis on the collective, fruitful understandings will be achieved.

Potential Solutions

American Indian researchers, with support from their communities, must challenge the political science discipline to correct the misinterpretations of tribal decision-making and political practices. Becoming more familiar with the tribal communities is crucial because political science has not engaged in a careful assessment of American Indian communities. In fact, the field has not been open to looking at the internal dynamics of tribes, yet many in the discipline spend hours browsing useless quantitative data and assuming causes and effects that may have little to do with tribes.

Another problem is internal colonization, which troubles Indigenous communities more than others. We must stay focused on our collective responsibility to our tribal communities and to the Indigenous knowledge we wish to manifest and protect. We must be critical enough about our past, present, and future to recognize when we have abandoned Indigenous knowledge for colonial reasoning. Therefore, my recommendations are not solely to the non-Indian researcher but are also directed to the Indian researcher who has assumed the philosophy of the colonizer. These individuals must also be obligated to accurately represent Indigenous knowledge.

Additionally, those who speak against colonial powers face a challenge unknown to those who support the status quo. Because American Indian practices and knowledge are a threat to the hegemony of Western European influence in the discipline, we face difficulty finding validation for these practices. Potential solutions to providing a safe place for Indigenous knowledge within the discipline will depend on the inclusion of those who maintain and practice Indigenous knowledge. We must diligently incorporate Indigenous knowledge into the social sciences by gathering and promoting Native voices such as those of tribal spiritual and cultural leaders. In addition, the field will ultimately have to acknowledge, in its attempt to understand Indigenous knowledge, that we Indigenous people do not compartmentalize our political understanding outside of religion, philosophy, and culture. Furthermore, tribal leaders must also be defined appropriately: just because one happens to be ethnically Indian does not mean one represents Indigenous knowledge. Nor does this mean that one has the foundational experiential knowledge found only by having an active ongoing role and presence within and American Indian community. Just because one happens to be a card-carrying member of a tribe does not mean that one understands the tribe.

What, then, is Indigenous knowledge? It is the established knowledge of the tribe, the tribe's worldview, and the customs and traditions that direct the tribe. We must not cower or rationalize when people point out that some American Indians do not fully know their tribal traditions. Instead, those writing and researching American Indian political practices must have a strong connection with the tribal communities they represent. Nor can we allow people to dismiss us as essentialists for wanting to highlight and incorporate Indigenous knowledge into the academy. Rather, senior American Indian scholars must be willing to encourage, defend, and support those now challenging the flawed investigations into American Indian communities. Many American Indian academics and researchers are fearful of challenging some of the research for fear of losing their employment. Establishing a cooperative of American Indians academics who share an interest in preserving Indigenous knowledge and incorporating this knowledge into the academy would provide a support system for all of us as well as aid in denouncing unproductive research. American Indian scholars must group together and not shy away from the political conflicts that so often exclude Indigenous knowledge from the academy.

Tribes must take a proactive approach by identifying and defining Indigenous knowledge and practices for themselves—and if they choose to borrow customs from other tribes, such as is a common practice with tribal court systems, they should not be challenged by academics or other outsiders for not being "traditional." Instead, tribal clarification should be relied on to offer insight into the "how" and "why" of such practices. Effective challenges to political science must arise from an activist or tribalist approach, which ultimately will challenge the academic status quo. Failure to do so increases the likelihood that research on American Indian political practices in political science will remain all but ignored, or worse yet, conceived and defined by outsiders.

Long-Term Goals

The field must be open to American Indians, and we must begin to ask the questions that incorporate areas of significance into tribal communities, not just appease the hypothetical discussions currently being pressed upon our communities. The narrow perspective of the questions the field currently attempts to answer does not encompass the complexities of American Indian society. I believe that including American Indian political practices in the various subfields of political science (such as comparative politics and theory) will broaden and academically validate the unique contributions Indigenous knowledge has to offer. Comparative politics can be an avenue for mutual appropriation of knowledge because it affords an opportunity to apply the variance and difference among tribes. Often, "minority politics" is found only in the subfield of American politics, where it offers simply an exterior review of American Indians. For example, in the subfield of American politics the focus is often on superficial examinations that simply count how many tribal issues have made it before the U.S. Supreme Court. Studies like this that serve to consider the issue do not allow for Indian perspectives and contributions. If Indians were asking the questions, I believe they would ask different questions because of their unique understanding and relationship to the culture, tribal communities, and Indigenous knowledge.

We must avoid trying to tailor answers to the theoretical models found in nonempirical social science. Instead, if we use a subfield such as comparative politics to examine the complexities among tribal nations, we may begin to illustrate how Indigenous knowledge has a place in the discipline. Additionally, Indigenous knowledge should also be included in political theory that searches for other conceptions of political decision making, outcomes, and processes. Most political theory courses compel students to analyze and critique only theoretical descriptions of behaviors and political institutions. Including Indigenous knowledge in political theory would challenge students and the discipline to examine cognitive and affective issues, consider alternative methods, and ultimately participate in determinations that positively affect the students, the discipline of political science, the academy, individual Indigenous scholars, and Indigenous communities as a whole.

Contributions to Nation Building
The important role political science plays in understanding justice, the state, and democracy are of immediate relevance to tribal nations. Political science can assist tribal nations in being more self-reflective about what is happening within the tribe, in addition to providing supportive approaches and possible resolutions to ongoing concerns. Dialogues may be encouraged that revisit traditional systems of governance, instead of dwelling on contemporary forms of government. Perhaps this might cause tribal governments to revert back to these established systems that have been long since challenged and dismissed by Western legal thought and legislative and judicial power. Since by its very nature political science is the study of politics, institutions, democracy, and justice, it should endorse the political nature of American Indians, especially in so far as they demonstrate these concepts. The focal point should be that of tribal sovereignty and recognition of tribes' unique political status. This can lead to a more beneficial discussion by tribes in the area of citizenship, governmental structure, and membership.

Moreover, empowering American Indians to assert our political status in a world that consistently tries to depreciate our status is of utmost importance. We must comprehend both how our tribal background and structure operates and how the American political system operates if we are to effectively deal with the rhetoric, policy shifts, and legal challenges that come our way. Providing a discipline that assists tribal leaders in considering and engaging Indigenous knowledge in policy making may provide for a more effective way to meet the needs of the community without challenges to a particular administration. Political science then may assist tribes and tribal leaders in providing a forum to analyze approaches, behaviors, and decisions that they may have otherwise ignored if they were not provided with an arena to address them other than in confrontational elections. This is not to suggest that all tribal governments are dysfunctional or ill-equipped to govern. On the contrary, I believe that tribal governments have functioned remarkably well given the foreign rules that have been forced upon them, especially in the area of governance and political systems. Rather than attempt to participate in contentious behavior within this foreign system, I believe it is important to understand the complexities of the system tribes now find themselves in and collectively resolve the disharmony before it consumes tribes to a point of collapse.

Political science can also highlight the advantages of including Indigenous knowledge by examining examples of good governance capable of dealing with the circumstances of contemporary politics. We must not allow ourselves to be restricted to "minority politics" and similar subcategories and the invention that Indigenous knowledge is based on sentiment rather than intellectual analyses. We must argue fiercely against the view of us as mere antagonists to the "dominant concepts" and demonstrate how our Indigenous knowledge is an integral ingredient in the study of political science. Providing an academic discipline that includes American Indian political practices is beneficial to everyone pursuing knowledge and also to the integrity of scholarship in the study of social sciences.

Notes

1. Ira Katznelson and Helev V. Milner, eds., *Political Science: The State of the Discipline* (New York: Norton, 2002).

2. Katznelson and Milner, *Political Science*, 5.

3. Deborah Stone, *Policy Paradox: The Art of Political Decision Making* (New York: Norton, 1997), 9.

4. David V. J. Bell, *The Roots of Disunity: A Study of Canadian Political Culture* (Toronto: Oxford University Press, 1992), 17.

5. DeLysa Burnier, "Constructing Political Reality: Language, Symbols, and Meaning in Politics," *Political Research Quarterly* 47: 239–53.

6. Robert R. Alford, *The Craft Inquiry: Theories, Methods, Evidence* (New York: Oxford University Press, 1998), 42.

7. Alford, *The Craft Inquiry*, 42.

8. Alford, *The Craft Inquiry*, 43.

9. Vine Deloria Jr., *Custer Died For Your Sins* (New York: MacMillan, 1969), 195.

10. Deloria, *Custer Died For Your Sins*, 193.

11. Deloria, *Custer Died For Your Sins*, 195. See also Vine Deloria, "Self-Determination and the Concept of Sovereignty," *Economic Development in American Indian Reservations*, University of New Mexico Native American Studies Development Series, No. 1 (Albuquerque: University of New Mexico, 1979).

12. Angela Cavender Wilson, "American Indian History or Non-Indian Perceptions of American Indian History," in *Natives and Academics: Discussions on Researching and Writing About American Indians*, ed. Devon Abbott Mihesuah(Lincoln: University of Nebraska Press, 1998), p. 23.

11. GRADUATING INDIGENOUS STUDENTS BY CONFRONTING THE ACADEMIC ENVIRONMENT

Joshua K. Mihesuah

"I should have stayed in school. I really messed up . . . I don't know why I didn't ask more questions when I was younger. Those old ones could have told me a lot of things."—My father, Henry Mihesuah, eighty years old and full-blood Comanche, in Devon Abbott Mihesuah, ed., *'First to Fight': The Story of Henry Mihesuah*

I composed this essay aloud as I drove my family through Oklahoma to visit relatives. As we entered the Quanah Parker Trailway west of Lawton, I recalled my father's words, which reflect both his continued concern about his lack of formal education and his deep desire to learn more about Comanche history, culture, and language. At age eighty, he remains emotionally torn between cultures, just like many Native students today. As we neared my parents' Duncan home, my wife and I discussed reasons why Native students, many of whom we know, fail to graduate from universities. The reasons are complex and not easily solved, and as usual we concluded that without institutional assistance, retention rates will decrease.

Although many of the reasons Natives drop out have been examined in numerous essays, the vast majority of those studies have been conducted by non-Natives far removed from the realities of Native life that have great bearing on students' success and failure rates. For example, instead of assuming that poor preparation is the only culprit, we should focus on the reality that many Natives return home or transfer to other schools because of unwelcoming university environments. Many dropouts and "stopouts" (those who leave for a while but return) choose not to conform to the values of the dominant society, and many remain frustrated because the academy does not meet their needs.

I agree with the comment made by Sioux educator and president of

Haskell Indian Nations University, Karen Swisher: "How can an outsider really understand life on reservations, the struggle for recognition, sovereignty, economic development, preservation of language and culture?"[1] As a Comanche who failed my first year at a university, who then returned to graduate with a master's degree, and who now has much administrative experience behind me, I have a unique perspective as to why Natives do not graduate in larger numbers. I don't have all the answers, but every day I work with Native students, collaborate with them, listen to their concerns, and assist them with their problems. Of course, Native students are not the only ones with academic difficulties, but they do have the highest dropout rates in comparison to other ethnic groups in the United States. Because of the unique cultural backgrounds that vary from tribe to tribe, physical location (often isolated from mainstream society), and positions as colonized peoples, they need specialized attention within the university. This is not, however, the same thing as "special education."

Interestingly, most of the same reasons that Native students who were forced to attend federal boarding schools suffered through their experiences are similar to the reasons modern Natives also dislike their experiences at university. Some aspects of Native students' educational experiences have not changed much since the 1880s. My grandfather, Joshua Mihesuah, was one of hundreds taken to Fort Sill Boarding School against his family's will. He told me stories of having his braids cut off and being disallowed to speak Comanche. Parents attempted to "kidnap" their children and take them back home, but because the school was guarded by the military, many Comanche children turned out like my grandfather: colonized, Christianized, and confused, stripped of their Comanche culture, but fortunately not of their NU MU NUU (Comanche) identity. While most Native students don't face this type of physical oppression they still face ideological oppression as they become immersed in environments that are often much different from their home communities. A Native student unfamiliar with mainstream life can become quickly overwhelmed when encountering large numbers of non-Natives with concomitant stereotypical beliefs about those outside the dominant culture, insensitive teachers and classmates, and the stressful university life, in addition to being forced to conform to differing worldviews, values, and social skills.

There still is a lack of respect among many university faculty, staff, and administrators for Native cultures. In Flagstaff, for example, despite the Navajo, Hopi, Walapai, Havasupai, and Yavapai Apache reservations' geographic proximity to the border town (there are twenty-two tribes in Arizona), it is surprising to learn that few faculty have visited those communities. Insensitivity and stereotyping, both blatant and subtle, of Indigenous peoples are pervasive in classrooms. "Given" tribal names such as Papago, instead of the self-determined Tohono O'Odham are still used by professors; Squaw Peak and Squaw Peak Parkway are names that persist in Phoenix (although they have been renamed after fallen Hopi soldier Lori Piestewa); and despite Natives' concerns about the ski resort on Natives' sacred Mount Humphreys in Flagstaff, plans are in the making to expand the resort by using reclaimed water for snowmaking (which many Natives and environmentalists fear will increase the number of ski runs). New legislative and congressional lines have been drawn to include Flagstaff and large portions of the Navajo and Hopi reservations. Natives have high hopes for more political clout, but many non-Natives are concerned that Natives will get more than their share of funding, although there is no historical precedent for this concern. These topics are debated in classrooms, and quite often, Native students are too intimidated to speak up to express their views and stance about the ignorance of their instructors and classmates. Students continually fail Gateway courses (basic math, English, and science) because professors tend to have a "cut it or you're out" attitude.

Professors often do not understand or appreciate Natives' need to hear tribal stories and to travel home to be near other members of their tribe. Many teachers do not want to—or know how to—discuss emotional, tribal, and cultural matters with students. Instead, they ignore, belittle, or patronize them. Students are uncomfortable in classrooms where professors spotlight individual Natives as experts on all cultures and expect Indigenous students to publicly present aspects of their tribe—and other tribes—on the spot. They are uncomfortable around students (both Native and non-Native) who assert that Natives should accept that "the past is gone," to "get over it," and to assimilate into mainstream society.

Many students are not equipped emotionally, socially, or academically for success at university because of poor preparation at local high schools and a lack of support or understanding of academic matters at home. Many mentally drop out long before physically leaving school, having isolated themselves without pursuing help. Eventually they leave and withdraw to the comfort of their homelands.

Many teachers and administrators are ignorant of Native students' special cultural concerns, such as their desire to attend ceremonies for rites of passage, cleansing, and healing. One example is that of a Navajo anthropology student who arrived to take her physical anthropology exam with the expectation that the bones she would identify would be replaced by her professor with plastic casts. She had arranged the bone replacement with her professor, but when she realized that the professor had not switched the bones as promised, the situation resulted in her frantic rush home to participate in a cleansing ceremony and two weeks of missed classes. The professor later remarked that he didn't think it a "big deal" for her to touch human bones, but the student was so traumatized that she eventually dropped out. Another example is when a student died in a dormitory and numerous Navajo students had to return home for advice and cleansing, also resulting in missed classes and lack of understanding from their professors.

One of the most pressing issues for a Native student is identity. Many Natives, even those who are full-blood, often have intense identity issues. Many may live on a reservation, but they often do not speak their language or know much about their traditions. Some Natives call themselves "traditional," but they misunderstand the term and become their own worst enemies when they try to "out Indian" other Natives. Their rationalization is that because they live on reservations, participate in powwows, and practice religious ceremonies not traditional to their tribe, they are somehow "more Indian" than Natives who do not do these things. Students who lack self-confidence and cultural pride often turn to using drugs and alcohol. Depression takes its toll on many Native students' families, which in turn affects the students, many of whom will not visit the counseling services on campus because there are no Native counselors. Internalized colonization (called the "boarding school syndrome" among many Native activists), is the phenomenon of believing that whites and their culture are superior, accepting negative stereotypes about Natives, not questioning biased classroom lectures, and acting negatively towards other Natives. This personal sense of oppression is prevalent among many students and their parents and is why we see so many students drop out instead of standing up for their rights. Indeed, Native students with confidence, a strong belief in the importance of their cultures, strong study skills, parental support, a desire to succeed, and plans to work within their communities and reservations are more likely to complete their degrees.

But not every student is academically prepared, confident, financially stable, or goal-oriented. Even universities with large Native student populations, counseling and retention offices geared specifically toward Natives, and sensitive professors, staff, and administrators face great difficulties in recruitment and retention of Natives. How can any university ensure that its Indigenous student population will grow and be retained?

Academic programs that focus on helping Native students develop strong self-esteem and a sense of empowerment are crucial. Supporters of the status quo, with their inflexible course requirements and standards, often discourage Native students from pursuing interests that focus on their tribes. Of course, not every Native student is concerned about their tribe because they either live far away from their community or are only marginally Native (that is, a small blood quantum combined with lack of family connection to the tribe) and are more interested in personal goals than their Nation's empowerment. For those Natives who hail from a reservation or tribal community, a sense of purpose as a member of that tribe and having outlets to express themselves are often important to their sense of identity. Because of the large Native student population and proximity to tribes, NAU established the Applied Indigenous Studies Department (AIS) in 2000 in order to educate students in areas of concern to their tribes, such as policy, Nation-building, economic development, self-sufficiency, and environmental protection.[2] Since its inception, the number of majors has grown from three to forty (and many more nonmajors enroll in the courses), and participants comment that the curriculum is just what they were searching for. Unlike other courses on campus, Native students are in the majority (sometimes comprising one hundred percent of the class enrollment; caps are usually set at thirty). In the first two years of the program, students spoke freely about tribal concerns, were exposed to Indigenous guest speakers including former tribal leaders, and pursued a course of study directly related to their tribe's needs.

Students were influenced by Native intellectuals who "practice what they preach." In my wife's classes, after listening to guest speakers in the spring of 2002—Angela Cavender Wilson, Michael Yellow Bird, and James Riding In—some students wept, and several remarked that consistent discussions of decolonization changed their lives. After several courses that emphasized empowerment, students organized a protest against an inadequate professor and temporarily convinced the administration to remove that instructor from classes that focus on Indigenous concerns. Time and again, I hear of students who enroll in AIS 101 with the attitude that they do not care about issues such as inappropriate and offending mascots or incorrect versions of history, yet they emerge at the end of the semester defining themselves as "activists" who want to combat these problems.

Sensitive and encouraging teachers are integral to the success of programs such as NAU's AIS, but they need to transcend the "do as I [teach], not as I do" philosophy. They also must show students by example how to become empowered, and they should demonstrate how to take charge of their lives without ethnocentric undertones (or, as I have seen too much of, heavy overtones). They need to continue to stress that tribes must work together and that no one tribe is "better" or "more Indian" than another. While Native students usually state that they prefer to be taught, mentored, and counseled by Natives, they also respond well to non-Native instructors who are knowledgeable about tribal issues and student concerns. Ultimately, professors who practice the activism they teach are the best role models; however, not all Native professors and staff members do.

Time and again, Natives who are in authoritative positions yet are unsure of their identities, who are frauds (passing themselves off as Natives), or who feel insecure and angry (at themselves and other Natives) influence Native students in the wrong ways. NAU had, in theory, a potentially dynamic AIS department; however, it has recently become confused because of the ideological differences among faculty who favor decolonization and empowerment strategies (and who at this writing are trying to leave the department) and the faculty in power who prefer mainstream education, that is, rejecting activism strategies, the "recovering Indigenous knowledge" focus, and the humanistic side of education that Native students require. Only time will tell how students will react to this dramatic ideological change.

A program focusing on Native needs should also provide a physical space on campus where students can see other Native students, speak their language without ridicule, receive academic assistance, and discuss tribal issues with other students and staff who share the same or similar concerns at another university. Natives often complain about racism in student housing, such as the time two Native female roommates taped an upside-down American flag on their door (a sign of distress) to signify their frustration with racism in student housing, which included arguments from the resident assistants that the roommates were imagining the problem. Instead of having the issue solved, they met with protests from other (non-Native) residents in the dorm.

Native students at NAU are divided over their feelings about segregated dormitories. Many Natives say they prefer to be desegregated so they can learn about other cultures, while others believe exclusive dorms are necessary. In fact, NAU is the second university (University of Arizona was the first) to organize Native fraternities.

Social events are necessary. NAU has a welcome picnic at the beginning of each semester specifically to introduce students to each other and to the faculty and support staff, while AIS and other programs also host barbeques. At the end of each semester, the Native American student services office and retention programs sponsor the Native American Convocation and Awards Ceremony, which highlights the graduates' accomplishments and honors their families for supporting them.

Effective recruitment strategies are imperative. Students want to see other Natives as recruiters, and they comment that they appreciate talking with seasoned Native students to better understand what to expect when they arrive on campus. They especially want to hear about success stories, that is, students who almost dropped out but persevered and are on their way to graduation. Students have stated that they don't want the "smartest" students to talk to them, because often they are too intimidating and use sophisticated jargon. They also want to have Native upperclassmen as mentors who can advise them about study habits, money management, classes to take (and avoid), and counseling services.

Tribal scholarship offices must be friendly, accessible, and accountable. Students often complain about ill-tempered office staff who appear unconcerned if students do not have timely funding. Students can identify by name helpful officers, and, conversely, they are not shy about verbally expressing their anger for unhelpful staff, because if funding for tuition, books, and housing is even slightly delayed, students often give up and return home. So, emergency scholarships must be made available for academic and living expenses. To illustrate the great need for these quick loans, during 2000–2001 the Native American Support Services (NASS) office used all of its five thousand dollar allocation from Fort McDowell casino revenues within a few days of each semester.

Native students require an office such as NASS where they can discuss tribal and personal matters that concern them and that can serve as an advisory office for both academic and social matters. One student comments that NASS is his home base, and he visits the office every day. Retention specialists, who must be committed to serving Native students and willing to work long hours as an intertribal team, have found it productive to seek out Native students by visiting them in dorms, at club meetings, and in classrooms. The specialists must be given the time to advise students about courses to take by assessing their backgrounds, potentials, and goals, something many mainstream counselors often do not take time to consider. The office also has established an Elder Program so that students will have a person on campus who can hopefully advise them on matters specific to culture and religion. NASS has created a unique Cohort Scholars Program for Hopis through the Hopi Foundation. It allows students to repeat failed courses, whereas students funded by the Bureau of Indian Affairs are not allowed to repeat courses. The Hopi Foundation also sponsors a graduate assistant who mentors students and assists them with study skills. NASS staff conducts sensitivity workshops for the campus in efforts to educate non-Natives about aspects of Native cultures that should be taken into consideration in lectures and student assessments. NASS also cosponsors a speaker series that features prominent Native intellectuals. We also sponsor an upperclassman Native mentor who helps incoming students as well as a website that educates the entire campus about our services and activities. During stressful times such as midterm and final exams, we have an open-door policy and stay late and open early. NASS has organized focus groups comprised of students, staff, and faculty to advise and assess our office and to raise issues, concerns, and successes. All these activities take much planning and organization, in addition to one of the most difficult aspects of managing an office: fundraising. But it is worth it. We have assisted hundreds of students every semester, they tell us that they appreciate the services and they continue to return.

Clubs and organizations such as the Hopi Senom Club, Native Americans United, American Indian Science and Engineering Society (AISES), and Native American Business Organization (NABO) provide opportunities for students to mentor each other, get to know upperclassmen, and develop leadership skills by becoming officers. Students have opportunities to plan events and activities and can come together in an otherwise comfortable environment situated in a predominantly white school. Clubs also give students the chance to organize political pressure groups to bring forth concerns to the administration and to learn about other tribal cultures.

Using the Native student population statistics to acquire grants that do not really assist Natives is a strategy quickly recognized and resented. Students at NAU comment that while they recognize the large numbers of Natives on campus, they also interpret some of the programs' brochures as being embellished. Conversely, grants used to improve programs are appreciated and respected by Natives and their parents. In my extensive travels to other universities, I have met only a few administrators and faculty who are truly motivated to provide assistance to Native students, and this attitude is reflected in their recruitment and retention statistics, in addition to the lack of implementation of rigorous assessment and evaluation of their Native academic and support services departments.

Directors and coordinators of Native programs around the country should try to work together in program development and mutual support instead of making competitive comparisons as to which program has the most Native students, which one graduates the most, and which one is "better." I hear various directors at conferences belittling other programs from hearsay. We need more cooperation between schools so each university can play up their strengths.

Finally, universities must stand behind the programs and the professors who work closely with Native students and are truly concerned about their welfare. No matter how much special programs and departments assist their Native students, successful retention comes from campus-wide efforts and commitments, in addition to family and tribe support, plus good, old-fashioned determination on the part of the students.

Notes

1. Karen Gayton Swisher, "Why Indian People Should Be the Ones to Write About Indian Education," in D. Mihesuah, ed., *Natives and Academics: Researching and Writing about American Indians* (Lincoln: University of Nebraska Press, 1998), 194.

2. For information on NAU's program, see http://www.ais.nau.edu. Nation-building as an academic focus and as a way to empowerment is discussed in Devon Abbott Mihesuah's *American Indigenous Women: Decolonization, Empowerment, Activism* (Lincoln: University of Nebraska Press, 2003).

12. SO YOU THINK YOU HIRED AN "INDIAN" FACULTY MEMBER?

The Ethnic Fraud Paradox in Higher Education

Cornel D. Pewewardy

Marketing the images of Indigenous Peoples of the Americas is an ongoing legacy.[1] Cultural exploitation and appropriation also continue, whether at powwows, mountain man retreats, pioneer and frontier days reenactments, art shows, music festivals, arts and crafts gatherings, sport mascots, Boy Scout summer camps, television commercials and sitcoms, Hollywood movies, in the writing of books, awarding of student college scholarships, or at college or when university faculty check the "race" box in applying for faculty positions in higher education. Cultural exploitation has found its way to American higher education, and the most prominent examples are individuals who self-identify as American Indian[2] by checking the appropriate race box. These frauds know that most higher education officials will never verify their tribal membership. This pattern of cultural exploitation and marketing is continuously perpetuated in a truly paradoxical form. I refer to this phenomenon as the Ethnic Fraud Paradox.[3]

Lévi-Strauss (1995) insisted that a myth could be translated only by another myth, never by a scientific formula. He posited that every myth is driven by the obsessive need to solve a paradox that cannot be solved. The self-identification of fraudulent "Indigenous Peoples" has prompted several organizations such as the American Indian and Alaska Native Professors' Association to construct a policy statement on ethnic fraud, which they did in 1993. Two public research universities (University of Oklahoma and University of Washington) have formal verification policies implemented by the university administration. It has also caused legitimate Natives to question more aggressively and openly the legitimacy of frauds. The paradox that will never be solved is that most frauds are comfortably ensconced in university positions and in the world of publishing where they are protected by administrators and publishers who have too much to lose if their frauds are exposed. Even though Native activists and our allies can expose frauds and create hiring guidelines for universities, unless universities are willing to follow those guidelines and unless tribes complain more aggressively when they discover someone pretending to be of their group, fraudulent behavior will continue and even proliferate.

Who is an American Indian and who gets to determine this identity has become an ongoing dialogue within the last few decades among legitimate (tribally enrolled) Native peoples. Ethnic fraud involves issues of tribal sovereignty, jurisdictional turf, and internal affairs of the U.S. federal government. It is about the deepest emotional feelings of belonging or not belonging to a tribal group of people.[4] Confronting ethnic fraud is also about interrogating the validity of the self-proclaimed definitions of who are Indigenous Peoples. Although the politics of cultural identity and the life experiences of Indigenous Peoples have been addressed more frequently in recent years by scholars, activists, and novelists, there is little discussion about how and why Indigenous Peoples make their identity choices.[5] Ethnic fraud is rarely emphasized in scholarly research and writings, and ironically, most of the writers who promote self-identification are not tribally enrolled. They are "honorary" members, close friends with frauds, or relatives by marriage of those people who proclaim the former two.

Expressing one's personal thoughts about sensitive subjects like cultural identity and ethnic fraud is difficult because in the academy, challenging frauds is the same as challenging the administrators who hired them and the grants and contracts offices that support their grants. Ultimately, however, the issue of ethnic fraud in higher education is also about honoring the tribal sovereignty of Indigenous Peoples of the Americas. Tribes are the official source to define who is and who is not a member of their tribes, and in the academy it is up to us—Native intellectuals and activists—to challenge frauds and their supporters and to serve as intermediaries between universities and tribes so that tribal councils will be aware of the ethnic fraud problem.

Ethnic Fraud

Ethnic fraud is the inaccurate self-identification of race by persons applying for faculty positions at mainstream colleges and universities, or for admissions into special programs, and for research consideration. Gonzales defines ethnic fraud as "the deliberate falsification or changing of ethnic identities in an attempt to achieve personal advantage or gain."[6] For example, ethnic fraud occurs when a student or faculty member falsely identifies himself or herself as American Indian to gain financial aid, employment, or professional reward. The process of ethnic fraud occurs when individuals consciously announce publicly or write on application forms that they are an official tribal member while the tribe they are identifying with does not recognize them as such. "Fraudulent Indians," therefore, are individuals who are consciously committing cultural theft.[7]

Ethnic fraud involves not only the person who makes the false statement, but also those who interview and hire the applicant on their word without asking for proof of tribal membership. It also involves individuals who know full well that their candidate is not Indigenous but hires them as a political move against real Natives (usually activists). While in most cases these university officials do not consciously commit fraud, they still become party to it by not attempting to verify the authenticity of such identity statements. The false claim and the support of it becomes a conspiracy of negligence between the applicant and the institution, a twist on President Clinton's phrase "Don't ask, don't tell." If the institution does not ask for tribal documentation or does not support the call for implementing a policy on ethnic fraud, then it is allowing the charade to continue, because often it has much invested in the fraud and exposure would put the institution in jeopardy. Both the institution and the individual benefit from this arrangement. The school gets diversity credit and satisfies the affirmative action office. The institution employs someone who is most unlikely to challenge the status quo. They acquire the quota without the problems. And, the individual has a better chance of getting the faculty position, research grant, committee assignment, or awards that she or he is seeking in higher education.

The possibilities of securing employment, receiving awards and incentives, receiving admission preference to academic institutions, receiving preference for financial assistance in higher education, and being placed in unique positions of entitlement enhances the temptation to take advantage of what has become in higher education a "luxury" of self-identification as American Indian. Clifton contends that the "academic Indian," a person in academe who claims tribal ancestry to gain a professional advantage in the promotion and tenure process, has emerged out of this momentum.[8] Sometimes the term "academic Indian" is interchanged with "paper Indian," meaning that the individual is only American Indian "on paper only" and not in their tribal philosophy, commitment to their struggle, and cultural lifestyle. These economic identities are strictly for economic purposes and outcomes. These individuals are not involved in traditional and cultural activities.[9] They usually do not run interference for Indigenous students in higher education. Rather, they prefer to play it safe by being silent—content to play the role of the "token" minority hire within a mainstream faculty. Others, however, play their role to the hilt and claim that they teach from a "traditionalist viewpoint." Students will suffer, especially the ones who want information that frauds simply cannot give them.

Fraudulent Indians engender several other far-reaching problems. One is monetary. Students and scholars who claim to be Indian in order to secure tuition, jobs, grants, and research funding may deprive deserving Indians. Another is that many fraudulent Indians and "New" Indians attempt to speak authoritatively about "their" tribe's history and culture, and many people believe them.[10]

Why is ethnic fraud a big deal, and why is it relevant to Indigenous Peoples? Many times is it the student or individual who needs it the most who is eliminated from consideration when institutions do not do their homework. Who is and is not an authentic Indigenous faculty member will become more important as the economy gets tighter, the new racial categories of biracial and multiracial become more prominent, and people believe that there is financial gain to be achieved by claiming to be American Indian. And, as discussed in chapter two of this collection, some of the most effective gatekeepers are frauds—not real Native activists—who are supported by administrators because the frauds in turn support the status quo.

"Indian at Heart" and Other Pseudo-Indian Terms

At the recent National Conference on Race and Ethnicity (NCORE) there was a special session on Indian identity titled, "A Dialogue on the Question: Are You or Are You Not an Indian?" Like a lot of conferences that discuss "who is and who is not Indian," this particular session was packed mostly with young graduate students. However, a few faculty members were in attendance. Almost every testimony was emotionally driven, with stories uncovering their Indigenous ancestry. One coed's story stands out as an example of the desire many academics have to be perceived as Native.

A young graduate student from the northeast coast talked about her family's and tribe's plight for federal recognition as a tribe, historically battling with the British, French, and Dutch colonists. The result of conquer-and-divide tactics by these Europeans, her tribe is now scattered throughout the northeastern United States. In short, she told the packed room of participants that the federal government may never recognize her tribe, but ultimately, she knew she was "Indian at heart."[11]

The significance of this testimony was when she concluded her talk by saying that she probably could not ever qualify for her tribe's enrollment criteria, but that she knew that she was ultimately "Indian at heart." Many other participants in the room were emotionally moved by her testimony and began to affirm this person as if they also knew what it meant to be "Indian at heart." A self-identified Anishinaabeg male instructor of Native American studies at a public research university consoled this individual by responding, "It doesn't matter what the color of your skin is or if you have a card or not, but how you feel inside of you. In your heart is how you identify." Not surprisingly, this "Indigenous" faculty member encouraged cultural appropriation after hearing the college student's "Indian at heart" testimony because she legitimized his claim to being Native. Like many other self-identified faculty members who play this game, this one missed an opportunity to deconstruct the colonizational process for the young student(s). The question becomes, What kind of scholarship are these self-identified Indigenous faculty members doing to assist their tribes? It is clear that a lot of these enabling faculty members focus on literature as their field of study because many can pretend to be Indigenous and knowledgeable about tribal cultures while evaluating fiction stories but not doing decolonization work.

After presenting at cultural diversity and multicultural education conferences regularly for the last fifteen years, I can attest that one becomes numb to hearing the different stories and definitions of who is and who is not "Indian." Many discussions at these gatherings seem to center on emotionally charged testimonies of their marginalized cultural identities. According to Womack and Cook-Lynn, "emotional Indians" are not doing literary criticism and writing book reviews to deconstruct European colonization. They are too busy trying to justify their tribal existence.[12] Frequent responses to an Indigenous identity by both college students and faculty are "I'm a watered-down Comanche," "I just found out that I have Native American ancestry and I think it's *real cool*," "We're all Natives anyway," "I'm a teenie-weenie Indian," "I'm part Cherokee," or those that take their identity conversations to experiences outside their current physical human existence (e.g., "Indian in a former life").[13] And, when authentic Indigenous faculty question self-identified faculty members to prove their identity claims (and that means proof of tribal enrollment), the latter launch into xenophobic-coded language like "politically correct," "reverse racism," "ethnic profiling," "ethnic cleansing," "identity police," and "purity cops,"[14] and of course, they threaten to sue.

Richard Allen explains that fortunately (or, unfortunately for them) Cherokees bear the brunt of humor at numerous tribal gatherings, both professionally and socially. For example, Allen explains that the nature of this humor plays out in the form of the stereotypical Cherokee princess syndrome[15]: "My great-great-grandmother was a Cherokee princess" or that they are the descendants of Chief John Ross or Sequoyah. Over the years, the "Cherokee princess" story has provided great sport for members of the tribe. It seems that wherever a Cherokee travels, there are always "Cherokee relatives" to be found, and it would seem that John Ross, Sequoyah, and this nebulous but fertile Cherokee princess grandmother were the only Cherokees to procreate.

Yallup asserts, "It's too bad that the way that a person accepts being Indian is by saying their great-grandmother was a Cherokee princess. Instead of telling everyone else that your great-grandmother was a Cherokee princess, or that you are one-sixteenth Cherokee, try this: Tell yourself. The pressure of being Indian is worth it."[16]

For the Umpteen-millionth Time, Not Another "Mixed-blood" Poem or Story!

Some colleagues have no patience for tribal identity explanations and discussions. As my friend Oklahoma Choctaw Grayson Noley told me, "You either know who you are or you don't—it's that simple." Womack explains that poems and stories read by writers whining about being mixed-blood continue to write on this topic for the "umpteen-millionth time!" Womack is concerned about how little formal discussion there is among Indigenous writers concerning who controls Indigenous literature, what is the purpose of Indigenous literature, what constitutes Indigenous literature of excellence, how such criteria should be determined, what set of ethical issues surround being an Indigenous writer, and what role tribes should play in the whole process. Literary criticism appears to be emerging as a "safe" field, one that supports anyone who claims to be Native.[17]

Identity discussions seem to arise in many professional conferences in higher education. For example, Cook-Lynn offers the following response at a Native studies conference. Because Cook-Lynn was not in attendance at this particular conference in Native studies, colleagues informed her about one presentation entitled, "My Multicultural Identity: Where I'm From and Where I'm Going." Cook-Lynn immediately responded, "Reminds me of that country and western song, 'Here's a quarter . . . call someone who cares!'" Another presentation was "Audible Vanishing American from a Crossblood Elder." And still another was "Looking for Buffalo Bill's Wild West." Ultimately, Cook-Lynn's response to these conference presentations was "Do we really need more Buffalo Bill stories?" Cook-Lynn summarizes this type of discourse as: "What I've been complaining about recently and especially in the decade of the nineties is this kind of tokenism, marginalization, domination, cooptation, and irrelevance in Indian Studies, because what it amounts to is the effort to honor irrelevance, and in the process ignore or discredit genuinely significant work."[18] Given the numerous definitions of who does and who doesn't have a legitimate tribal identity, that decision is to be decided solely by a tribal community and their specific criteria for tribal membership. Granted there is the issue of federal tribal recognition, which some nations have clearly unjustifiably been denied, but overall tribal sovereignty is the capstone issue. That tribes are ignored illustrates the dire need for Indigenizing the academy.

AI/AN Professors' Statement on Ethnic Fraud

In 1993, some concerned members of the Association of American Indian and Alaska Native Professors pushed for the development of recommendations for institutions to use to help them ensure and affirm American Indians in the hiring process. Most American Indian universities and tribal colleges have a verification form that applicants to their institutions must complete. It has been noted that American Indian individuals who have verification (i.e., an enrollment card or other documentation) are usually willing to provide them, because they are aware of their importance to these types of institutions.

Individuals who are reluctant to provide colleges and universities their tribal verifications immediately become suspect by Indigenous faculty who are comfortable with their tribal identities and find it very easy to validate their tribal citizenship. This phenomenon is similar to the Canadian version of Grey Owl (a white man posing as Canada's Noble

Savage), Canada's "Indian" environmentalist, philosopher, and gripping public speaker of the early twentieth century.

Even more curious is the seeming acceptance that Native Canadians of the time had for this obviously blatant imposter of their culture. Thus, some members of the Association of American Indian and Alaska Professors initiated the ethnic fraud discussion because many members of the organization perceived that there were so many "Grey Owl" situations in the midst of the academy (and in the organization) that they constructed the policy statement to bring awareness to this phenomenon and act according to their recommendations.

Excerpts from the Ethnic Fraud Panel

On Friday, February 15, 2002, Rosemary Christensen, Helen Long Soldier, and I were on a panel together to discuss issues of ethnic fraud in higher education at the twelfth annual American Indian/Alaska Native Professors' Association conference held at Arizona State University. The title of our panel discussion was "So You Think You've Hired an Indian Faculty Member?" We decided to organize this panel because many of the testimonies of Indigenous faculty provided case after case of examples of ethnic fraud at their respective institutions. I contacted the program committee via the Native Professors' listserve. My call for presenters on the ethnic fraud panel invited other Indigenous faculty to join me on this panel.

An immediate counterresponse to my panel proposal came to the listserve from Thom Alcoze, from Northern Arizona University. Identifying himself as a "mixed blood, Cherokee-Scotch/Irish/Delaware," Alcoze proposed a sequel to my ethnic fraud panel at the conference entitled, "So You Think You Were Born Indian?: Using a Simple Paradox to Keep Native American Nations Divided and Against One Another." Like many other nonenrolled "Natives," Alcoze defended his claim to Indianness by using a common tactic: he accused Native activists of falling prey to the federal government's ploy of "divide and conquer."

Upon reading Alcoze's email message responding to my initial proposed ethnic fraud panel discussion, respected (authentic) Indigenous colleague Grayson Noley's email fired off the following reply to Alcoze:

> I sit here *on the day before Thanksgiving* contemplating the irony of the message from Professor Alcoze and the prospect of giving my white clerical staff a half day off this afternoon so they might get a head start on this celebration of the invasion

of those seeking the same freedoms they denied to the original inhabitants of this land. I guess those of us who composed the Ethnic Fraud statement should have expected that *somewhere* down the line, someone would take offense. Contrary to what Professor Alcoze alleges in his sarcastic title for a sequel to Professor Pewewardy's proposed panel discussion, it is an attempt to bring people together that prompts the dialogue. The Ethnic Fraud statement was intended to assure that those representing themselves as American Indians were indeed such.

I have no concern about people who legitimately are tribal members and take advantage of the few opportunities to get ahead that *are there*. I only want to see that they do have the chance to do so and that their opportunities aren't limited by those *who want to be American Indian only* for the perceived benefits. That isn't tearing us apart. It is identifying those who are legitimate and making sure our many claims to heritage aren't torn asunder by those who profess falsely or greedily to be Indian and use up opportunities which should be reserved *for* those who have been discriminated against as Indians.

The fact is, I hope Professor Pewewardy does have his panel. If Professor Alcoze wants to sponsor an alternative view, then I would attend it as well. Another fact is, those who are American Indian in culture, commitment and philosophy *and* who make that fact known in hiring competitions in universities should not be embarrassed or offended by the Ethnic Fraud statement made by the American Indian Professors Association some years ago. Those who claim American Indian status for personal gain and are not American Indian in culture, commitment and philosophy should be embarrassed and ashamed of themselves.[19]

Long Soldier's response to the higher education institution's self-identification process was:

ETHNIC FRAUD IS A BIG DEAL!!!! It's a big deal because ethnic fraud impinges upon tribal sovereignty. Tribes are the ones who have the say who is a member of their tribes. It's important that we respect the authority of the tribes. Moreover, I see the issue of ethnic fraud as an act of cultural genocide. An example of ethnic fraud is when people come in from outside the circle (and they are marginal at best) and identify themselves as Indians and become spokespersons or infer certain types of cultural behaviors or cultural beliefs as being Indian. Most times, those inside the circle know they are not Indian.[20]

To better engage our colleagues in the panel discussion I initiated an "anonymous brilliance" exercise during our talks.[21] I asked the audience to take a few minutes and write down on paper their immediate thoughts and feelings about the issues of ethnic fraud in higher education today, especially as it relates to their respective institutions or particular situation. The audience represented both faculty and graduate students, but mostly tenure-track faculty members were in attendance.

Of an estimated fifty people in the large conference room, only twenty-two people responded to the "anonymous brilliance" assignment. Many colleagues wrote out their assignment, but interestingly chose not to turn it in to me when I asked them to return their papers. On the other hand, there were many in the audience who decided not to participate in the assignment. The number of people who participated in the assignment who did not turn in their papers is an indicator of "how uncomfortable" the subject is . . . to recognize it, to see it in a fellow professor or sadly, in oneself. "It is easier to pretend it doesn't exist, but it is an issue with many layers, and perhaps each layer should be examined to get at the real core of the issue."[22]

For the ones who did return their assignments, the following excerpts are offered to give the reader a sample of the ethnic fraud paradox in higher education. One response highlights the internal conflicts illustrated by the complex layers of bureaucracy in establishing an ethnic fraud policy in higher education. Their point of being outnumbered by nonenrolled faculty has become a power struggle in developing any type of ethnic fraud policy, simply because of resistance factors initiated by nonenrolled faculty:

> Too many individuals claim to be Native and are not—we know this. The problem—or one of them—with this, is they often are not questioned nor are required to produce documentation. Their word is enough. So—the major question is, what can be done? The AIAPA statement on fraud is important. How are you going to decide who is Native if they aren't enrolled, but have very long drawn out and usually fabricated family stories? The 'judges,' therefore, can only be subjective. They are influenced by politics, friendships, and threats. Another question—if this group can't make a profound statement to deal with this very real issue, then who can? It appears that those who are *not* enrolled have outnumbered those who *are*!

The following participant's comments contrast the ethnic fraud issue with other areas of Indigenous life, such as the speaker's bureau, the arts, writers, and so on:

> Consistency is needed among Native entities. Speakers, presenters, flute players,

one-man plays—any and all forums that are provided via our own conferences, workshops, edited books, etc. We should be requiring documentation, do a check on that documentation, before we advertise, introduce and otherwise grant exposure and indirectly add to their vitae as validating their claim. Just as important as BS, MS, Ph.D. [the entity] should be enrolled member of —— versus of —— heritage; daughter/son of enrolled member, perhaps in similar fashion as Native artists. Is education as important as art?

Similar to the problems of the Indian Arts and Crafts Act of 1990 problem, the issue of ethnic fraud in higher education comes down to "Who is going to enforce this law?" Because I am an artist (musician), many traditionalists have informed me that many fraudulent (so-called "Indians") get past the Indian Arts and Craft Act of 1990, which requires proof of documentation on tribal enrollment, by falsifying themselves when questioned at cultural gatherings and events. Many artisans manufacture their own tribal identification cards as a method of getting around the documentation procedure, because they know that many tribal officials will not take the time to verify their tribal membership.

Moreover, Arlie Neskahi suggests that fraudulent musicians should be placed on a national Web page labeled as "Non-Indian Musicians" or outright frauds. Neskahi's Rainbow Walker website (http://rainbowwalker.com) explains how some artists are trying to identify themselves as "Native" by labeling their music as "Native inspired" or "Native influenced." Neskahi contends that these non-Native musicians develop a musical genre derived from Indigenous forms. Neskahi posted his website to dispel any notions that these people are Native; to assist the consumer in knowing what is authentic Native American musical product; and to deter the exploitation of Native music, culture, and spirituality. Providing a website of outright frauds like Rainbow Walker (see, e.g., *ethnicfraud.com, scambusters.com, hoaxprofessors.com*) could be the model within other professional areas when dealing with the issue of ethnic fraud in higher education.

Another participant's comment is grounded in the frustration that they bear the social and professional responsibilities to mentor Indigenous students through their college or university studies: "Ethnic frauds add to my work. Many faculty who claim to be Indian do not mentor Native students, do not have 'feeds' for them, do not tutor them, and do not 'run interference' for them with administration." This comment suggests that fraudulent faculty members do not invest their time and energy into the movement or struggles of Indigenous Peoples on their respective campuses. Once these members are on faculty, they feel they are "off the hook" in mentoring Indigenous students. Many feel uncomfortable with themselves, avoid engaging with tribal communities, and essentially become part of the university baggage. And, if they do decide to mentor, they often give incorrect advice and information (such as teaching from the "traditional perspective"), which is even worse because students are the ones who suffer.

The participant's comment that follows becomes one of cultural awareness, or rather conscientisation to transformative praxis. Paulo Freire's notion that "the oppressed must also free themselves and that the oppressor alone can not free the oppressed"[23] has meaning in this statement: "I am in an AIS program (grad student) and was told by a university employee right at the beginning of my program that 'If you squeezed all the AIS professors together—you *might* get one Indian.' Sadly, this is true."

The following quote is typical of "Natives" who cannot prove it:

> How do questions of authenticity re: Native American cultural/racial identity apply to mixed bloods who aren't 'visibly' Indian, cannot document tribal affiliation and yet have been raised Indian? In the Southeast, for example, Native American cultural identity has survived within small family groups that have kept their Indian identities secret and undocumented, for reasons going back to the Removal period of the 1830s—survival based upon concealment, etc. Many of these can't produce documentation necessary to qualify for tribal membership and yet were raised in homes where Indian languages were spoken, Indian culture and Indian storytelling traditions were practiced. Granted, there is a problem with fraud, the Cherokee princess phenomenon, etc., but where do we draw the line on authenticity in such cases?

Indeed, some SE Natives may fit this description, but today, it appears that every member of a Five Civilized Tribe who cannot produce proof of tribal membership uses this as an excuse. How many of them were actually "raised Indian?" What does this mean?

Then there is the claim to being Indigenous by cultural osmosis—that is, by simply being closely associated with individuals who claim to be Indigenous. Here's one of my favorite true-life stories, in a comment from one of the participants: "In the past year, I have come across some doozies in the annals of self-identification. A twisted story comes from a student who applied to my program identifying herself as 'First Nations' by 'cultural osmosis'—based on the claimed fact that her adopted brother was (she thinks) part First Nations. I shit you not!"

This last participant seems to be self-actualized and very conscious of their Indigenous identity as well as the issues of ethnic fraud in higher education, and many participants had similar responses:

> Fraud, good term—becomes dangerous (posing as Indian) especially in academia because that person becomes an "authority" on Native Nations and speaks for us. From personal experience at a university this type of person created dysfunction within our Native student graduate community. These people are dysfunctional and manipulative and should be stopped. They spread their "infection" of dysfunction and create chaos by dragging people into their world of chaos. They also inhibit learning within a classroom setting because Indian students may not want to share information for fear of appropriation. These wannabees are also defensive and insecure and turn class discussions into personal issues. Keep it up!! Expose the frauds.

Recommendations

Given the numerous stories of cultural exploitation and marking of Indigenous Peoples, ethnic fraud adds to the long list of genocidal activities. Ethnic fraud occurs when applicants for faculty positions are given the opportunity to self-identify as belonging to a particular tribal group. Developing and implementing a policy that would require verification of tribal enrollment can address cases of ethnic fraud in which an individual claims to be an American Indian in terms of ethnic identity. I concur with Niles Bird Runningwater's[24] recommendations below for implementing a policy for higher education institutions dealing with ethnic fraud:

> Provide a space on the employment application for self-identifying individuals to list their tribal affiliation(s).
>
> Construct a heritage sheet that would accompany the employment applicant who is self-identified as "Native American," "American Indian," or "Alaska Native." This will allow the applicant an opportunity to provide verification of their tribal community involvement, tribal enrollment, social recognition, blood quantum, etc. This heritage sheet should also be accompanied with a statement by the institution regarding the ramifications of committing ethnic fraud.
>
> The policy should be enforced at the office of admissions level. There should be an administrator who is specifically assigned to handle the verifications of those self-identified as American Indian, and who should be granted the authority to remove any from the list who do not comply with the policy.

The verification policy must be a formal policy implemented by the institution. This will give it move validity and make it more enforceable.

These recommendations offer a mechanism for preventing ethnic fraud. They also honor tribal sovereignty and the right of tribes to determine their own membership criteria.

Conclusion

In contemporary times, perhaps more than ever before, the question of belonging to an ethnic group is controversial in American society, especially within tribal communities. Some tribes stretch the protections of sovereignty governance to exclude some of the their own people. At the same time, urbanized Indigenous Peoples appear to be returning to their tribal homelands in increasing numbers. Dwindling social services in cities, as well as the sometimes improving tribal economic ventures, drive this return to the reservation or tribal communities. According to Taliman, resource allocation is foremost in driving the recent tribal conflicts over membership. Consequently, cases that fight over tribal resources have disenrolled or evicted former tribal members and other residents of tribal communities.[25] Overall, disagreement about the standard of proof a tribe must meet to be recognized is a central question. Power and control lies in consciously influencing others. Most individuals are unaware that they are subjected to the art of influence every day. Whether by the mainstream news media, Wall Street, domestic politicians, or international propagandists, the effects of these influences are visible, if not always clear. Hidden agendas, subterfuges, and ploys are part of the art and science of influence technology. Influence technology is a serious and potentially dangerous game.

Over the years, I have come to know that the true source of power and control is the ability to convince people that their experienced reality is real. This is precisely why we see so many non-Native scholars situated in cushy university positions as "Indian scholars": they play on white guilt and white ignorance (and in many cases, Native guilt) and are able to convince administrators and colleagues that their claims to "Indianness" are real. It is also why it is so crucial that authentic Natives be able to question the frauds about their claims, and that administrators support the concerns of authentic Natives. This kind of cultural awareness is based on a Freirian notion of self-awareness of the social and cultural context of the nature of oppression suffered by disempowered people.[26]

As an Indigenous intellectual and activist, my focus is to more precisely understand the "change" potential of Comanche and Kiowa theory and praxis as well as to use these understandings to inform and expand the transformative potential within other Indigenous contexts. In this respect this essay concludes that as Indigenous scholars we need to move beyond merely engaging in "conscientisation,"[27] "decolonization," and "political literacy" initiatives to focus more sharply on transformative action and outcomes.[28] To work toward this transformative praxis, sometimes we (as Indigenous scholars) have to redefine our roles as scholars in academe to become involved as facilitators and informants in the process of tribal community empowerment. To take on only the role of facilitator is to deny my own activism. I must recognize that my own liberation and emancipation in relationship with my tribal community are at stake, and that continued marginalization and subjugation are the perils. Thus, by seriously examining issues of ethnic fraud in higher education, many critically conscious Indigenous scholars are calling for the reexamination of one's identity and place within the higher education context of privilege and power.

I agree with Sofia Villenas that "we scholars/activists of color need to understand the ways in which we manipulate our multiple, fluid, clashing, and colonized identities and how our identities are manipulated and marginalized in the midst of oppressive discourses."[29] My response to the ethnic fraud paradox in higher education is that I will not stop at being a public translator and facilitator for my communities, but that I speak through the voices of my tribal people as an activist seeking liberation from my own historical oppression in relation to the multiple communities for which I now engage. Thus, I see that the work of Indigenizing the academy evolves in the domains of conscientisation, resistance, and transformational praxis.

Unfortunately, issues of ethnic fraud strangle the chances to move toward Indigenous conscientisation. Ethnic fraud can also be especially challenging to Indigenous professionals whose job it is to address acts of discrimination and bias, whether overt or systemic. Concerns surrounding how one defines one's tribal identity are an ongoing paradox within the Indigenous Peoples' community, particularly within academe. As one can see from reading the excerpts from the ethnic fraud panel at the American Indian Professors' conference, the issue of an Indigenous identity is simple for some, yet complex for most people. Unless ethnic fraud policies are implemented in higher education institutions, ethnic fraud is more than likely to infiltrate further into higher education. As Indigenous academics, we must do a better job of empowering ourselves through strategies such as these if we wish to survive as Indigenous Peoples in academe and succeed in higher education institutions.

Notes

1. Previous research focusing on aboriginal peoples in the United States has used the terms "American Indian," "Indian," and "Native American" as the nomenclature for this population. This chapter subverts this tradition by instead using the term "Indigenous Peoples." This term is capitalized because it is a proper noun (particular persons) and not an adjective (a word describing a noun). It is also capitalized to signify and recognize the cultural heterogeneity and political sovereignty of Indigenous Peoples in the Western Hemisphere. See Michael Yellow Bird, "Indian, American Indian, and Native American: Counterfeit identities," *Winds of Change* 14, no. 1 (1999).

2. Like Michael Yellow Bird ("Cowboys and Indians: Toys of Genocide, Icons of American Colonialism," unpublished essay), I do not use the terms "Indian," "American Indian," or "Native American" in this chapter for the Indigenous Peoples who reside in what is now referred to as the United States of America. I, too, consider these names to be counterfeit, colonized identities imposed by European Americans who attempt to keep Aboriginal Peoples in a perpetual state of colonization through the use of these racist labels. Instead, I use the terms "First Nations Peoples" or "Indigenous Peoples" interchangeably throughout this chapter. Also in this chapter, I use "Indian" as a term of subjugation.

3. Claude Lévi-Strauss, in *Myth and Meaning* (New York: Schocken Books, 1995), touches on all great methodological paradoxes: the parallel tensions between myth and science, myth and history, myth and music, and "primitive" and "civilized."

4. J. Barreiro, "First Words: Identity in the Crucible," *Native Americas* 19, no. 1/2 (2002): 2.

5. D. A. Mihesuah, "American Indian Identities: Issues of Individual Choices and Development," *American Indian Culture and Research Journal* 22, no. 2 (1998): 193–226.

6. A. A. Gonzales, "Urban (Trans)formations: Changes in the Meaning and Use of American Indian Identity," in Susan Lobo and Kurt Peters, eds., *American Indians and the Urban Experience* (Walnut Creek CA: AltaMira Press, 2001), 169. See also A. A. Gonzales, *American Indian Identity Matters: The Political Economy of Ethnic Group Boundaries*, PhD diss., department of sociology, Harvard University, 2002.

7. D. A. Mihesuah, "Introduction," in Devon Abbott Mihesuah, ed., *Natives and Academics: Researching and Writing about American Indians* (Lincoln: University of Nebraska Press, 1998).

8. J. Clifton, ed., *Being and Becoming Indian: Biographical Studies of North American Frontiers* (Chicago: Dorsey, 1989).

9. S. B. Pratt, "Quest for an Identity-Indian Youth in a Non-Indian World: Cultural Identity and How It Affects Native Youth," paper presented at the Conference on Mental Health Issues for the Emotionally Disturbed North American Indian Child and Adolescent, Tulsa, OK, 1990.

10. Mihesuah, "Introduction," 19.

11. The phrase "Indian at heart" is a conundrum. Frequently used by individuals trying to claim their Indian identity—for whatever reasons—who cannot be citizens of their announced or self-identified tribes. Using the term "at heart" is associated with feelings of the heart or being heartfelt, thereby presenting oneself to be moved by human emotions more than by official tribal membership criteria.

12. E. Cook-Lynn, *Anti-Indianism in Modern America: A Voice from Tatekeya's Earth* (Urbana: University of Illinois Press, 2001); C. S. Womack, *Red on Red: Native American Literary Separatism* (Minneapolis: University of Minnesota Press, 1999).

13. The phrase "Indian in a former life" usually refers to individuals who believe that they existed as an Indigenous person sometime in their past lives. See C. D. Pewewardy, "Will the Real Indians Please Stand Up?" *MultiCultural Review* 7, no. 2 (1998): 36–42.

14. These are xenophobic words and terms created to keep one away from their sociopolitical struggle(s).

15. R. L. Allen, "Creating Identity at Indian Expense: Public Ignorance, Private Gain," paper presented at Native Stories and Their Keepers: Telling the Public, Sequoyah Research Center Symposium, University of Arkansas at Little Rock, November 15–17, 2001. Cherokee princess syndrome describes individuals who claim not only Cherokee ancestry, but that their ancestral lineage is linked to royalty like a European princess.

16. A. C. Yallup, "Not Indian Enough," *Red Ink* 9, no. 2/vol. 10, no. 1 (2001): 15.

17. Womack, *Red on Red*.

18. Cook-Lynn, *Anti-Indianism in Modern America*, 179.

19. Grayson Noley, e-mail posted on American Indian/Alaska Native Professors' Association listserve, 2001.

20. Helen Long Soldier, e-mail posted on American Indian/Alaska Native Professors' Association listserve, 2002.

21. The anonymous brilliance assignment was an idea that was shared with me by an award-winning classroom teacher at the University of Kansas. Now at the Arizona State University, Dr. Michael Yellow Bird has his students write on a clean sheet of paper (with no names to identify the author) a response to any particular hot topic in his courses. After allowing enough time to respond, he collects the papers from the entire class (papers are folded in half so as not to identify the penmanship of the writer). He then places the papers in a bag or box and starts shuffling them up, as in shuffling a deck of playing cards. Once thoroughly shuffled, he redistributes

the papers to the class, hoping that none of the students get their own papers. After reading someone else's paper, he engages the class in a larger discussion on the topic.

22. Juanita Pahdopony, personal communication, September 15, 2002.

23. Paulo Freire, *Pedagogy of the City* (New York: Continuum, 1993).

24. Niles Bird Runningwater, "Exploring Ethnic Fraud: An Analysis of Verification Policies for American Indians in Higher Education," MPA thesis, University of Texas at Austin, 1996.

25. V. Taliman, "Termination by Bureaucracy: Membership Denials in the New Economic Era," *Native Americas* 19, no. 1/2 (2002): 8–17.

26. C. Delgado-Gaiton and H. Trueba, *Crossing Cultural Borders: Education for Immigrant Families in America* (London: Falmer Press, 1991).

27. The term "conscientisation" refers to learning to perceive social, political, and economic contradictions and to take action against the oppressive elements of reality. See P. Freire, *Pedagogy of the Oppressed*, revised 20th anniversary edition (New York: Continuum, 1993).

28. G. H. Smith, "Beyond Freire's Political Literacy: From Conscientisation to Transformative Praxis," paper presented at the American Education Research Association Conference, New Orleans, 2002.

29. S. Villenas, "The Colonizer/Colonized Chicana Ethnographer: Identity, Marginalization, and Co-optation in the Field," *Harvard Educational Review* 66, no. 4 (1996): 711–31.

13. NOT THE END OF THE STORIES, NOT THE END OF THE SONGS

Visualizing, Signifying, Counter-colonizing

David Anthony Tyeeme Clark

Responding to an overabundance of negative news stories featuring "Indians," *Grand Forks Herald* columnist Dorreen Yellow Bird recently challenged individuals she named "big-city reporters" to consider the possibility that "there is another story to be told about the people on reservations." Referring to the examples offered by her Sahnish grandmother and an aunt, Yellow Bird advised her readers that "There are many older people on the [Fort Berthold Lake Indian] reservation . . . who have a greater understanding of life and the world around them than even the great philosophers in history. They have learned to live with what was dealt them, and they handle it quietly with courage. Many of these older people have a rich knowledge of healing, culture, and ways of life."[1]

Yellow Bird's rebuke of mainstream journalism, as well as her prescription for locating the wellspring of Indigenous knowledge on the other side of popular stereotypes about "Indians," is unambiguous. Using plain language, what Yellow Bird elucidates are ways of knowing and being that have contributed to the survival of Indigenous Peoples through the settler wars of aggression, compulsory assimilation, forced terminations and relocations, and relentless resource hoarding. Her concern aimed at the journalistic production of one-dimensional meaning about "Indians" is a concern shared by the contributors to this volume, whose attention is focused more comprehensively on the production of meaning about and sometimes by Indigenous Peoples in the academy.

Contributors to *Indigenizing the Academy* fundamentally are concerned with the survival of Indigenous Peoples.[2] When comprehended as a dynamic course of action, to think about indigenizing the academy is to imagine the academy as a location from which Indigenous Peoples appropriate research, writing, and other non- (and sometimes anti-) Indigenous educational resources to seek justice for past and enduring crimes, to combat unyielding colonization, to safeguard treaty rights, and to advance general well-being among Indigenous communities. In order to bring about the necessary and radical sorts of transformations encoded in the phrase "indigenizing the academy," contributors to this volume propose that Indigenous academics and our non-Indigenous allies labor to reconfigure both the colonial structure of the academy and the colonizing frames of mind affecting our consciousness.[3] The argument emerging here is that the authority for Indigenous studies must be located prominently among Indigenous institutions and rooted in Indigenous ways of knowing and being. From these essential sources of authority, Indigenous scholars and our non-Indigenous allies rightfully are empowered to discipline the disciplines and to subject Indigenous studies to the concrete needs of Indigenous Peoples.

With authority located among Indigenous Peoples, contributors to this volume suggest three wide-ranging areas of concern for the futures of discipline-specific and interdisciplinary Indigenous studies. First, everyone here agrees, at least for now, that to decolonize what currently is widely accepted as knowledge about "Indians" is crucial. Second, a consensus emerges in these pages around the need to theorize, conceptualize, and represent Indigenous sovereignty so that our people may live well into the unforeseeable future. Third, contributors to this volume argue for the necessities of producing indigenous knowledges *for* Indigenous Peoples rather than primarily as subjects for non-Indigenous curiosity.

In the remainder of this closing chapter, as an aid to the reader, I will read back through earlier chapters to illustrate these three intellectual concerns more fully. Before doing so, I review the several recommendations contributors advance in these pages as a comprehensive response to institutional anti-Indianisms in the academy. To indigenize the academy means by necessity that Indigenous scholars and our non-Indigenous allies must identify and overpower anti-Indianisms.

Many readers will associate the term "anti-Indianism" with Elizabeth Cook-Lynn's recently published collection of essays entitled *Anti-Indianism in Modern America*. First, Cook-Lynn counsels us,

> Anti-Indianism is that which treats Indians and their tribes as if they do not exist, the sentiment that suggests that Indian nationhood (e.g., tribalism) should be disavowed and devalued. Second, Anti-Indianism is that which denigrates, demonizes, and insults being Indian in America. The third trait of Anti-Indianism

is the use of historical event and experience to place the blame on Indians for an unfortunate and dissatisfying history. And, finally, Anti-Indianism is that which exploits and distorts Indian cultures and beliefs. All of these traits have conspired to isolate, to expunge or expel, to menace, to defame.[4]

Reading the academy through these four traits positively results in naming a broad accumulation of social activity that daily devastates the security and interests of Indigenous Peoples. Such activity engenders numerous problems for Indigenous students and professors making their way into and through the academy.[5]

Among the several structural anti-Indianisms that demand our immediate attention, perhaps the paramount institutional obstacle to indigenizing the academy is that social activity Devon Abbott Mihesuah properly names "academic gatekeeping." Gatekeeping might be understood as the enduring and now thoroughly institutionalized manifestations of an earlier backlash, the reactionary posture assumed thirty (and more) years ago by non-Indigenous scholars like Wilcomb Washburn irritated by the introduction of contemporary concerns in American Indian studies and forced unwillingly into positions of sharing their authority with activist Indian professors such as Vine Deloria Jr. Gatekeeping, too, might be understood as a consequence of the bureaucracy and compartmentalization in higher education that, according to Keith James, nourishes rigid and sometimes hypercautious thinking and behavior, as well as cultivates the sorts of "corrupting influences" that make the academy and its surrogates unfriendly places for Indigenous students and employees. Finally, we might acknowledge gatekeeping also as the unchecked consequence of what Deloria identifies as the submarginalization of Indigenous Peoples and persons (a condition wherein, in Deloria's words, "the Indian as a positive person becomes reduced to a submarginal existence in many people's consciousness") and what Joshua Mihesuah identifies as "the large numbers of non-Natives with concomitant stereotypical beliefs about those outside the dominant culture." As bearers of the anti-Indian status quo today, gatekeepers, Devon Abbott Mihesuah cautions, "take advantage of [and still contribute to] the oppression of Indigenous peoples." Customarily jealous and habitually selfish, gatekeepers use their prevailing authority to manage and shape the face of future faculty, the production of knowledge about Indigenous Peoples, what students learn, who is recognized and promoted, and what intellectual work is published and rewarded.

Academic gatekeeping certainly is not the only problem formed in and produced by ever-dividing and routinely divisive non-Indigenous institutions. Closely related to and functioning as a rationale for gatekeeping are the institutional demands placed upon Indigenous faculty. Such demands, as Deloria and other contributors warn us all, both compel Indigenous faculty to meet the expectations of non-Indigenous entities (such as state legislatures, governing boards, professional organizations) and to produce knowledge academic gatekeepers validate, as well as to teach subjects and in ways non-Indigenous students acknowledge as suitable for their often selfish and narrow but high-maintenance needs. Accepting as appropriate and valid these institutional demands on the inadequate time we are allowed as Indigenous professors means little time is left for the research and writing, and the outreach and relationship building, that actually might work in the interests of Indigenous communities.

Another problem related to academic gatekeeping is the complicated matter of what Cornel Pewewardy in plain language names the ethnic fraud paradox. The bottom line, as Pewewardy and many others see it, is that persons falsely identifying themselves as "American Indian" when applying for college and university admissions, fellowships, and other financial support, as well as for faculty positions in higher education institutions, should (or must) be understood as a matter that forcefully and damagingly effects tribal sovereignty, the sovereignty of what in U.S. Indian law are named "Indian entities," the sovereignty of Indigenous tribal nations. Said candidly, ethnic fraud is a suffocating form of cultural genocide; in Pewewardy's words, "Ethnic fraud adds to the long list of genocidal activities." "Had it not been for the historic lessons derived from the lives of those who previously engaged in political battles and struggles for the sovereign rights that Indigenous Peoples now have," Pewewardy counsels, "we might not now have a viable path to continue the struggle for survival as sovereign tribes." Citing the 1993 statement on ethnic fraud issued by the American Indian and Alaska Native Professors Association and to the verification forms used by most American Indian universities and tribal colleges, Pewewardy dares mainstream higher education institutions to recognize tribal sovereignty by supporting tribal communities and their specific criteria for tribal membership (or citizenship) in admissions, financial rewards, and hiring.

To indigenize the academy, as the contributors to this volume suggest, necessarily means that Indigenous students and scholars and our non-Indigenous allies must respond truthfully *and politically* to institutional anti-Indianisms. As a collective means for combating anti-Indianisms, Deloria forcefully argues for developing "new alliances" and "mutual assistance pacts" among Indigenous professors that eventually could work outward from the academy to embrace what he names "the national Indian community." To indigenize the academy probably also means that we must not only expect but demand a radical redistribution of social and educational resources in the direction of Indigenous students and the needs of Indigenous communities. Calling on Indigenous communities, separately and cooperatively, in his words, to "put their resources behind pushing higher education institutions to serve their needs," Keith James encourages a specific response from Indigenous communities, tribal colleges, and professional organizations of Indigenous scholars. "Native communities," he advises, "need to, individually and collectively, demand that higher education assist them with their goals and needs, especially state schools and especially land-grant institutions. . . . Native communities need to define what they want and need and systematically communicate it to higher education institutions, their governing boards, and media." James urges Indigenous faculty and professional organizations to form independent accreditation boards; such entities might, he recommends, "develop and apply standards for certifying inclusion of Native perspectives (including cross-area synthesis), existence of Native supportive climates and systems, and attention to Native community goals and needs."

Other straightforward, plain-speaking responses to institutional anti-Indianisms are necessary, too. Joshua Mihesuah outlines, specifically, what he has observed, as a university administrator of student services, to be the different needs of diverse Indigenous students that institutions can and should (or must) address. "Academic programs focused on helping Native students develop strong self-esteem and a sense of empowerment," he proposes, "are crucial." Greater flexibility in meeting the demands of standardized curricula and individual course requirements and standards, taught by, in his words, "sensitive and encouraging teachers," Mihesuah proposes, also are necessary. Indigenous students additionally need physical meeting space *on campus*, a location within which what Keith James refers to as "boundary-spanning activity" might develop and radiate outward and back again, where, in the words of Joshua Mihesuah, "students can see other Native students, speak their language[s] without ridicule, receive academic assistance, and discuss tribal issues with other students and staff who share the same or similar concerns."

Thus, indigenizing the academy is not only, or perhaps even primarily, the rather simple (but difficult) matter of exchanging ideas. Visualizing an indigenized academy is not utopist, the stuff of unrealistic dreaming; rather, visualizing an indigenized academy free of institutional anti-Indianisms most likely is a matter of no-nonsense, matter-of-fact politics. Indigenizing the academy, *importantly*, is a matter of generous and meaningful redistributions of material resources toward the needs of Indigenous students and employees—including the particularized needs of those teaching professors engaged in research and who write.

It is from this subject of teaching professors who are engaged in research and who write that I return now to examine more closely the three intellectual concerns I have identified as central ones shared, at least for now, by contributors to *Indigenizing the Academy*. These three central concerns consist of the interrelated matters of decolonizing research methodologies, theorizing sovereignty, and producing knowledge. In addition to radical redistributions of material resources, indigenizing the academy in these three ways probably requires sweeping reallocations of intellectual resources ranging from who is admitted into and advances in (and through) graduate programs, what gets published and rewarded, and who colleges and universities hire and promote. In addition to these three material manifestations (or signifiers) of an indigenized academy that nourishes and promotes communities of Indigenous scholars and our non-Indigenous allies, what I am thinking about when I write the words "intellectual resources" are what we might agree to think about as the first origins for ideas about the world, about human beings, and about relationships.

Currently dominant inside the academy are ideas that not only are anti-Indian, even racist, but ideas with inexcusably exclusive non-Indigenous origins. From an Indigenous point of view, perhaps, knowledges interchangeably referred to as "Western civilization" and "education" do not simply dominate what counts inside the twenty-first-century academy; they constitute almost all of what counts still as the only widely available knowledge. Countless efforts today are supported that translate knowledges produced in and exported from Europe and that mark those translated and transferred knowledges as native, even indigenous, to "America." Looking at course required readings, course descriptions, and degree requirements at just about any U.S. college or university, on the other hand, convincingly and profoundly argues that there is little exchange of languages and ideas taking place among non-Indigenous populations and Indigenous Peoples in most universities right here in this country. There currently are far more international students than Indigenous students active in graduate programs; there is much more energy being invested in academic conferences and exchange programs with European populations than there are with the Indigenous tribal nations. What contributors to this volume argue for in response to these selfish exclusions is a meaningful exchange of *indigenous* ideas, a return to roots of our Indigenous traditions, an exchange of ideas with the intention of bringing into being a new framework for a decolonized future, exposing historical and ongoing colonization, and returning well-being to Indigenous Peoples.

Contributors advance a number of proposals and suggestions that call for indigenizing the academy by redisciplining the disciplines. Fundamentally, this redisciplining minimally moves in the direction of showing concern for the Indigenous communities scholars research and write about. Devon Abbott Mihesuah, for instance, argues for going well beyond the appearance of concern, the pretense of being correct, that has followed in the wake of a growing number of Indigenous historians and our allies currently present and active in the academy. She argues for affirming the field of Native history by decolonizing the methods that disproportionately have informed its intellectual production of knowledge allegedly about Indigenous Peoples. Historical methodologies reoriented with the needs of Indigenous tribal peoples in mind, according to Mihesuah, feature contemporary tribally located concerns, centrally include Indigenous voices and perspectives (and move away from manufacturing meaning about the past exclusively out of archives), and are by definition interdisciplinary.

Mihesuah, the historian, is not alone in advocating disciplining (or indigenizing, or interdisciplining) specific academic disciplines whose practitioners long have demonstrated considerable narcissistic resistance. Joseph P. Gone, for instance, pulls together a case for making what he names "professional psychology" relevant to Indian Country by, in his words, "transforming the conventions of mental health service delivery in Native communities on the one hand, and transforming the conventions of academic training in psychology on the other." Joely de la Torre argues for using political science in ways that "assist tribal nations in being more self-reflective about what is happening within the tribe, in addition to providing supportive approaches and possible resolutions to ongoing concerns." Andrea A. Hunter, citing a detailed undergraduate cultural resource management curriculum that combined resources at two universities (one in Arizona and another in Australia), calls on stubborn archaeologists to reconsider their hostility toward the current repatriation laws and to reconsider their antagonisms in response to even the suggestion of incorporating strong Indigenous voices in their classrooms. She hopes archaeologists might sometime soon accept the relevance of tribal knowledges and oral histories, particularly oral migration and origin histories.

This long and difficult process of decolonizing the methodologies that claim to produce meaningful knowledge about Indigenous Peoples is a central project among Indigenous intellectuals across the lines of academic disciplines. Without exception, the contributors to *Indigenizing the Academy* authenticate the power potential of Indigenous epistemological and ontological first origins. Cornel Pewewardy, for instance, explicitly affirms "the 'change' potential of Comanche and Kiowa theory and praxis." He advocates using "understandings [informed by Comanche and Kiowa theory and praxis] to inform and expand the transformative potential within other Indigenous contexts." Taiaiake Alfred makes the point about decolonizing research methods that produce "knowledge" about Indigenous Peoples this way:

> We will begin to make meaningful change in the lives of our people as a whole only when we first focus on making real change the lives of our people as individuals. . . . In our minds and in our souls, we need to reject the settler's control and authority, their definition of who we are and what our rights are, their definition of what is worthwhile and how one should live, their hypocritical and pacifying morality. We need to rebel against what we've become and start remembering and acting on who our ancestors were, what they were like, and the things they believed in. This is the spiritual revolution that will ensure our survival.

Angela Cavender Wilson suggests that "the strategies that we develop as Indigenous people of North America toward decolonization and empowerment must be distinct to us and developed from the guiding principles that allowed us to live a sustainable existence for thousands of years."

Clearly, I think, the concern with decolonizing research methods is closely related to and overlaps with the project of theorizing and conceptualizing and representing Indigenous sovereignty. Theorizing Indigenous political sovereignty and economic self-determination in legal contexts have long been critical projects among political leaders and activists.⁶ More recently, influenced in no small way by Robert Allen Warrior's work on intellectual sovereignty, Indigenous scholars have been theorizing and continue to conceptualize rhetorical, cultural, and even semiotic sovereignty. In this volume, just to cite to one example of the manner in which scholars are indigenizing discussions of sovereignty, Daniel Heath Justice proposes understanding sovereignty as more than simply a legal concept. "Sovereignty and self-determination," Justice suggests,

> require more than just a redefinition of political and legal relationships between Indigenous nations and the nation-states of the Invaders; they also require a reimagining of ourselves beyond the antiquated artifacts that the Invaders insist we become. Our traditions, families, and nations all contribute to that reimagining, and so too do the literatures we craft in response to this challenge. With each poem or story or novel or song or other text that emerges from Indian Country, we assert the enduring Indigenous presence in this hemisphere. . . . Words matter. . . . For many of us art is an essential mechanism for the liberation of our nations.

Regardless of their specific disciplinary homes in the academy, contributors to this volume concur on this matter. Decolonizing research methodologies and theorizing Indigenous tribal sovereignty are projects aiming at what Justice names "the liberation of our nations."

Among the contributors, wide-ranging agreement emerges on the importance of producing Indigenous knowledges for Indigenous Peoples rather than to satisfy the fantasies, desires, and curiosities of non-Indigenous persons. There is *much* at stake in this project. Vine Deloria Jr., for instance, implores the current generation of Indigenous scholars to respond aggressively and collectively to what he refers to as "absurd anti-Indian theories . . . offered without the slightest hesitation and apparently with the full support of the academic community." Citing the inadequate works of James Chatters, James Clifton, Elliot West, and Shepherd Krech, Deloria calls on Indigenous scholars to research and write about, in his words, "how Indians treat their lands" and to challenge the framing categories of knowledge production that "might be regarded as a mere classification system devoid of valid observations."

Deloria is alone neither in criticizing the prevailing non- (and sometimes anti-) Indigenous production of knowledge about and sometimes by Indigenous Peoples nor in offering suggestions that relocate the purpose of and authority for knowledge production among Indigenous Peoples. Angela Cavender Wilson argues for "Indigenous scholars to put forth stories from our oral traditions that will undoubtedly challenge the myths of America and provide alternative perspectives largely unavailable in written documents." Daniel Heath Justice, working from the proposition that "Indigenous literatures are grounded in the cultural survival of the communities from which they emerge," rightly points out that "the institutional mechanisms of the academy often fail to recognize the intellectual work that takes place in our communities."

In place of knowledges that not only are *not* useful for Indigenous Peoples but, worse, labor to overpower our freedom to exist as Indigenous Peoples in almost every sphere of our existence, contributors to this volume advocate recovering, rejuvenating, and holding in the highest regard the importance of Indigenous languages. Working from the premise that "our first obligation as Native scholars engaged in this kind of work is not to the academy, but to our nations," Angela Cavender Wilson, just to cite to one example, sketches comprehensive possibilities for recovering and producing Indigenous knowledges through language revitalization. Certainly, when the academy becomes a safe place wherein scholarly attention is devoted to studies of Indigenous governance, languages, oral histories, technologies, and sciences, as well as to historic and sacred site protection, community health, and treaty rights, then, in those moments of knowledge production, the academy will be indigenized.

Indigenous studies, one might say, are purposely and perhaps inescapably "political." Ten years ago, to mention just one additional wellspring of these "politics," members of the Indian Nations at Risk Task Force produced their final report, entitled *Indian Nations at Risk*. Citing considerable testimony from Indigenous parents and educators, numerous school site visits, and well in excess of forty papers commissioned from experts in Native education, the authors of the report concluded that schools failed to educate Indigenous children.[7] Sixty-five years earlier, in 1926, then U.S. Secretary of the Interior Herbert Work ordered a survey of Indian affairs. Among the findings of a survey team that included the educator Henry Roe Cloud and the scholar Arthur C. Parker, and whose members cited deficient nutritional programming, excessive dormitory overcrowding, and substandard medical attention, was the striking incrimination that "The work of the government directed toward education . . . is largely ineffective. . . . The survey staff finds itself obligated to say frankly and unequivocally that the provisions for the care of the Indian children in boarding schools are grossly inadequate."[8]

During the interim, in those sixty-three years between publication of *The Problem of Indian Administration* in 1928 and *Indian Nations at Risk* in 1991, legislation designed by members of the U.S. Congress to transfer growing numbers of Indigenous children from U.S. government "Indian" schools to integrated public schools failed miserably in winning over a critical mass to the idea of sharing educational resources in a manner that advocated the exchange of languages and ideas. One response to these persisting failures, from an angle of vision with a legitimate sense of abiding urgency, means, in the words of Elizabeth Cook-Lynn, "Native studies is politics."

The "politics" to which Cook-Lynn refers are ongoing attempts that contemplate seizures of non-Indigenous state power in the interest of and security for Native tribal nations. These seizures of state power include the appropriation or reorientation of education at all levels. Such politics express the widely shared wish to redirect social resources in a manner that enables schools, for instance, to be transformed into powerful sites for educating Indigenous young persons in the ways of knowledge practiced among their People and not only in the ways of "Western civilization."

The state of affairs generally *today* for Indigenous young people trying to go to school and learn subject matter designed to form obedient U.S. citizens and productive, docile workers may translate as outrageous. Consider, for instance, a joint report released in October 2001 by the Minneapolis Public Schools, the Minneapolis Foundation, and the Greater Minneapolis Chamber of Commerce. In 2000–2001, according to the report, entitled *Measuring Up*, twenty-four percent of all American Indian students in the schools were suspended, compared with twenty percent in 1998–99.[9] In Minneapolis, public school functionaries, overwhelmingly non-Indigenous, suspended one out of every four students in schools with declining American Indian student enrollments, with dropout rates among American Indian students that consistently exceed twelve percent during the time that elapses from the opening of fall semesters to the end of annual academic calendars, and where achievement as measured by the Minnesota Basic Standards Test is lowest among American Indian students. Even outside the schools, these kids are not on a level playing ground. In 2001, the Children's Defense Fund of Minnesota, using data gathered from the 2000 U.S. Census, state government agencies, and private research groups in Minnesota and nationwide, reported that American Indian children in Minnesota fared significantly worse than white children in various measures of well-being related to matters of health and family finance.

Minnesota may not be typical when compared to other states, but Native children attending U.S. government schools similarly struggle with the effects of decisions mandated by the non-Indigenous majority. Congressional investigators for the Government Accounting Office (GAO), the investigative apparatus of the U.S. Congress, reported in 2001 that roughly 50,000 students in the 185 schools managed by the U.S. Bureau of Indian Affairs scattered across 23 states (more than seventy percent of which are in Arizona, New Mexico, North Dakota, and South Dakota) underperform on standardized tests and college entrance exams when compared with their tribal and public school counterparts.[10]

These examples powerfully propose that Indigenous students resist what amounts to mind-numbing conformity. This resistance points to effective Indigenous parenting. Unfortunately, and at the same time, these examples suggest that non-Indigenous educational apparatuses, as they currently are managed and funded, cannot contribute as effectively as they might to Indigenizing the academy. Not only are the official curricula of these schools notoriously insensitive, as well as obviously hostile to, Indigenous students (in spite of the largely unrecognized efforts of Indigenous school educators), but the means of marking academic success for admissions into colleges and universities leave even those young people who somehow navigate the antagonistic terrain of the schools disproportionately on the outside of the academy. Either these schools staffed by functionaries who are credentialed by higher education faculty must be reconfigured thoroughly in the interests of Indigenous Peoples and with our active and meaningful participation, or the shaping of Indigenous intellectuals must continue in some other space, in some other way.

There is hope for the future in 2004. Cook-Lynn offers one possibility for moving forward. "It is our responsibility," she contemplated in a published version of a lecture delivered in 1998, "to continue the [earlier] struggles toward a decent future for Indian people and the empowerment of Indian nations. In our twentieth century, the antagonists, the enemies of our nations, the thieves who want our land and water and other resources, they are still out there. I believe the 1990s task force on Indian education, which says that our nations are at risk, is something we should take very seriously."[11] Reflecting on the origins of what she names the "Indian Studies Era in the universities of America," Cook-Lynn further proposes that at their headwaters Indigenous studies were

> meant to develop not only the tribal intellectuals but also a system for the study of native societies from the inside, the study of language, culture, historical and legal relationships with the United States as nations-within-a-nation. It was meant to have as its constituencies the tribal nations of America, and it was meant to have as its major intent the defense of lands and resources and the sovereign autonomy of nationhood. . . . it was meant to counter the related disciplines that have been in the business of colonizing the natives. . . . The challenge today is to remember that our constituents are not now and have never been just students, many of whom can fend for themselves, not just faculties, many of whom compromise for personal gain, not just universities, notoriously self-serving and Euro-centered. The challenge today is to remember that the focus of Native American Studies was in the beginning an attempt to create a mechanism in defense of the indigenous principles of tribal sovereignty and nationhood in a democracy like the United States, with whom the tribal nations signed solemn treaties.[12]

Indigenizing the Academy is not an exception to Cook-Lynn's intimation that studies of Indigenous Peoples are (or can be) political in these ways.

The academy, if indigenized, might offer important resources for restoring well-being to our nations. "There are an infinite number of problems facing Indians that would welcome intellectual input," Vine Deloria Jr., suggested in a recent forum on sovereignty. "Traditional people were and are natural philosophers," the senior Deloria Jr. reflected in 1998. "If we look closely at their words, we find deep insights described in the simplest of language."[13] In ways that Dorreen Yellow Bird asks "big-city reporters" to look to tribal peoples for real news about "Indians," it is to these deep insights Deloria mentions that an indigenized academy would look, too. Like Deloria, the other contributors to this volume are fundamentally concerned with the question of major redistributions of "cultural capital" in curricula and in pedagogies, which regulate access to critical literacy and competence and to the practices of knowledge production and critical thinking.

Wa a o, wa be ski na me ska ta; mo ko ma na, *do you get it*? Are you listening?

Notes

1. Dorreen Yellow Bird, "Real Stories of Reservation Life Lie with People," *Grand Forks Herald*, January 4, 2003.

2. When using the words "Indigenous Peoples," here, I am thinking of those human beings who are related in some way to the hundreds of distinct families, groups, kinship communities, clans, tribes, bands, councils, reservations, colonies, towns, villages, rancherías, pueblos, confederacies, and nations who/that trace their ancestry back well before 1492, from a linear, chronological angle of vision, and since the beginning of time, from others, in what at this moment likely is that contested geography claimed by the United States. For Indigenous Peoples, certain areas along the international borders separating the United States from Canada in the north and from Mexico in the south are their homelands that transcend the surveillance apparatuses of just one nation-state. For a recent response to persons wishing to know what to call Native/Indigenous/First Nations individuals, see Suzan Shown Harjo, "What Do You Want to Be Called?" *Indian Country Today*, 25 July 2001, A5. See also Michael Yellow Bird, "What We Want to Be Called: Indigenous Peoples' Perspectives on Racial and Ethnic Identity Labels," *American Indian Quarterly* 23, no. 2 (spring 1999): 1–21; and Gerald Vizenor, *The People Named the Chippewa: Narrative Histories* (Minneapolis: University of Minnesota Press, 1984), especially 13–36.

3. Unfortunately, even after decades of laboring to reverse the devastating consequences of colonial education, as several of the contributors to this volume suggest, still there are Indigenous folks who in their lives have been educated by the same mass media communications–mediated material that authorizes a sometimes unmarked white supremacy as normal and universally human. Certain persons have internalized false and self-defeating notions in ways that, for them, it seems, the racist "Indian" products of the non-Indigenous imaginary have become at some point authentic and real. Following Frantz Fanon, a Comanche brother names this "cultural schizophrenia"; it is a malady that requires immediate intervention.

4. Elizabeth Cook-Lynn, *Anti-Indianism in North America: A Voice from Tatekeya's Earth* (Urbana: University of Illinois Press, 2001), x.

5. To focus only on the academy may underappreciate locations where knowledge allegedly about Indigenous Peoples has considerably greater, far-reaching implications. It is through the making of meaning about invented "Indians"—through orientalizing forms of redface—that anti-Indianisms are formulated and supported *even inside the academy*. Beyond offering external support for a recreational culture that blunts the formation of counterhegemonic politics, redface not only participates in making public policy that likely does not enrich life among the critical mass of Indigenous folks, it also reveals a disturbing pattern of understanding that enriches that way of thinking about and ordering the world we might agree to name white supremacy. Redface at once applauds and lampoons Indigenous cultures, ways of being, and ways of understanding and knowing. Its various manifestations through children's toys and games, through scouting, through athletic mascots and sport fan

antics, through schools and into the academy underwrite the envy as well as repulsion, the sympathetic identification as well as the fear, the attraction as well as the guilt that disciples of white supremacy and their oblivious allies manifest through hierarchically unequal relationships with the masses of Indigenous Peoples.

6. See, for instance, the relevant sections of Vine Deloria Jr., *We Talk, You Listen: New Tribes, New Turf* (New York: Macmillan, 1970).

7. Terrel Bell and William G. Demmert, *Indian Nations at Risk: An Educational Strategy for Action* (Washington DC: U.S. Department of Education, 1991).

8. Lewis Meriam and Henry Roe Cloud, eds., *The Problem of Indian Administration: Report of a Survey Made at the Request of Honorable Hubert Work* (Baltimore: Johns Hopkins University Press, 1928), 8, 11.

9. Carol R. Johnson et al., *Measuring Up 2002: A Report on the Minneapolis Public Schools* (Minneapolis: Minneapolis Public Schools, 2001).

10. To read the entire report, see "BIA and DOD Schools: Student Achievement and Other Characteristics Often Differ from Public Schools," GAO report #GAO-01-934.

11. Cook-Lynn, *Anti-Indianism in Modern America*, 151, 158.

12. Cook-Lynn, *Anti-Indianism in Modern America*, 152–53, 178.

13. Vine Deloria Jr., "Intellectual Self-Determination and Sovereignty: Looking at the Windmills in Our Minds," *Wicazo Sa Review* 13, no. 1 (spring 1998): 27, 25.

APPENDIX

Questions for Reflection

1. Why are supporters of the status quo often offended by the concerns of Indigenous scholars over the way Native peoples are researched and written about?
2. What does Indigenizing the academy mean to you? Why is it important?
3. Why is Indigenizing the academy a political act?
4. How has colonialism impacted the academy in general and your discipline specifically? What suggestions do you have for decolonizing your discipline and institution?
5. What is the background of professors who engage in Indigenous studies research and writing at your institution? Are they involved in contemporary Indigenous struggles? Is their work useful to Indigenous communities or is it exploitative, intended to satisfy the needs, curiosities, and interests of the dominant society?
6. What are the links between the struggles of Indigenous peoples and other marginalized populations in this hemisphere and throughout the world? How can we work toward solidarity that acknowledges our differences (including the reality of colonialism) while fighting for our shared concerns?
7. How can concerned allies assist with Indigenizing the academy?
8. What were/are the politics, social climates, and motivations affecting the authors who construct stories of Indigenous peoples and their pasts, including chronicles of Indigenous/white relations?
9. If there are no Indigenous administrators at your school, then how are Indigenous voices included in your school's decision-making processes? How does your school know what Indigenous peoples need?
10. Given the recommendation of the American Indian and Alaska Na-

tive Professor's Association on ethnic fraud in higher education, what can you do to insure that mainstream colleges and universities are honoring tribal sovereignty by respecting tribal enrollment criteria? To whom should the enforcement of policies be assigned, and what should consequences be for ethnic fraud infractions?

CONTRIBUTORS

Taiaiake Alfred (Kanien'Kehaka) is currently the Indigenous Peoples Research Chair at the University of Victoria and holds the Joe DeLaCruz Chair for Indian Government Development at the Center for World Indigenous Studies in Olympia, Washington. He is the author of *Heeding the Voices of Our Ancestors* (Oxford, 1995), *Peace, Power, Righteousness* (Oxford, 1999), and *Wasáse: Rites of Resistance and the New Warrior Creed* (Oxford, forthcoming).

David Anthony Tyeeme Clark (Mesquakie and Potawatomi) is a Ford Foundation Dissertation Minority Fellow in American Studies at the University of Kansas. He is the co-editor of *Counting Coups: A History of "Indian Mascots"* (Nebraska, forthcoming) and *The Roots of Red Power* (Nebraska, forthcoming). He edited *The Power of Many Voices: Readings in North American and United States History, 1550–1865* and *1963–1970* (Copley, 1995).

Vine Deloria Jr. (Standing Rock Sioux) is a professor of history, law, religious studies, and political science at the University of Colorado, Boulder. His numerous books include *Custer Died for Your Sins* (Avon, 1969), *God is Red: A Native View of Religion* (Grosset and Dunlap, 1973), and *Evolution, Creationism, and Other Modern Myths: A Critical Inquiry* (Fulcrum, 2002).

Joely De La Torre (Pechanga Band of Luiseno Indians) is an assistant professor and former department chair (on leave 2002–03) in the department of American Indian studies at San Francisco State University. She currently serves as the special advisor to the lieutenant governor of California on California Sovereign Nations. She is completing her forthcoming book entitled, *American Indian Political Power in the New Millennium*.

Joseph P. Gone (Gros Ventres) is assistant professor in the department of psychology (clinical area) and the program in American culture (Native American studies) at the University of Michigan in Ann Arbor. His research interests include cultural psychology and American Indian mental health. He may be contacted by email at jgone@umich.edu.

Dr. Andrea A. Hunter (Osage) is associate professor in the department of anthropology, director of the North American division of the Laboratory of Paleoethnobotany at Northern Arizona University, Flagstaff, and chair of the Native American Repatriation Review Committee at the Smithsonian Institution. Although relocated in the Southwest, her archaeological and paleoethnobotanical research emphasis has focused on the Osage Tribe in Missouri. She is currently preparing an edited volume on the Osage at the time of European contact.

Keith James (Onondaga) is professor of organizational psychology in the department of psychology at Colorado State University and director of the Alaska Native/Native American psychology program at the University of Alaska. He is the editor of *Science and Native American Communities* (Nebraska, 2001). His work focuses on Alaska Native/American Indian community development; approaches to integrating Native perspectives, goals, and needs with mainstream science and technology; creativity and innovation in organizations; and social and organizational influences on physical health.

Daniel Heath Justice (Cherokee) is assistant professor of Aboriginal literatures in the English department at the University of Toronto.

Devon Abbott Mihesuah (Choctaw Nation of Oklahoma) is currently professor in the new Applied Indigenous Studies Department, Northern Arizona University. She serves as editor of the award-winning journal *American Indian Quarterly* and edits University of Nebraska Press's book series "Contemporary Indigenous Issues." She is the author of dozens of essays and books on a variety of topics, including *American Indigenous Women: Decolonization, Empowerment, Activism* (Nebraska, 2003); *'First To Fight': Henry Mihesuah NU MUU NU* (Nebraska, 2002); the novels *Roads of My Relations, The Lightning Shrikes,* and *Ahni micha chukka (Hope and Home): Three Tales of Choctaw Survival*; and is editor of *Repatriation Reader: Who Owns American Indian Remains?* (Nebraska, 2000) and *Natives and Academics: Researching and Writing About American Indians* (Nebraska, 1998).

Joshua K. Mihesuah (Comanche) is director of Native American student services (NASS; see the website www2.nau.edu/nass for more information) and is a former assistant dean of students at Northern Arizona University (which has over thirteen hundred Native students enrolled and the largest Native graduation rate in the country). He is the founder and first chairman of the Coconino County Intertribal Council and is president of the board of the Native Americans for Community Action (NACA). He is a former president of the Flagstaff United School District Board.

He won the 2002 award for outstanding contribution to Native American student communities presented by the Native American Network, a part of the American College Personnel Association and the Committee for Multicultural Affairs.

Cornel Pewewardy (Comanche-Kiowa) is assistant professor in the department of teaching and leadership, school of education, at the University of Kansas. He is the co-editor of *Counting Coups: A History of "Indian" Mascots* (Nebraska, forthcoming). His research agenda is studying the psychological impact on children's academic achievement caused by ethnic stereotyping. He serves as the key consultant for the National Collegiate Athletic Association's (NCAA) study for the elimination of "Indian" mascots from member institutions as well as an educational consultant to numerous school districts across the country on improving the academic achievement of underrepresented populations in education and faculty curriculum development.

Angela Cavender Wilson (Wahpetunwan Dakota) is assistant professor of American Indian history in the history department at Arizona State University. She is the author of *Remember This: Dakota Decolonization and the Eli Taylor Narratives* (Nebraska, forthcoming).

INDEX

academic cults, 56
academic gatekeeping, 4, 31–44, 220–21
activists, 38
Adair, James, 149
Adisa, Gamba (Audre Lorde), 110
African Americans, in academia, 31, 44n4
Alcatraz, 41
Alcoze, Thom, 207, 208
Alexie, Sherman, 120n11
Alfred, Taiaiake Gerald, 42, 71–72, 73, 75, 76, 114, 115, 145, 155
Allen, Paula Gunn, 1, 104, 120n11
Allen, Richard, 205
Almanac of the Dead (Silko), 105
American Indian and Alaskan Native Professors' Association, 200, 206–7
American Indian history, 143–57; authors of, 144–45, 156; "facts" in, 148; Indian perspectives of, 146; need for, 146, 154–55; patterns of, 149; as political, 146; powerhouse repetitive works of, 152; tribal versions of, 148–51
The American Indian Mind in a Linear World: American Indian Studies and Traditional Knowledge (Fixico), 47
American Indian political practices, 174–75

American Indian psychologists, 124
American Indian Quarterly, xi, 1, 3, 39, 42
American Indians (Shoemaker), 41
American Indians in American History, 1870–2001 (Evans), 42
American Indian Studies programs, 3, 113
American Historical Association, 12, 156
American Political Science Association (APSA), 176, 178, 183, 184
American Political Science: The Discipline's State and the State of the Discipline (Katznelson, Milner), 177
American Society for Ethnohistory, 3, 46n18
anonymous brilliance, 208–9, 216n21
anti-Indian attitudes, 21, 23, 219–20
anti-Indian theories, 20–22
Apess, William, 118
Applied Indigenous Studies (AIS), 195–96
archaeology, 169–72
Armstrong, Jeannette, 118
Asian Americans, in academia, 32
authors, as gatekeepers, 40–43
"Aversive Racism," 53
Awaikta, 118

INDEX

award committees, 37, 38
Axtell, James, 8, 77
Ayahuasca, 83

back cover blurbs, 43, 47n20
Barclay-Kerr, Hoturoa, 164
Battle of Little Big Horn, 151
behavioralism, 177
Beier, Paul, 46n14
Benedict, Jeff, 118
Benjamin, Walter, 31
Bering Strait migration theory, 20–21
"best friend" relationship with an Indian, 24–25
Bilias, George A., 149
Bin-Sallik, Mary Ann, 164
Biography, 143
Bird, Gloria, 106
Black Elk, 24
Blackwell Publishing, 40, 42, 43
Blair, E. J. April, 164
blood quantum, 76
boarding schools, 41, 81
book reviews, 39
Brant, Beth, 104, 109, 116
Brooks, James, 41
buffalo, 20–21
Buffalo Wars (1870s), 22
Bukey, Evan B. 156
Bull Lodge, 126, 130–33
Bush, George W., 8

Caytes, 152
Ceremony (Silko), 105
Champagne, Duane, 1
Chatters, James, 19, 226
Cherokees, 41, 154
Cheyennes, 22
Children's Defense Fund of Minnesota, 228
Choctaw Genesis (Galloway), 42
Choctaws, 41, 42, 46–47n18

Christensen, Rosemary, 207
Chronicle of Higher Education, 4
Chrystos, 104
Churchill, Mary, 106–7
Clearing a Path (Shoemaker), 40–42, 46n13, 47n20
Clendinnen, Inga, 158n19
Clifton, James, 21, 29, 36, 40, 226
Clinton, Bill, 202
Cloud, Henry Roe, 227
Cody, Iron Eyes, 22
collectivism, 53
collegiality, 38
Collingwood, R. G., 149
colonialism, 9, 31, 44, 70, 89–91, 112, 151
colonized Natives, 76
Columbus, 82
Comanches, 22, 151, 152, 192
"comfy history," 42, 47n19
A Companion to American Indian History (P. Deloria, Salisbury), 40, 146, 149–50
conference committees, 37
Conley, Robert, 123n33
"conscientisation," 214
contribution history, 156
Cook-Lynn, Elizabeth, 74, 110, 113, 204–6, 228, 219, 229, 230
corrupt academic systems, 48–67
Cox, Brent, 100
Cox, James H., 105
cronyism, 52, 63
Cruikshank, Julie, 41
cultural exploitation of Natives, 200
Custer Died For Your Sins (V. Deloria), 29
Custer, George Armstrong, 151
"cutting edge" research, 40

Dakota language, 72–73, 81–82
Dances with Wolves, 111, 151
Darko, Thomas, 108

decolonization, 42, 43, 70–72
De La Torre, Joely, 73
Deloria, Phil, 40, 41, 42, 80, 146–47, 149–50, 156–57
Deloria, Vine, Jr., 114, 144, 157n1, 181, 220, 222, 226, 230
DeMallie, Raymond, 87n30
diabetes, 83
Diagnostic and Statistical Manual of Mental Disorders, 127
divide-and-conquer tactics, 61
Dorris, Michael, 120n11
Dragging Canoe, 100
Driskill, Qwo-Li, 119n1, 119n6, 121n15
Duncan, Patti, 6
DyLsa, Burnier, 179

The Ecological Indian (Krech), 22–23
Ecuador, 83
egalitarianism, 41
empiricist scholars, 147
empowerment, 43, 71; strategies for students, 195–99
Erdoes, Richard, 24
Erdrich, Louise, 105, 120n11
"essentialist," xi
ethnic fraud, 34; in academia, 200–215, 221
ethnohistorians, 146
Evans, Sterling, 42, 46n16

Fanon, Frantz, 69, 70
favoritism, 52
Fixico, Don, 40, 78
fellowship committees, 37, 38
Ferris, Jeanne, 4
fiction, 3, 10, 38
First Nations? Second Thoughts (Flanagan), 118
Flanagan, Thomas, 118
Fort Sill Boarding School, 192
Foster, Morris, 45

Foucault, Michel, 145
Fourth World, 117
Frazier, Ian, 35, 118, 152–53
freelance writers, 24
Freire, Paulo, 36, 69, 70, 85n3

Galloway, Patricia, 42, 46–47n18
gatekeeping strategies, 32–47, 144, 148
gays in academia, 32. *See also* Two-Spirit sensibilities
"genetic Indians," 76
genetics, 50–51
Ghost Dances, 101, 103, 112
Glancy, Diane, 120n11
Gould, Janice, 101
Gould, Stephen Jay, 19
Government Accounting Office, 229
Grand Forks Herald, 218
"grazing," 59
Greymorning, Stephen, 81
Grey Owl, 206–7
Grob, Gerald N., 149
Gros Ventre, 127, 130–33

Hamilton, Allen Lee, 151
H-Amindian Web site, 3
Hanta Yo (Hill), 3, 35
Harjo, Joy, 106, 113
Harring, Sidney L., 42
Haskell Indian Nations University, 192
Haudenosaunee, 82
Havasupais, 193
Herring, E. Pendleton, 177
Highway, Tomson, 104
Hill, Ruth Beebe, 3, 35
historians: as creators of history, 148–49; responsibilities of, 50
History of the American Indians (Adair), 149
Hobson, Geary, 108–9
"honorary" Indians, 201
Hopis, 45n8, 193, 198

242 INDEX

Howe, Craig, 40, 41
Howe, Leanne, 40, 46
Hudson, Charles, 106–8

images of Indians: as buffoons, 156; as ecological destroyers, 23; as ecologically responsible, 22, 156; as friends of animals, 40; as having no common sense, 23; as ignorant about their cultures, 20; as inferior candidates for positions, 36; as informers for whites, 24; as violent, 151–52, 156; as "window dressing," 44
Incas, 152
Indian Arts and Crafts Act, 210
"Indian at Heart," 76, 203–4, 216n11
Indian Nations at Risk, 227–28
"Indigenizing the academy" (ideology), 5, 14, 88, 101, 134–35, 169–71, 218–19, 221–31
Indigenous (term), 44n2, 85n1, 98
Indigenous health and diet, 82–83
Indigenous knowledge, 182, 186–88; recovery of, 45n5, 73–74, 75, 77, 82–84, 155–56
Indigenous language loss, 81–82
Indigenous perspectives, 42, 144
Indigenous scholars: alliances between, 26–27; as gatekeepers, 37; problems faced by, 17, 18, 71; responsibilities of, 93, 95–97, 99, 110, 150, 185–90
Indigenous students, problems faced by, 191–99
Indigenous thinking, 93
Indigenous women, 153–54, 155
individualism, 53, 93, 97
Ingrates at the Gate: People of Color Confront Higher Education (Duncan), 6
internalized colonization, 41, 72–73
International Plant Medicine Corporation, 83

interpretive arguments, 179–81
The Invented Indian (Clifton), 21, 40, 41
Iroquois, 152

Jackson, Andrew, 154
James Mooney Award, 46n18
Jessel, Penny, 40
Johnson, Troy, 41

Kanien'kehaka, 98
Katznelson, Ira, 177
Kaye, Frances W., 105
Kennewick Man, 3, 19–20
Kenny, Maurice, 104
Key, V. O., Jr., 177
King, Thomas, 113
Kiowa Education Fund, 43
Kiowas, 22
Kipp, Darrell, 81
Krech, Shepard, 22–23, 29, 226
Krupat, Arnold, 105, 108, 121n13

LaFleshe, Francis, 16
Larson, Sidner, 116
Lassiter, Luke E., 43
The Last of the Ofos (Hobson), 108–9
Lévi-Strauss, Claude, 200
literary critics: as "lit-critters," 38; role of, 108
literary studies, Native, 100–119; problems with, 105; role of, 109; suggestions for, 102–3
Little Bear, Leroy, 98
Little House on the Prairie (Wilder), 86–87n24
Long Soldier, Helen, 207, 208
Lorde, Audre (Gamba Adisa), 110
Louis, Adrian, 118
Love Medicine (Erdrich), 105

Mails, Thomas, 24

Malotki, Ekkehart, 36, 45n8
Manifest Destiny, 79, 87n24
Manuel, George, 114
manuscript reviewers, 39–40
Martin, Paul, 20–21
Mato Nunpa, Chris, 81
Matthews, John Joseph, 16
Matthiesson, Peter, 24
Mayas, 152
McCormick, Peter, 43
Mead, Margaret, 18
Measuring Up (report), 228
Memmi, Albert, 97
merit committees, 38
meritocracy, 49
Mexican Americans, in academia, 32
Mexicas, 152
The Middle Ground: Indians, Empires and Republics in the Great Lakes Region, 1650–1815 (White), 42
Mikaere, Martin, 164
Miller, Jay, ix, x
Miller, Loren, 83
Miller, Susan, 1, 42
Milner, Helen V., 177
"Modern Racism," 52
Momaday, Scott, 16, 113, 120n11
Moore, David, 105
Moraga, Cherrie, 115
Mormons, 30
Munslow, Alan, 148

Nanih Wayah, 41
National Conference on Race and Ethnicity, 203
National Geographic Explorer, 143
National Indian Organizations, 27
National Indian Youth Council, 75
National Museum of the American Indian Act, 160–61
nation-building, 42
Native (term), 44n2

Native activists, 2–3, 5, 9
Native American (term), 44n2
Native American Graves Protection and Repatriation Act (NAGPRA), 161, 171
Native American Student Services (NASS), 198
Native American Studies Association (NASA), 176
Native intellectuals, x, 3, 7, 8, 9, 12, 14
Native languages, 106, 121n15
Native psychology, 224–25
Native scholars: demands on, 27–28; as sell-outs, 114. See also Indigenous scholars
Natives and Academics: Researching and Writing about American Indians (Mihesuah), ix–xi, 1, 2, 4, 40
Native students: suggestions for empowerment, 222. See also Indigenous students
Navajos, 36, 193
Neihardt, John, 210
nepotism, 52, 63
Neskahi, Arlie, 210
New Age groups, 76
Newberry Library, 20
"New Indian Historians," 77
"New Indians," 17
Ngugi wa Thiong'o, 14
Nietzsche, Friedrich, 146
"The Noble Nine," 105, 120n11
Noley, Grayson, 205, 207–8

objectivity, in research and writing, 20, 107, 112
On the Rez (Frazier), 35, 118, 152–53
Ortiz, Simon, 113
Owens, Louis, 120n11

Parker, Arthur, C., 16, 227
Parker, Quanah, 151

Parks, Douglas, 87n30
Peace, Power, Righteousness (Alfred), 155
Perdue, Theda, 77
Piestewa, Lori, 193
The Pleasures of Academe: A Celebration and Defense of Higher Education (Axtell), 8
Pleistocene Extinctions (Martin), 20
Policy Paradox: The Art of Political Decision Making (Stone), 179
politically correct (term), 146
political science, 174–90
Political Science: State of the Discipline, 176
politics, in academia, 25, 27, 29, 36, 92, 107, 112, 146
postcolonial (term), 141
postpositivism (term), 178–79
Powell, Malea, 107
Power/Knowledge (Foucault), 145
The Power of Kiowa Song (Lassiter), 43
pre-application strategies, 62–63
"privileged information," 78
The Problem of Indian Administration, 228
professors, as gatekeepers, 34–37, 59–60, 196
promotions committees, 38
psychology issues in the academy, 124–40
publishers, as gatekeepers, 38, 40–43

Queer sensibilities. *See* Two-Spirit sensibilities

race, as data-determining criteria, 19
racism, x, 13, 18, 27
Rainbow Walker, 210
"Real Indians," 148
red-tailed hawks, 40, 46n14
"regenerated racism," 7, 20

repatriation of human remains, 160, 161–62
retaliation, against activists, 44
Rethinking American Indian History (Fixico), 40
Riding In, James, 3, 195
Riggs, Stephen R., 82
Roa, Tom, 164
Robinson, Eden, 120n11
Robyn, Linda, 164
Rose, Wendy, 113
Ross, Chief John, 205
Routledge, 40, 47n20
Ruoff, A. LaVonne Brown, 105
Runningwater, Niles Bird, 212

Salisbury, Neal, 40, 146
Sanders, William, 120n11
Santa Clara v. Pueblo, 186
search committees, 33–34, 45n6, 48
self-determination, 75
Sentinel of the Southern Plains: Fort Richardson and the Northwest Texas Frontier, 1866–1878 (Hamilton), 151
Sequoyah, 205
Seventh Generation, 94, 103
sexism, x
Shoemaker, Nancy, 40, 41, 42, 46n13
Silko, Leslie Marmon, 105, 120n11
Sioux, 152
Smith, Linda Tuhiwai, 2, 6
Smithsonian Institution, 161; Native American Repatriation Review Committee, 161, 162, 171
The Southeastern Indians (Hudson), 106–7
Southwest State University, 82
sovereignty, 114, 115, 118
Spivak, Gayatri, 80
status quo, 2, 4, 5, 7, 8, 13, 38, 41, 44n5
Steiner, Stan, 24
Stone, Deborah, 178–79

strategies for communities, 63–64
Swisher, Karen, 192

Tapahonso, Luci, 120n11
targets of opportunity, 26
Taylor, Drew Hayden, 118
tenure committees, 38
terminology, 44, 85, 215, 231
territoriality, 39
theories, non-Indigenous, 40–42, 46n13
Tohono O'Odham, 193
traditional tribal diets, 82
Trask, Huanani-Kay, 72, 111, 113, 122n26
tribal colleges, 64
Tsiyu Gansini, 100–101, 116
Tupinambas, 152
Turner, Frederick Jackson, 35, 153
The Turn to the Native (Krupat), 106
Two-Spirit sensibilities, 104, 120

University of Oklahoma, 200
University of South Australia, 162
University of Washington, 200
U.S. Information Agency Multidisciplinary Indigenous Program, 162–69
U.S. Patent and Trademark Office, 83

values, differences between Natives' and non-Natives', 33, 51, 53
Van Camp, Richard, 120n11
Villenas, Sofia, 214
Vizenor, Gerald, 113, 117, 120n11

Walapais, 193
Wallace's strategies, 64–67
Warrior, Clyde, 114, 115
Warrior, Robert, 75, 113
warrior scholars, 9, 96
Washburn, Wilcomb, 220
Waters, Frank, 24
Welch, James, 120n11
West, Elliot, 22, 226
Western Michigan University, 77
Wheeler, Winona, 71
White, Hayden, 145, 157
White, Richard, 42, 77, 78, 148
"white Cherokees," 154
white scholars, demands on, 28
Wilde, Oscar, 108
Wilkins, David, 183
Wilson, Angela Cavender, xi, 1, 45n11, 145, 148, 183, 195
Wilson, Norman J., 147
Windschuttle, Keith, 152, 158n19
Without Reservation (Benedict), 118
Womack, Craig, 104, 117, 121n13, 204
Worcester, Donald, ix
Work, Herbert, 227

Yallups, 205
Yavapais, 193
Yellow Bird, Dorreen, 218, 230
Yellow Bird, Michael, 3, 176, 215n2, 216n21
Young Bear, Ray, 118, 120n11

IN THE CONTEMPORARY INDIGENOUS ISSUES SERIES

Indigenous American Women: Decolonization, Empowerment, Activism
By Devon Abbott Mihesuah

Indigenizing the Academy: Transforming Scholarship and Empowering Communities
Edited by Devon Abbott Mihesuah and Angela Cavender Wilson